Jacklin

Jacklin

MY AUTOBIOGRAPHY

TONY JACKLIN

with CURTIS GILLESPIE

**SIMON &
SCHUSTER**

London · New York · Sydney · Toronto

A CBS COMPANY

First published in Great Britain by Simon & Schuster UK Ltd, 2006
A CBS COMPANY

1 3 5 7 9 10 8 6 4 2

Simon & Schuster UK Ltd
Africa House
64–78 Kingsway
London WC2B 6AH

www.simonsays.co.uk

Simon & Schuster Australia
Sydney

A CIP catalogue record for this book
is available from the British Library.

ISBN 0-7432-6882-2
EAN 9780743268820

Typeset in Sabon by M Rules
Printed and bound in Great Britain by
The Bath Press, Bath

The publishers have made every effort to contact those persons having
rights in the material reproduced here. Where this has not been possible, the
publishers will be pleased to hear from anyone who recognizes their work.

Picture credits

1, 4: *Daily Express*; 2, 3, 5, 14, 18, 20, 22, 24, 29, 31–4, 37: Author's
collection; 6: Colorsport; 7, 8, 10, 15, 36: Empics; 9: *Daily Mirror*; 11, 16,
17, 19, 25: Popperfoto; 12: PA; 13: Frank Carroll; 21: Ian Joy; 23: Hailey
Sports Photographic; 26: David Cannon/Allsport; 27, 28: John H. Paul; 30:
David Steen; 35: Jim Hill; 38: Jim Mandeville

*To Astrid, whose love and strength
made my life whole again*

*And to my children: Bradley, Warren, Tina, Anna-May,
A. J. and Sean who, in this crazy world, have all
turned out to be exceptional human beings*

With thanks also to Curtis Gillespie for his great talent, and to Cynthia Dillane for her observations and support

Jacklin

Introduction

If you bought this book thinking it was simply another tale about a golfer and his exploits on the course, then I may have to offer an apology. Of course, golf is everywhere throughout this story – and is clearly the reason I can write a book like this – but the game of golf is really only the frame for the picture I'm going to try to paint for you. Because to me, and I hope to you, this book will tell a story that is all too human, a story about a person who has lived the most extraordinary life, but who has also been touched by the common experiences we all go through. My life has been crammed with high achievements and devastating losses, with fierce determination and grievous incident, with the gratification of trusting the right people and the despair of trusting the wrong ones. It's had it all, from the heights to the depths and everything you could imagine in between. Hardly a day goes by in which I don't stop at some point and think, *My God, what a life I've had!* And that's not even taking into consideration the two or three things most people will probably remember me for: the two Opens; the Ryder Cups. Yes, I achieved some extraordinary things in the game of golf; I'm proud of those things and always will be. That won't ever change. But it's not what this story is really about, at least not to me. This is a story about a person whose life has had everything in it – and I mean *everything* – and who has gone about his business from Day One with as much passion and intensity as he could command.

I come from a northern English background that was dire in many respects. It might be only natural to play that down a bit, to be polite towards my birthplace or to the memory of my parents. But what's the point in that? It was a bloody hard life I had growing up, and I don't want to say otherwise. We were poor. My parents struggled with it. To call my upbringing 'humble' would move it more than a few notches up on the social scale. I was thinking about this when I was back in the north of England just this past winter, visiting Wigan to watch some football with my friend Dave Whelan, the owner of JJB Sports. Dave is a northern England man through and through. We were reminiscing and I told him how my granddad used to tell me to pee on my hands to harden up the skin – God knows if it would have worked or not – so that they'd be more suited for working in the mines or the steelworks. Dave laughed because he instantly, instinctively, knew about the times and the world I was talking about. He said when he was growing up in Wigan it was so damn cold all the time his dad used to tell him to pee on his hands, too, but that was just to keep them warm! They were hard times in postwar northern England.

Things changed when golf became the way I was able to express my personality, when through resolve and single-minded determination I was able, working pretty much alone, to unlock the secrets of the game, or at least those secrets that were going to work for me. My success as a very young man brought wealth and fame. I married a perfect woman, Viv. We had a wonderful family. It might have been reasonable to assume life was well on track, but how could we have known the roller-coaster was only just leaving the gate? A few years after scaling the one peak I'd always set my sights on – the Open Championship – my professional life became a source of bitter frustration and plummeting self-esteem. I will try my best in this book to explain to you how golf soon became the only thing in my life – really, the one single thing – that made me unhappy. The Ryder Cup captaincy gave me new life and a new reason for being, but then in the middle of the second phase of my life tragedy struck and I was left utterly, shockingly alone. The words don't exist to convey the emptiness, the pure anguish of what my children and I went through.

It signalled the start of a new life, a second act. I met Astrid not long after the bottom fell out of my first world. We started our own life together, and what a gift it has been. We've been through our own share of difficulties, not the least of them financial, but I often wonder how I could have been so lucky. To think that there might have been only two women on the planet I was utterly meant to be with, and I managed to find them both in my lifetime. Astrid is the kind of woman who could be a role model for any young lady growing up nowadays, possessed as she is of such intelligence, such a sound ethical sense, such a sense of humour and great self-respect. I love her dearly and together we have created the kind of life I've always wanted. A life of comfort and security, yet brimming too with challenges and fascinating projects (like The Concession, the golf course and housing development in Florida that Jack Nicklaus and I recently partnered on, which celebrates our shared Ryder Cup moment at Birkdale in 1969).

In this book I want to share with you what it was like to go through the astonishing things I've been through. Not just what happened, but why it happened, how I made it happen, and how these things made me *feel* as I was experiencing them. Because what life is all about is not so much what happened to you, as what kind of person you became through it all. This to me is the essence of my story – you have to discover who you are, and then live with passion and honesty every single day, so that you can lay your head down at night and say, 'I did my best today and I was true to myself, and if I made a mistake, how can I learn from it?' That's the real voyage to me. Where you go *inside*. I am an enthusiastic, emotional person. I live in the heart, I always have. I just don't see the value in pretending to be something other than what I am; I never have and never will. And because I am who I am – no apologies, no excuses – when I was flying high it was the most glorious, extraordinary life. But when I was at my lowest, life almost didn't seem worth the trouble. That's just the truth.

This is the story of my journey, and it's going to be the last time I'll tell it this way. I want to share it with you as best I can. The passion. The pain. The determination. The victories. The setbacks. The fullness of a life I feel incredibly fortunate to have led.

1

Why not begin with the day it all changed? The day when my world shifted from dream to pursuit. It's a subtle difference, you might say – can't you pursue a dream? Fair enough. But to me it was profound, because it was the day I went from a kind of hazy daydreaming about winning the Open to the belief, the *knowledge*, that I was now chasing something I could actually achieve. It was an exhilarating and, truth be told, almost terrifying day; exhilarating for the buzz of the achievement, terrifying because now I knew I had it in me. It was a new kind of pressure, but I thrilled to it. It was a wonderful pressure. This is something you can only know inside you, and which is difficult to explain – that moment in your life when you know pressure is going to be your friend, not your enemy. That you perform best under pressure, and that others don't. What a powerful feeling this is. Jack Nicklaus once said about winning Majors that they were the *easiest* tournaments to win, not the hardest. He felt this way because he knew inside that 90 per cent of the field wouldn't be able to handle the pressure. He *could* handle it, and so he only had to worry about the very few players able to match both his golfing ability *and* his ability to cope with the strain. There might have been only a dozen or so players at every Major he had to compete against. Think about that. It's brilliant, is what it is. Not only was he right, but it also has to be one of the greatest examples of positive thinking in sports history. He took the intense scalding pressure of Major golf, and made it work for him, made it his ally. I know that feeling. When I was at my best, this was how I felt. Pressure was my friend.

I was sixteen when I first took this knowledge fully inside myself. The Lincolnshire County Championship was being played at Holme Hall Golf Club, my home club at the time, having switched over from the Scunthorpe Golf Club. My father, Arthur Jacklin, had become quite a handy player by that time, and he'd also entered. This was the Open county championship, meaning it was a full field of amateurs and professionals. I'd won the county Boys championships three times already, but had never entered, let alone won, a tournament with professionals in it. The morning was breezy but playable, and I went out in 74 to share the lead with one of the pros (my father shot 77 and was tied for second). Over lunch the weather broke open and turned around, violently, as the weather so easily can in the north of England. A massive gale-force wind came in. Lincolnshire is renowned for the flatness of its landscape: once the wind gets up there's nothing in the way to stop it. 'You could lie down on that wind,' my father said later. Suddenly, it became a day not for scoring, but for survival. I wondered if the other players were getting nervous about it, because it sure wasn't going to be any fun out there. But to me, it was *Game on*. I went out in 35, and came home in 36 for a 71. I had won the tournament, nine shots clear of the best professional and twelve clear of the next best amateur. 'A tremendous performance,' my father said later, amazed. Part of me couldn't believe it, either, though another part – the emerging side of me – was thinking, *Well, this is just what you do if you want to win. You just play golf and get on with it and make a score.* I was impressed by my play on the one hand, but unimpressed on the other – wasn't this just what good players did, what they were *supposed* to do? If you didn't expect to play great, odds were it wouldn't happen too often. Still, I had won, on a nasty day, against real competition, playing golf precisely the way I wanted to play it. It took a few days to process, but soon enough I knew what it all meant to me. Everything had changed. I had a path. I had confidence. My instinct had been right. I had a way out.

Anyone who doesn't know me personally would probably automatically associate me with golf. That's normal, to be expected. Nothing wrong with that, and of course I'm not at all bothered by it. *Tony Jacklin equals golf: two Opens, Ryder Cups galore, world player, and so on. End of equation.* But I don't look at it that way, and never really have, because long before golf came into my life my personality was formed and fairly clear to me. I know it for a fact now, but I think I was aware even as a youngster that golf – as much as I have always loved the game – was only ever an outlet for my competitiveness, indeed for my whole personality. It was never the other way round. I used golf and my eventual gifts in the game to voice who I was. It was not golf that created the person I grew into. A great game, golf, the greatest, but all the same it's only ever been a vehicle for me to say something about my own character, an outward expression of the person I was inside. I don't think golf creates character, so much as reveals it. But when I was winning Opens, playing and captaining in Ryder Cups, dashing all over the globe with a golf club in my hand – in other words, when I was on top for my golf – I don't think I was ever fully comfortable explaining (if anyone cared, that is) who I was: that sense of being a person driven to move beyond his upbringing. I wanted to better myself, and I saw early on that I was either going to do it through golf or I wasn't likely to do it at all. Hunger. Desperation. Desire.

Drive. Destiny. Call it what you will, but I was a young man in Scunthorpe, ten years old, twelve, thirteen, almost on fire with the need to get better at golf, to raise myself to the only level that I knew would carry me out of Scunthorpe, literally and symbolically. Only the highest level was going to do. Even at that age I was intensely committed to reaching it. It was a story of pure resolve.

Let me draw you a picture of the Scunthorpe of my childhood, or at least the picture as I remember it today. It'll be hard to do because any attempt to really capture the hardness of it, the poverty and overall blight of the place at that time, might come off as sounding a bit over the top. But make no mistake; these postwar years were very, very rough times. Imagine grey overcast skies. Street after street, mile after mile of cramped terraced housing, of buildings crammed up close as tight as fence boards. Three huge steel works (Appleby Frodingham, John Lysart and Redburn) skirting a hard north of England industrial town. A time when all the men would wear their long grey woollen overcoats if they went out and every lady a hat if she went down High Street. A life's work for most was the mine or the steelworks or the dockyards, a visit to the pub, a trip to the seaside now and then, nothing like central heating, and not two pennies to rub together for anything other than the most basic living necessities. Nobody had *any* money. None. This was Scunthorpe, Lincolnshire, post-World War Two. Hardship was all we knew. We were flat broke all the time. I was born into this world, this way of life, on 7 July 1944, and I grew up in Scunthorpe, loving it in a way – there are some fond memories, certainly – yet somehow always feeling it was a place I needed to escape.

Of course, you never can fully escape, can you? Even if that's the right word. We're all shaped by our childhoods, by who raised us, who loved us and who didn't, by the immediate world around us. I'm no different from anyone else. We're formed so deeply by the people around us when we're young, most obviously our parents. I think it took me a long time to realize just how much I'd been moulded by my parents. Or at least, that what I wanted to make of my life was in many ways a reaction, a kind of response, to who my parents were and the circumstances in which I was raised. Through my early years as a professional golfer I can tell you that I was a deeply driven person, almost to the point of losing balance. Sure, you can say it has to be that way, that any major figure in any field has to bring a kind of obsession to what they do, whether they tee it up at the Open, step onto the pitch in the World Cup, or sing their lungs out at Covent Garden. But over the years I've come to question that. I suppose part of me always wondered if it was the right way to go about things, and maybe that's why when I achieved what I achieved at such a young age – the Open in 1969 and the US Open the year after – there was a great sense of accomplishment, but also a sense of something like emptiness or even fear. Like a voice inside my head was saying, *Right, I've done it . . . and this is all there is? What now?*

Who am I? This is the one question I've been trying to answer all my life, and I suppose to one degree or another it's the question we're all trying to find the answer to, isn't it? It's only human, but that's what has always fascinated me about living in this world – trying to understand other people, as well as myself. Golf has been easy by comparison, but you could fairly say that golf and people are two things you'll surely never get to the bottom of. Not that that ever stopped me from trying.

My days on the golf course as a young boy were full of discovery and fun – it was a great way to spend my time. Whether I ended up winning the Open or not, it still would have all been worth it because I was mad for the game and there were a lot worse things I could have got up to, trust me.

But I look back on those days now and I see that I was also at the golf course dawn to dusk for reasons other than my sheer love for the game. Certainly, I was anxious to make something of myself, to make a name in the world, and I thought golf was the likeliest avenue for me to do that. Yet I think my home life had something to do with it, too. It wasn't that ours was not a loving household. In some ways it was, though I would have to say that the more loving side of my father's nature didn't come out until later in his life. He was also a bit of a disciplinarian, though again, this was just part of his own upbringing, rather than something he'd thought through entirely. I remember, for instance, that I wasn't allowed to sit down at the dinner table until I was about five years old. I stood for every meal. Can you imagine? It seems extraordinary in this day and age that such a thing was 'normal', but I don't think I ever questioned it. It was the way his father had treated him, so it was the way he treated me. I'm not criticizing or judging him, only telling you that this is one of the things I remember about growing up in our house. I don't even recall if I disliked it or thought it unfair. It just was part of life: you accepted it and got on with things.

My father worked at a few different jobs when I was growing up, driving a locomotive at the steelworks, then driving a lorry. When I was about eight, we moved 10 miles or so out into the country, to a village named Winteringham. It was a chancy thing to do, but I suppose it was a way my parents thought they might bring in a few extra pounds here and there through the fish and chip shop attached to the place. I'm sure they put in a bit of money, and my mum's parents would have put in some, too. There were two houses beside each other with the chip shop at the front, and we all went in on it together. We lived in one of the houses, my grandparents in the other, and my mum and dad ran the chippy. It was hard, because my dad was still doing all his shifts at the steel works. It was just this extra thing they hoped would fly; times were so hard and money so tight, even a few spare pennies here and there could make a difference. My dad once said to me, 'If I ever earned twenty pounds a week I'd be the happiest man in the world.' He never came close to that, and when I won the Open in 1969 I started sending him a cheque for twenty-five pounds every week just so he wouldn't have to worry about money the way he always had.

Since my father still had his shifts to do at the steel works while we ran the shop, we had a fellow named Ernie Button – a good-hearted bloke who suffered from a mild mental handicap – helping out when Dad had to be away for his shifts. Ernie helped light the fires under the chip pans where the fat used to harden every night, and sometimes would freeze in the winter; he was friendly, old Ernie, and my sister Lynn and I used to get piggy-backs from him. I look back and hope we didn't take advantage of Ernie's rather simple nature; we certainly liked his company and he seemed to like ours. We moved back into town after about a year because my mother contracted meningitis. More to the point, she simply didn't like living in the country. She saw herself as a person of the city, and I think she just felt herself to be above 'country living'. Those were mostly happy days in Winteringham, though I remember the very first day we opened the shop for business my mum very publicly made me go and stand in the queue to get some fish and chips. Back of the line. I suppose she thought she was being clever, or that she was teaching me some sort of life lesson, I don't know. All I know is that it was humiliating to me as an eight-year-old. She did it in her wisdom, or as a bit of fun; she wasn't being nasty, I think. But it's lodged in my memory as something that humiliated me.

In any case, we were always moving; at least that's how it felt. We had lived in seven different houses by the time I left home in my teens. I imagine there was a bit of the gypsy in the Jacklin genetic code, a piece of DNA that didn't hurt in the life of a professional golfer.

The further I get away from those years, however, the more clearly I am also able to see who my mother was, and the ways she influenced me, in what I suppose was not always a positive way. She was a strong-willed woman, and had a wonderful singing voice (whatever talent I have for belting out a tune on or near key I got from her). She sang with the local Scunthorpe Operatic Society, and always seemed to manage to secure herself the leading role. She was very, very good, and I'm not just saying that. Though I didn't quite see it that way back then, I think she felt tied by her life, her station, as it were. I suppose you could say she always felt she'd married beneath her. And I know she also felt that having children hindered her. She even admitted as much once when she was interviewed for a book ages ago, and she said, 'I've never voiced it before in the family, but I can say now that it was hard for me seeing Tony going forwards . . . it was frustrating [to not go there myself] because the potential was there.' She was a very emotional person (as am I) and it was easy for us to clash, probably because we were alike in some ways. She loved it that I succeeded, but I know how much it frustrated her, too, because there just was nowhere for her to channel her own drive, her motivation, her talent.

It's a hard truth, but I think my mother was something of a selfish woman. My father was a guy who persevered and kept on with his life and his marriage because that was what people did. The thought of separation or divorce would never have entered my father's head, but I don't imagine the concept of romantic love did either. My mother was the type of woman who would put out the full spread for tea on Sundays if we were having company, and would make a big show of it, but if it was just us, we usually had to fend for ourselves. She simply wasn't interested.

I don't blame her for it. She was who she was. The saddest part of it all is that she was never able to change in the same way my father did. He always remained a simple and humble man (though too stuck in a rut for his own good), but he came out of himself as he got older, as I got more successful. He was able to enjoy what I achieved, and he loved meeting Nicklaus, Palmer and Trevino. He had great fun at tournaments, and always seemed to have a smile on his face. But my mother didn't change. Not a bit. There always seemed to be an air of bitterness around her as she got older, right up until the day she died of stomach cancer in 1992 at the age of seventy. I loved my mum because she was my mum, but I never did admire the way she went about living her life. A hard thing to say, but it's what I feel.

The real character in my life when I was growing up was my grandfather, David Jacklin, my father's father. I can honestly say I never met anyone like him, in all my years trotting around the globe. He worked at the Immingham docks, and worked so hard it's difficult to imagine nowadays; a seventy-year-old man out there with men one-third his age, shovelling iron ore. Unless you've done it, you can't know how backbreaking and relentless this kind of labour was, and to do it at his age was a certifiable miracle. He retired in Killinghome (east of Scunthorpe, near Immingham; which was where my father was brought up) and even then he'd zip around on a little motor scooter I'd bought for him, off tending to various odd gardening jobs he'd taken on to subsidize his pension and keep food on the table.

I also have very vivid memories of our family's 'allotment', which was a garden, basically, something that a lot of working-class families had. It was a small bit of land, tiny, really, that you could rent for a few shillings a month, quite some way from our house. I was very young then, but I remember so vividly the potatoes and other vegetables my dad used to grow there. I used to go with him and dig up the ground, prepare it all, put in the seeds. This was life, and this was how we managed to have a few fresh vegetables. It was a longish ride to get to the allotment, and he used to put me in the barrel on the back of the bike, a kind of a wheelbarrow trailer thing. If we'd picked some vegetables, I'd sit in the barrel with the potatoes and sweet peas and lettuce on the way home.

We lived in such a tiny house, such close quarters. And it wasn't just us, of course; for a whole class of postwar Britons this was simply the way it was. Terraced housing. Two up, two down. A poxy little kitchen the size of a modern walk-in wardrobe. I used to hate bloody Mondays, because that was wash day when all the clothes and bedsheets in the house got washed. I'd come home from school for lunch, and there'd be this huge great pile of steaming laundry drying out in the front room in front of the hearth. The sheets and clothes were strung up on this giant wooden folding rack, and what with such terrible weather all the time, which meant you couldn't dry them outside, it made the front room an awful place. And don't forget we're talking about a minuscule room. I mean, when my dad sat in his chair and stretched out, his feet would practically touch the hearth.

It was always cold in the house. If my dad was working the night shift, though, he'd put a fire on in the hearth when he got home about half past six in the morning, so that when I got up to do my paper round the front room would be all warm. Dad would be fast asleep in his chair. I'd go out and do my papers and come back, and there would be some toast and dripping under the grill, waiting for me. We used to eat a lot of pork dripping and that sort of thing. I remember my grandfather always had pigs around his garden, but they weren't pets. His front room was hardly what you'd call under-used. It was where he sat, but it always had salted hams and the like hanging from hooks in the ceiling.

These were hard times, and to say people had no money is hardly the point – everybody accepted that and lived with it; there was also no *hope* of having any real money. I don't think my father ever gave my sister Lynn or me anything like what we would call an allowance today or any pocket money at all. There simply wasn't any to give. My father made ten or twelve pounds a week most of his working life. Any money I ever found in my own trousers got there because I'd worked for it, that was all there was to it. I did a paper round for years, first thing every morning. After finishing the round, I would march over to the steelworks and sell papers at the gate to the tired, dirty, grey men in their flat caps leaving the factory. As they bought their papers, these men, who'd just toiled through twelve-hour shifts in punishing heat, would say to me that I'd have to be mad to do as they had done and get a job at the works. It would be an understatement to say their gruff advice left an impression on my eleven-year-old mind.

On the weekends I worked down at the Scunthorpe market with Irving Ballante, the auctioneer, helping sell all kinds of household articles, cheaply made towels, bedsheets, clocks and the like. I would stand beside him, passing him these items which he barked out were being sold at 'knock-down' prices. Every now and again, he would shout himself hoarse or the crowds would just die down, and then he'd let me take over doing some of the shouting and selling.

Between this work and the paper round I managed to squirrel away maybe a pound a week, which was not much but at least it gave me something to spend on myself. It was such a tight atmosphere for money in those days. I smoked a bit here and there back then, but could never afford a pack of Woodbines; I'd buy rolling papers and then subtly (I hoped) collect the butt ends and left-behinds in the ashtrays at the club, so that I could shake out the tobacco to cobble together a few free cigarettes. I remember my father was always – and I mean always – up to some scheme to make a little money here or there, like buying an old car, for instance, and fixing it up, then reselling it to make a few pounds. He had a few Ford 8s and Austin 7s, cars I'm sure were built in the Thirties. He'd buy them for maybe a tenner, but then he'd spend half his life underneath these things, trying to fix them up, make them run properly. If he could do that and sell it for £12, well, that was two pounds profit, even it took him a month of labour to fix the thing. I remember helping him out, and being in charge of the starter, standing outside at the front of the car. He'd be inside, working away, and I'd be out the front giving it with the starter, worried about it kicking back and breaking my bloody thumb. The starting handles were always just pieces of shit, to be honest. I remember it like it was yesterday, standing out there with him. He used to talk about cars as if they were people, *Oh, she's a lovely one, this*. It would drive you mad.

He'd get one fixed and we'd drive it somewhere, to Maplethorpe, perhaps, where my granddad on my mum's side had a caravan. It was only 60 miles away but it took us two hours to get there, on those old awful roads in a crappy little car. And the back seats of those cars always had an appalling smell to them, that mix of old leather and fumes leaking in all over the place because the carburettors were such disasters. God, you can't tell anybody what that smelled like. I lost count of the number of times I was car-sick in those old traps. Every trip was a nightmare, but there was Dad in the front seat, always prattling on, *Oh, she runs lovely, doesn't she?*

I remember once when I was about fourteen, we went to South Wales on holiday. We'd planned to leave at four in the morning because it was a ten-hour drive then, what with no motorways. If you got behind a tractor, you took your chances, that was it. Anyway, we got all packed up and then realized we couldn't leave until it was light outside because the luggage rack at the back of this dinky little car was so full it covered the back lights. It was another universe back then, and you can't tell anyone what it was really like unless they were there and lived through it.

If it wasn't cars that Dad was trying to make a couple of extra pounds from, it was moving house half a dozen times in Scunthorpe – the deal was that my parents would buy a house, work like mad on fixing it up here and there (my mother was a good seamstress and would run up some curtains; my father would do some handiwork, and give it a bit of paint and wall-paper), and then they would resell it to pocket fifty or a hundred pounds, and then we'd be on our way to the next house.

It was just that sort of time: if granddad, at seventy shovelling iron ore down at the dockyards, came across a stray lump of coal, into his pocket it would go, back to the house and into the coal bin, as anyone else would have done. Even that much, something as small as a lump of coal, was worth the effort. It was life. Nobody knew any different. Nobody could see the end of it or any way to get out from under it, and this kind of upbringing shaped me, for better and for worse.

Having said all that, I worked so hard for what little money I had that I let myself enjoy a bit of it now and then. I was particularly keen on snooker in those days, and with one chum or another I would nip down to Binns snooker hall, a great old place, upstairs, with about twenty tables, where the lights were always on and it was sevenpence a frame. We'd while away the hours I wasn't on the golf course or at school (which wasn't much of a priority for me, I'm sad to say). I loved snooker and was not so bad at it, and football was another love of my early teen years, but neither came close to touching golf. I suppose if I'd been gifted in some way in football or snooker, I might have taken those up more seriously, might have pursued them the same way I pursued golf. But it was always going to be golf for me, even if there might have been times I wasn't as good as I thought I was. Often I played golf with members other than my father, and there was usually a little something at stake on the side.

I remember at one point I was enough in debt from my golf money matches that I took a micrometer (a tool used for measuring the thickness of steel) down to the second-hand shop in town to try and barter it off. I knew it was worth three pounds, and I hoped I'd get two. I can't honestly recall if I sold it or not, but I suppose I got the money from somewhere because I still kept on playing in similar matches. Trying to sell the micrometer felt like a necessity at the time, just a thing I had to do because I was desperate to pay up and therefore keep playing (though I didn't often let myself get into debt). But looking back on it now I can see it also represented something pretty significant about who I was at that age – I'd already decided in my heart I was not going to follow the path my parents wanted for me, which was to get a job at the steel foundry and collect a weekly pay packet. My uncle had given me the micrometer because my family thought – not unreasonably, I suppose – that I would finish off at school and become an apprentice fitter at the steelworks. I knew that was not going to happen, though I never spoke of it to my parents or anyone else. Perhaps I never even said it out loud to myself. I sure as hell never told my parents or my uncle I'd tried to sell the micrometer.

My dreams were not about the steel works or shovelling coal or driving a lorry. The respect I have for my father and my granddad, for the exhausting labour they put in day after day, decade after decade, is enormous. But I was meant for something else, that was all, and it was as if I knew it even then. My dreams were about golf, but not just the game itself – I was set on becoming a professional. The excitement I felt as a thirteen-year-old is something I still recall, even though there wasn't much to get excited about purely from a results point of view. I was a good player then, even if I hadn't done much in tournaments. But it was the range of possibilities that so entranced me as I lay in bed imagining what might happen if I dedicated myself and got a bit of luck. I wanted to be a pro, wanted to go to America, wanted to prove myself against the best in the world. That was my dream. But it's important to really underscore that it wasn't *just* a dream. I was a passionate, driven person even as a child. When I say it was my *dream* to play professional golf, to play against the best, I don't mean that I was sitting around day-dreaming, my head filled with fuzzy maybes. I was even at that age aware of a drive inside me, a need to prove myself, to be great. There was a hunger there. And once you know that impulse is inside you, it never goes away. I wanted to be the best golfer in the game, period. In a way, I was already past dreaming about it – I was pursuing it.

2

Golf came into my life by the purest chance. It was the summer of 1953. I was perhaps eight or nine years old and we were in Scunthorpe down on Collinson Avenue. Our neighbour, a man named Eric Markee, thought he ought to give the game a try, and one day he asked my father to go along with him. I've no idea where my father got golf clubs from. Borrowed Eric's, probably, until he got hooked and went to get his own set. But the simple truth is that he was mad for the game from Day One. In fact, I often wondered in the years that came and went if he wasn't more in love with the game than I was. For the first little while that he played I caddied for him, and after he finished he would pull out an old cut-down ladies three-wood and let me hit a few shots. Once it was clear I was smitten with the game, we went down to the second-hand sale room in town, the shop run by a member of the Scunthorpe Golf Club, Tommy Francis, where I got some old hickories. It was the same shop, frankly, where we acquired practically every single thing we owned – I don't recall us purchasing even one new thing the whole time I lived at home. It wasn't just big purchases, either; it wasn't until I was fifteen years old that I first ate in a restaurant. Anyway, they were grotty old things, these hickories, and I remember I used to have to stand them in water when I wasn't using them because the wood shrank and warped so badly if I didn't.

When I was growing up there were two golf courses in Scunthorpe, but I had very little idea about the game, and the game didn't have much of an idea about me, either. I didn't even know where the courses were. We lived on the kind of street where golf was not a way you imagined you'd spend your free time. And though I did start to play when my father played, I never came into possession of my own full set of golf clubs until I was eighteen years old. Can you imagine? At the age of eighteen I was starting to shoot real numbers in serious tournaments, I'd secured myself a job as an assistant at Potters Bar, and, in fact, I was only seven years from winning the Open . . . and yet I didn't even have a full *set* of clubs, let alone new clubs. I was a *professional*, and I had hand-me-down clubs! I suppose this illustrates a few different things, all of which say something about me and my upbringing, the obvious one being we didn't have the money for me to have decent clubs. Second, I was (and would always remain, truth be told) a natural player, a player who lived and died by feel and touch and confidence and inspiration, as opposed to mechanical repetitiveness. I grooved my swing in those early days, make no mistake about it, and my mechanics were becoming increasingly first-rate, but having such substandard equipment for so long, and excelling with it, left me in no doubt that if you've got a golf swing, you've got a golf swing. It's a lifelong thing. (Putting is something else entirely, but we'll come to that later, don't fret!)

The early days of my playing, the summer I turned nine, involved primarily going off with my father's clubs when he wasn't playing, just to hit some shots here and there, though I did get the hickories in short order. I was always very careful to practise out of sight of the clubhouse, since most of the members were not too keen about some boy thrashing around the course.

Many of the same members who turned a dark eye on me when I was having trouble getting the ball airborne were among the first to run up and pump my hand when I returned to the club years later with the Claret Jug. 'Twas ever thus, and a shame it is, because if there is one thing that golf needs, it's steady and genuine encouragement of youngsters. Not pushing them, mind you. Just encouragement. Letting them be. Giving them time and opportunity to play. Offering some decent teaching. (And tossing in a little etiquette training, wouldn't hurt, I suppose.) I try to do that with my son Sean, our youngest, who will soon be fifteen. He's got a hell of a swing, and he's crazy about the game, but I don't push him. What good would that do? If I pushed too hard he might become a slightly better player, but then he might hate the game by the time he turns twenty. Who would that benefit? I know in my heart that I was crazy for golf when I was young, and that my parents never once forced it on me, even when it was obvious I was more than just handy with the game. Of course, knowing my parents and myself (the way I came to know this as an adult), if they'd been pushing me to get out there and seriously practise my golf I'd probably have said *Stuff it!* If they'd done that maybe I'd be using that micrometer today.

Those early teen years at the club were fantastic. I didn't care much about anything except whatever was going on at the Scunthorpe club. Ted Muscroft – a lovely gent – let me work as his man about the place (since he acted as the greens keeper in the morning and the pro in the afternoons). I did everything: drove the tractor, cut the greens, whatever it took to be around the club, and then had the opportunity to go and hit golf shots when I was done with my jobs.

A year or two later I made a good chum in Frank Barclay, and we played a lot of golf together over the next few years. What a treat it was to have such a good pal to do these things with, someone to enjoy the game with, to compete against. He was a year older than me. It was through playing loads of matches against Frank that I started to understand something about myself, something quite central, though I had no real idea then what to call it or how to phrase it. I think it has to be something any athlete who eventually reaches the pinnacle of their sport must feel growing out of him- or herself as he or she is learning how good they are as youngsters. I'm talking about enjoying the feeling of winning. I liked to win. I liked to beat Frank. I'm just being honest. We were competitive, we kept score, and winning was something that felt good and which I found gratifying. It was important to me, and would become more so as I began to imagine myself making a living as a pro, or even more than that, that someday I might win the Open.

Of course, I was also intrigued by the golf swing, and spent hour after hour trying to develop something that would work, something that would allow me to score. Because that's the key isn't it? How many perfect, fluid, gorgeous golf swings are there out there? Thousands. Just take a look at the American college tour. Every swing is perfect, and let's face it, most of them look the same, too. But not many of them are going to go on and be world-beaters. The game is about scoring, nothing else. I got that even as a teenager.

While I was trying to come up with a golf swing that let me learn how to score, and win, I read as many magazines as I could get my hands on. But the funny thing is that I never had what you'd call a formal lesson. My father never bought me any sort of instructional manual. I just learned by doing what instinctively felt right to me, and from watching others, though even this presented a few challenges. The lowest handicap at the club, dear old Teddy Muscroft, was a seven or an eight, but I had to be careful not to watch him since his action was such a terror to behold. I think it would be a bit too harsh to call it an aversion, but I certainly don't have a library full of instructional books. I never did and never will. I remember reading somewhere a few years ago that I used to hear of people who even carried around books like Hogan's *Five Lessons* in their golf bags. How ridiculous is that? As if they could just whip it out of the bag when a problem comes up, so they could consult the thing. There's no surer way to cock up your game than trying to fix something in the middle of a round. So much of what we might call the 'teaching industry' nowadays is almost fraud – it's nothing but a cash cow for the 'teachers'. You hear about the one or two good players these massive teaching factories produce, but you never hear about the thousands and thousands of youngsters who pay a small fortune and then disappear.

For me, learning the mechanics of the swing was about trial and error, and I was fortunate to get it right, to have an intuitive feel for the game that allowed me to understand the complex chain of events that go into a golf swing. I don't think there's much use denying that what you learn as a youth will probably be with you for ever, so it's best to learn decent fundamentals from the start. I don't think my golf swing has really changed all that much from then. Of course, I'm not the green sapling I once was, so I can't go at it like I used to. There isn't the same flexibility to get right to the back of the swing. But the basic brushstrokes haven't changed much.

Some will argue that a player like Tiger Woods has already changed his fundamental swing a couple of times in his still young career. I think this is true, but only partially. He hasn't changed his grip, and he's always had exquisite posture. Those things haven't changed. But in any case he's not the standard to be used in a discussion. The man is simply outrageously gifted, and works hard to boot. Harry Overcoat who plays twice a month isn't going to have the same chance of changing his swing around, trust me.

So as a self-taught golfer I went and beat balls, and dug it out of the ground, to use the old Hogan phrase. I was full of intensity and resolve every time I went to the range. It was serious, and I wasn't there just to screw around. Also, I watched and copied. I would study any player I thought was good, to see not just what I could learn from them technically, but anything else in their game that I could use. I sometimes offered to caddy for decent players who came around for a match against a Scunthorpe player, mostly so I could watch and learn from the way they acted and reacted to whatever happened on the course (though I only did this for a few players, like the Grimsby club member John Elmore, a one-handicapper who was a big noise around the county). Nowadays, the geniuses on television call all this *course management*; back then, it was called using your head.

But it was during those hundreds and hundreds of hours standing by myself on the range that I came to know the simplest things are what count. I knew – almost by instinct, I suppose, since no one told me so – that without solid fundamentals there was no hope, none, of being the golfer I wanted to be. Did I know this even as a twelve-year-old, as a thirteen-year-old? Absolutely, I did. The grip, the stance, the ball position, the posture – those things that can't change under pressure. I was driven, *obsessed*, to learn it myself, to get it right.

After mastering some of the fundamentals it seemed to me that the key concept I always wanted to keep in mind – now commonly called *swing thoughts* by the gurus out there – was to control my swing speed. Tempo. Rhythm. These were what controlled the golf swing, or mine anyway. I wasn't in the game to get lucky, or to hope things came out right without knowing why – I wanted to do it right, and to know *why* I was doing it right. And to me it was always about keeping the fundamentals tight and then learning to control the tempo of my swing when I got under pressure, so that all those nerves, that adrenalin, that excitement, my *emotions*, weren't controlling the tempo. So, from the age of about twelve or so, this was my life. Practice, focus, determination, desire. I was on a mission. I knew it and wanted it, and my life was devoted to collecting information, experience and knowledge about golf and the golf swing. It didn't matter what it was. If it had anything to do with golf, I would soak it up . . . on purpose, mind you. I was after something here.

Bobby Locke made one of the first great impressions on me. It was something you couldn't ever forget, no matter how long you lived. He came to the Scunthorpe Golf Club when I was thirteen, just to play an exhibition with Teddy Muscroft, the pro with the eight handicap. Such a lovely man, Ted, but a crap golfer. Anyway, I was going to be Locke's caddy for the event, but before they went out he gave a little exhibition for some of the members. Unluckily for me, being his caddy, I had to be the one legging it out to the other end of the practice ground to pick up his balls and stuff them back in his practice bag. He started with an 8-iron. It had been raining, and the first ball he hit plugged in the ground. I eased it out with my finger and wiped it on the towel. He said something to the crowd, turned around and hit another 8-iron. It went straight into the plug hole his first ball made. Can you imagine? Astonishing. You can't invent something like that. It was too incredible, and I'm telling you it made a pretty heavy impression on me. *Goddamn*, I thought, *how good is this guy?*

Oh, I almost forgot; I was in school, too, during these years. How could I have neglected to mention that? I hardly cared, I'm afraid to say. I went to the Henderson Avenue infant school and then to the Doncaster Road secondary school (fifty-three students in my class, and the only thing you could rely on getting out of it was a clip on the earhole delivered just in case you did something). The happiest day of my school life was the one when I walked out the door for the last time. Some classes I was competent in, like maths and carpentry (and I love wood-working to this day), but I left school when I was fifteen years old.

Leaving school was no tragedy for me. I was so anxious to play golf, and to do anything that had anything to do with golf, that my parents never had a single fear about where I might have been when they hadn't seen me for twelve straight hours. I was down at the club. To this day I'm a morning person, and I was even as a child. Every day I could I'd be up first thing, do my paper round, get home, do myself a sandwich, hop on my bike, and go over to the club (which was never quite as quick as it all sounds – through all our various moves in Scunthorpe we still never lived closer than 4 miles from the course). If it was summer I might be there for twelve hours a day, and in the middle of winter during school holidays I'd arrive when it was dark and leave when it was dark.

I was never bored with golf, never ever. I could spend hours doing the smallest little things, as long as they had to do with golf, and as long as they had to do with me improving. I remember I used to do this drill for my short game where I would take an umbrella and just poke it in the ground. Then I would sur-round the umbrella with pieces of firewood I'd brought from home so as to create a circle, my own sort of archery board, I suppose. The circle was perhaps 20 feet in diameter, and I'd step 70 or 80 yards back with my bag of fifty or sixty balls, and wouldn't allow myself to leave until I'd hit at least half of them into the circle. It was great fun, but for a lad like myself – a boy with a rather vivid imagination, it has to be said – it was also a chance for me to work on something else, something that today the gurus call 'visualization' or 'mental training'. As I hit ball after ball I imagined that Ben Hogan or Sam Snead was standing over my shoulder, watching me, seeing me perform, examining my mechanics. And they were always talking to me, too. I wonder if I talked back!? It makes me laugh, but, who knows, perhaps that's why the members left me alone out there, that strange, daft little boy who was always babbling to himself. Some of the neighbours at one of the houses we lived in might have thought I'd gone mad, too, because I once rigged up a makeshift practice area in our tiny back yard where our 8-foot-high back gate opened onto a small lane. I would aim at the wooden gate and whack little chunks of thick industrial hose at it (since I couldn't afford to ruin the golf balls I had then). *Bang. Crash. Slam.* Poor bloody neighbours. I'd probably been driven to practise at home after I accidentally smashed one of the Scunthorpe Golf Club windows whilst practising flop shots one day beside the practice green. The ball crashed through a window and came to rest on a snooker table. The club captain, Jack Webster, located me, drily asked if the ball was mine, and then dressed me down so severely and in such graphic language that I ran home in tears.

In any case, the words I heard in my head as I practised, whether from Sam or Ben, were a huge part of my motivation. I could imagine Hogan saying, without a smile, 'No, that's not quite right.' Or Snead drawling, 'Not bad, kid, not bad, but that won't cut it on tour.' I was desperate to impress these ghosts, though it was always somehow a bit hollow in the end, because when I went to pick up my shag bag full of dirty old golf balls (and increasingly with my goals for the target achieved), there was never anyone standing there to congratulate me, except for myself. I sometimes fantasized this or that great person, or even my father, had been standing there to say, 'Forty out of sixty inside fifteen feet! Well done, Tony!!' But in fact it was good there wasn't anyone there. This is the golfer's truth, particularly the golfer who rises to the heights, who plays as a pro, who, imagine!, goes on to win a Major or two.

You are alone out there.

Surrounded by thousands, but alone.

You have to learn that lesson early, that there is only one person whose opinion matters, only one person you can truly rely on in that crucible of pressure. You had better learn to like and trust that person, because you are stuck with him for ever. You have to get comfortable being alone, and pretty much have no choice but to accept it. Otherwise, you're just out for a walk with your mates at the local municipal. If you can't trust the person inside you, if you can't rely on him under pressure, don't bother reaching any higher than playing a five-dollar nassau, because you'll never make it. To win a Major, that self-belief has to be total, complete, *absolute*. I'm not here to judge anyone, or say it has anything to do with being a better or worse person; please understand that. All I'm doing is telling you the way it is, the way I know it to be. It's not about right or wrong, or better or worse. It's about performance, and it is what it is. It's fact.

My game improved steadily in the early years, though when I was eleven or twelve I found it desperately difficult to break 90. One morning, astonishingly, I broke through that barrier by miles, shooting an 84 while playing on my own. My delight and amazement was so great I wanted to tell someone right away, and I burst into the pro shop to tell Ted Muscroft. The air was let out of my tyres when he said he didn't believe me. Can't say I blame him, since I'd not yet even broken 90. But I played again that afternoon with Ted, and somehow I managed to do it again, to shoot exactly the same score, an 84. It was a miserable afternoon, raining so hard our time might have been better spent rounding up pairs of animals to save from the flood. But despite the grim weather, I was so determined to show him I was no liar, and, more importantly, that I was learning this bloody game, that I slogged through to that 84. What a great feeling it was.

The next year, when I was thirteen, I broke 80 for the first time, and wasn't often over 80 afterwards. I felt on my way. It was time to put in a handicap card, so that I could begin playing in tournaments, and testing myself against other players, which is really what I was after. Even then I was hungry for the competition, so anxious to have the chance to test myself that I almost laugh now looking back at how obsessed and singular I must have been.

Still, it was not the easiest time or place to be a talented junior. To start with there was no such thing as junior ratings; there was one handicap system and that was for the senior men. A junior player had a handicap and played under this system, or he didn't play tournaments. I'm delighted to see that the attitude of the adults in the clubs now has begun to change, so that they are starting to embrace juniors; it only makes sense. It's the only way the game will grow and flourish, and I think it's obvious the reason the United States has become ascendant in golf – the sheer depth of talent in America is astonishing – is because they have always had better junior programmes than we've had here. (You can even see the difference in results between us and great junior programmes in smaller countries like Australia and Sweden.) There has always been something of the view in Britain that those who come after us shouldn't have things any easier than we did. It's not a healthy attitude. What's the point of subjecting people to misery just because you had to go through it yourself? It's stupid shortsightedness.

But despite whatever obstacles there were at Scunthorpe (and there were a few members who didn't like a junior kicking their arse), I did manage to get my handicap card, which meant I could start competing in county tournaments. And as I said, that's what it was really about for me: competing. Getting the chance to prove, to myself as much as anyone else, that I had it in me, whatever that 'it' is, that special something that makes you rise to level after level of achievement. When I take a moment or two now (as I stroll down the beach on the Gulf Coast of Florida on a hot sunny day, so many millions of miles from grey old Scunthorpe), I do sometimes wonder how I managed to stay with the game. I wonder this not just because of the financial, physical or competitive hurdles I faced – though there were plenty – but because of the grief my father (unintentionally, I think) gave me on the golf course. I suppose I got my stubborn I-know-myself-best attitude from him, but we locked horns from almost the minute we stepped onto the course together. God help me, I can hear us arguing right now, as if it were yesterday, about anything, but mostly about him always feeling as if he had to give me incessant bits of advice. It used to drive me daft! Okay, he was my father, and I respected him, but when it came to golf, I bloody well didn't need him telling me what to do. By the time I was in my early teens I had a strong sense of what I was up to technically, not to mention what was probably a cocky little swagger to me. When my father would say things like 'nice and smooth now' just as I was about to hit the ball, it sometimes made me want to turn around and aim it at him. Not really, of course (well, I don't *think* I would have ever done it). But I don't think my father ever took me seriously as a golfer until I started to beat him regularly. Luckily for both of us, that happened pretty early on.

I find it ironic looking back, given how central the Ryder Cup has been to my life, that it really was the Ryder Cup that brought out in me the desire and determination to become a golfer. I was only thirteen. It was 1957, and the Cup was being played at Lindrick, which is about 60 miles from Scunthorpe. My father wanted to take me. I was beside myself with excitement, and was bouncing off the walls for days beforehand. To that point in my life I'd had no real 'live' contact with a golf pro of any sort. Teddy Muscroft tried hard as a player, but he just never had it. I always hoped the British Tour (which wasn't much of a tour, sadly) would come Lincolnshire's way so that I could see some actual players competing for a living. But it wasn't until the 1957 Ryder Cup that I had the chance to watch great players close up.

The captain was Dai Rees. The players included Peter Alliss, Max Faulkner, Eric Brown, Christy O'Connor, Bernard Hunt, Ken Bousfield, Harry Weetman. I remember them all. The Americans, led that year by captain Jackie Burke, brought over players like Dow Finsterwald, Dick Mayer and Tommy Bolt (the great, unique, Tommy Bolt, who I enjoyed crossing swords with when I finally made my way to America a decade later).

These were just names in my head until that point, names I read in the papers. At Lindrick (which Great Britain won, by the way – perhaps it was also here I got the idea in my head that the Americans were beatable!) they became flesh and blood. I was enthralled. I watched them perform, walked close along with them, and began to fantasize that one day it was going to be me walking on the other side of the ropes.

I'm not a hero worshipper by nature, and have never been one for getting autographs, though I've spent countless hours signing them, which I never resented or found tiresome. It sounds rather funny now, but I never actually liked my name when I was a boy. Tony Jacklin. Tony Jacklin? *I hate that name*, I would complain to my parents. *Why did you give me that name?* I remember moaning about it at dinner one night. 'Ben Hogan, Sam Snead, Arnold Palmer,' I whined to my mother and father, who must have had to work hard to keep the grins off their faces. 'Now those are great names.' They calmly responded that Tony Jacklin could be a great name, too, some day. My mother had actually planned to use Anthony, full out, but within a day or two of my birth a nurse picked me up and couldn't believe how heavy I was. She declared me Ten Ton Tony on the spot, and Tony stuck, though thankfully the Ten Ton didn't, in name or fact.

Great name or not, I wanted it under golf's brightest lights. The very day my father and I returned from Lindrick there was still enough light to squeeze in nine holes, and I was so inspired by what I'd seen that day that I proceeded to record my best ever nine-hole score. That day was a great leap forward for me, since I was finally able to see close up, in person, what it looked like to play the game properly. I saw myself reaching for that level. I'm not just saying that. I really did. And not only did I see myself as aspiring to that level, I believed I had it in me. Going to Lindrick reinforced the passion I had boiling around inside me.

The Scunthorpe Club had done its job for me to that point, but I was starting to get to the level where I needed real competition, some honest opposition in the form of better players to both learn from and test myself against. The only place that could be found in our area was at the Holme Hall Club. The club had some handy players, and they were willing to let me be part of their regular games – which always had a little extra riding on them. The amounts at stake, usually something like half a crown, seemed like astronomical sums to me then, but it sharpened my focus, I can tell you. I remember playing money matches against fellows like Frank Cottingham, who made washers and driers, Bill Empson, a car dealer, and another gent named Alan Williamson. I lost every now and then (hence the micrometer sale!), but I was winning more than losing. More importantly, playing so often with older men helped me mature as a person and as a player. I had to learn how to conduct myself on the course, and how to compete. By the age of fifteen, I began to feel in my bones that my destiny was to be a golfer of international stature. It was something I wanted, something I felt, something I could almost imagine touching. But my parents had other ideas.

Strangely, my parents couldn't see my bright, shining future. The trophies. The achievement. The fame and fortune. They didn't see the certainty of it all. Can you imagine? Seriously, who can blame them for not saying, *Okay, Tony, you have our blessing to chuck away school and a steady job so you can chase an itinerant lifestyle that's pretty damn unlikely to succeed?* In their world view, they may have believed I had some native golfing ability, but there was no way they felt it was enough to encourage me to try and turn it into a career. Turning a lathe at the steel works was more like it; it was tangible, visible, something you could count on in hard times. There was a pay packet in it, money you could see and touch. Not to mention that they knew chasing a golf ball around for a living would mean I'd be leaving Scunthorpe sooner than later. And so at their urging I went to work at the steelworks, apprenticing for a trade as a fitter.

One of my favourite comedy skits of all time is Monty Python's Four Yorkshiremen, the one where the four old Yorkshire codgers sit around trying to top one another with tales of hardship and woe in their childhoods. *We used to dream of living in a cardboard shoebox . . . would have been a palace to us. I used to have to get up half an hour before I went to bed,* and *pay mill owner for permission to come to work. And when we got home our mother and father would slash us in two with bread knives and dance about on our graves singing Hallelujah.* My God it's funny, and every time I hear it or think about it, it makes me tear up with laughter – not just because it's funny, either; the sense of humour is so much part of the north of England, that ability to seriously overstretch whatever the nugget of truth was to begin with.

I think this is the biggest reason why I feel so instantly

comfortable whenever I return to the north of England. I'm with my own. It's not so much the landscape, and it sure as hell isn't the weather. It's the sense of humour that's just so unique to that part of the world. It's embedded in my character, it truly is. It's part of who I am, that humour that comes out in every situation. It's all about painting pictures, about word play, about exaggeration, about puncturing any kind of pretension. And it's constant, in every walk of life, from Dave Whelan at JJB to the guys down at the local pub. There's always somebody just absolutely reducing me to tears. That's what I miss most about England, and I know the minute I go back north I feel at home. I've often wondered what it is about this particular part of England that makes its sense of humour so unique, this sardonic, almost bleak world view. It's hard to explain, but it must have a lot to do with basic survival. There are the mills, the steelworks, so much hardship, particularly in generations past. The weather was always so awful, everyone so poor. People basically had to find a way to get on with it and try to make light of things. Otherwise, it'd all be just a bit too grim. What's the old saying, You have to laugh otherwise you'd cry? That northern black humour was the only way to keep your chin up, really.

And so getting back to my earlier point, that's why I love that Monty Python skit so much – because it's funny but also because there's more than a nugget of truth to it. Life *was* relentlessly, numbingly hard. So you'll have to forgive me just a little if I start to sound like one of the four Yorkshiremen when I talk about those early days in Scunthorpe. Especially at the steelworks. God, I hated it.

I've said that my father worked as a locomotive driver for a time at the steelworks, and though I never doubted that my parents had my best interests at heart in wanting me to have a good solid trade to fall back on, the hours I spent in that dirty noisy factory were just about the least happy of my life, before or since. Every single day I simply couldn't wait for the moment to come when I was freed from it, so that I could sprint off to the club and start playing golf. I stood there all day, *itching* for quitting time. There were other complications, too, when it came to the steelworks, though I'm really only comfortable talking about it now that my father has passed away. When I was about twelve years old, he used to cycle back and forth to work. One day, he and a few other men were caught with lumps of coal in the saddle bags on their bicycles. This was something that was not at all uncommon, and we were just so poor that nicking a lump of coal here and there from a huge factory where it was just lying about the floor must not have seemed much of a crime to them. But they were caught and sacked immediately, and his name was in the paper for it. He was at the Scunthorpe Golf Club by then, and it was embarrassing all round. This was why he ended up driving a lorry for a haulage company.

In any case, although I was earning nearly £4 a week (two-thirds of which I gave to my mother to help out with household costs) my total unhappiness with it all must have got through to my parents. I don't think this took much insight on their part; I'm sure I was sulking and whinging the whole time. They figured out that I simply wasn't going to last: that if there was to be a happier conclusion I had to move on. I made it through a year. After enquiries and discussions it was agreed I would work instead in the solicitor's offices of Eric Kemp, a member at Holme Hall. Thank God for it. I acted as a kind of delivery boy for him, working through the morning, available for other deliveries and reception and odd jobs in the early afternoon, and after that I was free to go straight to the golf course, which I did every single day. I was happier no matter what the pay might have been, but the fact that he was paying me close to double what I'd been making at the steelworks was a godsend.

And my game was really starting to show signs that I wasn't

a complete dreamer after all, that maybe I did have some real talent to go along with desire and intensity and a serious work ethic. When I was thirteen years old I won the Lincolnshire Junior Championship for the first time. I won it again when I was fourteen, and yet again when I was fifteen, shooting 81, 66. This was a tournament open to any golfer up to the age of eighteen – I was the youngest player ever to win it. Winning the Junior Championship was a nice feather in my cap, of course, but it didn't represent much of a challenge. Junior tournaments were often very small then. One year the County Junior Championship had just eight entries. Of course, it's different now. The game has grown so much, and the talent pool has become so deep (much more so in America than the UK, as mentioned) that any even halfway decent junior tournament nowadays will feature dozens of scratch players. I like to think that I might have progressed even more rapidly as a player had I had that kind of competition to line up against, but who can know?

I did gain a few worthwhile lessons along the way in the matches I played around town. I was probably about fifteen when I learned to be an assassin on the golf course, that you really and truly have to be the last man standing to win regularly. I was in a county match that year, against a gent whose name I've forgotten, though I never forgot how he managed to beat me. We were playing a match at Holme Hall, and early on he was chatty and friendly, treating me very well indeed, and I remember thinking, 'What a perfectly nice fellow this is. He's lovely.' I got one up on him, then two up, and he kept on chitchatting away. I found him quite interesting, and soon I wasn't really paying attention to the match. *Bingo, bango, bongo.* He won 2&1. I was stunned, and afterwards I still didn't quite understand what happened. But once I realized that he'd killed me with kindness – and knew what he was doing as he was doing it – I never forgot it. It was a perfect lesson. I learned to keep my antennae up and use moments like that.

I also benefited from the advice and encouragement of people here and there. Playing County golf on the men's team was John Elmore, a teammate who I'd actually caddied for in previous years. He was a fine man, and was always looking out for me, always cared to ask what I was up to. One day he recited a bit of a poem that I liked and I asked him if he could get me the rest of it. He brought it to me the next day printed out on a little sheet of paper (that very page is now in the World Golf Hall of Fame). The poem, by Walter D. Wintle, said much to me as a youngster.

If you think you are beaten, you are;
If you think you dare not, you don't.
If you'd like to win, but think you can't,
It's almost a cert you won't.
If you think you'll lose, you're lost,
For out in the world we find
Success begins with a fellow's will;
It's all in the state of mind.

If you think you're outclassed, you are;
You've got to think high to rise.
You've got to be sure of yourself before
You can ever win a prize.
Life's battles don't always go
To the stronger or faster man;
But sooner or later the man who wins
Is the one who thinks he can.

A bit simplistic and sentimental it might be, but it made a great impression on my young mind, especially because I really did want to *win*, which wasn't always the most British way to be. Yet I wanted to be a good person too. This poem almost seemed to me to say that you could strive to win, want to win, and yet stay decent, too. I never let that poem, nor its message, leave my side. It was important, and has always remained so, to be driven *and* decent. I was determined to get to the top, but how we're treated and how we treat others is what we're left with, is *all* we're left with, at the end of the day.

So I kept on, playing against the best I could find in my area. The summer I was fifteen I was a decent enough player to be included in the county side that competed against Yorkshire, Northamptonshire and Norfolk. The chance to play fabulous courses like Brancaster and Hunstanton was a treat for me, but I was always worried about the money side of it (a kind of feeling that, with my upbringing, I don't think ever left me in life, no matter how much I made or lost). Expenses weren't covered for team members in those days, but I was fortunate in that Bill Bloomer, a Grimsby Golf Club member and father of the famous English tennis player Shirley Bloomer, was almost always good enough to take me back and forth between county matches in his Bentley. I never forgot the smell of the leather seats, the sheer quality of the automobile; I know I dreamed of owning a car like that one day.

At sixteen, I won the Lincolnshire Open I referred to at the start of the book, a win that truly lit the fuse under me. I knew I was good. My game was getting steadily better, and I was growing steadily more frustrated with my station in life, even though I was still only in my mid-teens. But I was so ambitious. You can't know how hungry I was, how anxious to prove I could be great. I was a racehorse dancing in the gates, desperate for the sound of the starter's gun. I wanted to be out in the world, making my way, showing what I was made of. And despite the love I came to have for the place, particularly in later years when I came back to visit, I knew I wasn't going to do it in Scunthorpe. When I was seventeen I wrote off to a club in California applying for an assistant professional's job, but never heard back, which was hardly a shock. I never told my mother and father about this, but I was brimming over with energy, confidence, a bit of cockiness. I was always leafing through the pages of *Golf Illustrated*, scouring the advertisements for any sort of opportunity.

Then one day I saw the advert that would change the tack of things, would set me on my way. I wasn't to know it then but it would also lead to two years of what nowadays we would call a love/hate relationship; back then it was just an incredibly irritating if ultimately necessary apprenticeship. In fact, it might have been more of a hate/hate relationship. It probably came close to double homicide on occasion, both of us guilty, toe-tagged and flat on the slab. Still, I know I would not have developed the same way without this man's influence on me; the same way, I suppose, a bushel of wheat can't be made into a loaf of good bread until you first beat the chaff out of it. I was the rough wheat, and I took some serious mental and emotional thrashings over the next couple of years. The brute working the thresher was Bill Shankland, the head professional at Potters Bar Golf Club, where I began my career as a professional golfer.

3

Bill Shankland, or Shanko as we called him, had captained his Rugby League side back in his native Australia, and his strong blunt physique suited his temper. To say he had the disposition of an angry pit bull is to slander the name of pit bulls everywhere. The man was a tyrant to his employees. He always did manage to put on a pretty good front for the members – he kept good stock, ran a nice shop, was a good teacher – but many saw through him, saw what a hard taskmaster he was, and that the man was as tough as old boots. I suppose I could look back now and say that his tutelage – if that's what you want to call it – was an ingredient in my eventual success, but I wouldn't put my worst enemy through it. Honestly. He was a mean bastard, end of story.

I was seventeen years old when I first stepped into Shankland's shop, and from that second on it seemed there was nothing I could do right. He was the kind of man who would come into the shop and run a forefinger along the length of a shelf looking for a speck of dust. I'm not making that up. He did this sort of thing all the time. But it could have been any number of tests. A pile of shirts I'd folded? *Disgraceful, that mess.* Just in from winning an assistant's tournament? *You did all right, but you were lucky, weren't you?* The floor freshly swept? *You missed that whole bloody corner!* Shanko was paying me £6 a week, plus half of whatever I made from my teaching and playing. This seemed all right to me at the time, but sometimes I wondered if he wasn't paying me £6 a week simply to retain me as a target. The man made my life hell. He could be a bastard when the mood was on him, which seemed to be pretty much every time he laid eyes on me.

Not every aspect of my new world was punishing, however. There was one immediate positive to my move to Potters Bar, and that was the delightful digs I found with Mr and Mrs Baker. She owned a house not too far from the course, and the bottom of her garden backed right up against the main rail line that ran north, a line that also ran right past Potters Bar; the house would rattle and shake as trains rumbled by, but I was quickly used to it and it never bothered me. My rent was to be £3 15s. per week. This included breakfast, meals that alone would have justified the amount I was paying her. When I'd first signed on with Shankland, I naturally felt unsure about my new world; that included a place to stay. Mrs Baker's husband, Fred, caddied at the club during his spare time, and when I arrived he suggested they might be able to take me in for a week. It started out as a temporary arrangement, but I ended up staying there off and on for the next six years! It was my base, my home away from home. I was comfortable with the Bakers, and ever grateful for their kindness and flexibility. Thank God for them; if I'd had a landlady near as hard to deal with as Shanko, I might never have made it out of my teens.

I have very fond memories of Mrs Baker. I suppose in some way she was a kind of mother to me in the way that I felt I didn't have back home. I must have wanted a bit of spoiling or something. I'd never been doted upon by my mum, but I was certainly spoiled by Mrs Baker. She was a delightful and kind-hearted woman who always seemed to be wanting to take care of the people around her. It's no surprise that as soon as Vivien and I were married, we stayed with Mrs Baker for a short time, that's how comfortable I was there. (We all have regrets here and there in life, and though I'm not one to dwell on what's lost or hasn't happened, I do wish that she'd been part of the shooting of the *This Is Your Life* programme, hosted by Eamonn Andrews, that featured me shortly after winning my two Opens. It was a terrific experience, and it surprised the hell out of me – they grabbed me just as I was leaving Buckingham Palace after the Queen had given me the OBE. The problem, though, is that you don't really have any input into how those shows get done – it was primarily my parents who advised them on who to include in the show – and so although it was a wonderful moment, and a really well done show, I wasn't able to say to anyone that Mrs Baker ought to have been part of it. That would have only been fair, because she was a lovely woman.)

It's funny; upon reflection I can almost look back at those years living in her house and say they were among the happiest of my life, at least up to the years when Vivien and I were able to have a family. Mrs Baker had a son who was about ten years older than I was, and he and I often went down to the local pub to throw some darts. We even played on the local team together. Mr Baker was also a fine person, a quiet gentleman, and he ended up driving over a million miles while working for London Transport. He passed away well before Mrs Baker. There was always such a nice spirit in their house. They were interested in other people. I certainly never felt like complaining that Mrs Baker treated me like a long-lost son, spoiling me, looking out for me, fussing over me. I was a very fortunate young man to find such a home from home as a seventeen-year-old.

Of course, I desperately needed that kind of affection and attention, simply as a shield to the Niagara Falls of abuse that

Shanko poured over me every day. I often wondered if he didn't get up every morning, brush his teeth, wash his face, and comb his hair, all while standing in front of the mirror asking himself the question, 'Now let's see, Shanks old man, what fresh hell can we make of that little git Jacklin's life today?'

I started in Shanko's shop in January of 1962. He had two assistants at the time, Colin Christianson and Dennis Scanlon, but both left later on that year, after which I was on my own. By 1963 he had a few other assistants working for him, but they were all part-time; it was still me who opened the shop, did most of what needed doing every day, swept it out at the end of the day, locked it up and set the burglar alarm. All for six pounds a week. It was pure agony at times, yet although I hate to even admit it even to a minor degree – I can hear my teeth grinding even now as I say it – Shanko did help me in one way. Not with my game, it's important to note. In the way that one might occasionally say, *Okay, let's just pop down to the range and have a look at your swing*, he would spend time with me, but I found his teaching maddeningly inconsistent. One day he'd be telling me to do something one way ('No, no, hit through from the right, Jacklin, that's the only way you'll get any real power') and then a week later he'd utterly contradict himself ('Keep the right side quiet for God's sake and pull with the left, pull, don't hit'). In the end, I got so confused that I had to stop listening to him as if it all made sense; I approached him with my own sort of golfing-brain gold pan, sifting out a nugget here or there and tossing the rest aside. What else could I do? If I had done everything he'd told me to do, he'd have had me folding sweaters for a career. Perhaps that was his goal all along. Nothing would have surprised me with him. The truth is that there weren't that many nuggets, either. I was observant, and it had become obvious to me pretty quickly that I ought not to listen too much to what he said about my game from a technical standpoint, if anything at all. I already had a very solid sense of what I was up to with my golf swing, and I didn't need him messing it up.

No, it wasn't anything to do with the swing that he helped me with. What he did do was make me even more determined than before. The man was such a bastard that he forged an even hotter determination within me to succeed. I became resolute in my desire to show him what I was capable of, and I think it's possible that if I hadn't hated him so much I might not have done what I did in golf. That was the guts of my relationship with Shanko: 'You bastard, I'll show you.' I've always been a passionate and intense person, in every walk of life, not just on the course. It's who I am. And it was certainly the case when I was a teenager. I had enormous self-belief, not just in my golf game, but in my whole person. Decisions were not stresses I shied away from. Speaking the truth and offering my opinions did not frighten me. So it was only natural that part of me hated Shanko. Why? Because the man did not respect me. Or at least, he couldn't show it. Some small part of him must have seen the core of who I was, but he was such a hard-hearted bugger the only way he could show his respect for me was to abuse me. Not that I could look at things this way at the time.

But whatever it was about him, I responded to his competitiveness with my own version of it. It was a backlash effect to begin with, in that I used him as a negative motivator. *I'm not going to let that bastard crack me.* Not the healthiest frame of mind, perhaps. But it became a positive thing – unconsciously, since I was not really aware of it at the time – once I started playing tournament golf as a professional. I suppose what I'm trying to say is that it became a positive thing when I could turn it outward, rather than inward or at Shanko. I always had an intense desire to succeed, from Day One, not to mention the innate ability to compete, but having that hunger to prove Shanko wrong did bring into focus some of that competitiveness. I *desperately* wanted to show him I was a player, and a person, he ought to respect. It was almost urgent, this need to prove I was better than what he'd pegged me for.

Isn't it strange? That a man I really didn't care for, a man with whom I had no real emotional connection, became someone who signified so much to me. He represented something, I suppose, something I didn't want to become – namely, a talented player working in a shop. My guess is that this had to be part of the reason why he was so hard on me. Shanko was a fiercely competitive man. Perhaps he got it from his days in Rugby League, perhaps from having to come all the way from Australia and establish himself as a golf professional and businessman. I don't know. I never asked him. It's not irrelevant, either, that he was not just any old golf pro himself, but had once been a fine player. He finished third in the Open Championship three times, in 1939 at St Andrews, in 1947 at Hoylake, and then again in 1951 at Royal Portrush in Ireland. He'd come close, but hadn't finished it off, and he once told me, in a weak moment, I'm sure, that he could have, *should* have, won the Open, but that he'd crapped himself. The pressure had got to him.

This is one thing the vast majority of golfers do not know, and can never know – that there are levels to golf, and you have to play at these levels to understand the pressures that go along with them. I've had so many amateurs and even pros ask me, *Do I need to work on my short game? Do I need to drive the ball better? What's the key to scoring?* There are various answers to these questions, but the point is that it's all about *competing* at the next level. It's almost purely about handling the pressure. Let's face it, there are hundreds of thousands of players in the world who hit it as well as most tour pros. None of them are ever going to win or even play on tour. Why? Because of the pressure. You either handle it or you don't. Having said that, it is also true that the ability to handle pressure is born of confidence, of self-assurance. I never passed off a win as a fluke, or a lucky streak, or as someone else handing it to me. After I won the Lincolnshire Open as a sixteen-year-old by nine shots, I didn't tell myself I won it because everyone else played badly, or because I was lucky. I told myself, 'I won because I'm good.' I'm not boasting. I'm just telling you what I thought.

This is how you handle pressure: self-assurance. It all circles back to what I was talking about earlier, that to get to the heights of achievement you bloody well have to *expect* to get there. It isn't done with mirrors. There's no faking it. You have to have the talent, but you have to absolutely, fundamentally, *want* it. Nothing will get in your way – you won't allow it to – because you have only one destination and you expect to get there.

Shanko undeniably made me an even more competitive person than I already was. Not that I was lacking in the desire to better myself. After all, I'd arrived at his shop on the 1st of January 1962 with everything in one suitcase: a grey suit my cousin had given me, a couple of pairs of slacks, three or four shirts. That was it, except for the five-pound note in my pocket. As luck would have it, there was a ridiculous blizzard the first week I was there, so there was nothing to do in the shop and there sure wasn't anyone out playing golf. My parents had driven me down from Scunthorpe that day, and by the time we got to Potters Bar there were two feet of snow on the ground. It looked more like bloody St Moritz than north London. Shanko, of course, didn't want to pay me to be working for him when there was no work to be done, so he told me to clear off and come back the next week. But that was never going to happen. My dad was a working man, and he'd taken time off work to do that four-and-a-half hour drive in his shite little car. He wasn't going to do it again the next week. We'd already had our emotional farewell. My dad simply told Shanko, *We can't take him back, he's here to stay.*

'I've left home,' I said. 'This is it. I'm here.'

There was no chance, none, that was I was going to get in that car and go back to Scunthorpe.

Shanko grunted and accepted it, but he still didn't give me anything to do, so I played snooker for the first week of my life as a golf professional. They let us play snooker in the clubhouse that week because of all the snow, but normally only the head professional was allowed in the clubhouse. There wasn't any other way to occupy my time. The next week, my term in hell began. What a miserable old shit he could be. He was so rotten that myself and the other assistant, Dennis, would sometimes take brand-new shirts right out of the packages, put them on, go out to the pub or the snooker hall, have a night on the town, and then replace the shirts in the packages before Shanko came in to the shop the next day. It was low-down behaviour on our part, but I was a teenager after all, and spite, sadly, sometimes motivated me to get back at Shanko the only way I thought I could. Not that it made me feel any better. No matter what I did he always made me feel a bit inferior, and I would lay awake at nights, staring at the ceiling, practically grinding my teeth at my own state of unhappiness. Many a night I vowed I was going to get up in the morning, pack my clothes and clubs, and catch the main line going north right from the bottom of Mrs Baker's garden. That was it. Enough was enough! I was packing it in. But morning would come, and I would stay. It was pride, pure and simple. I just could not go back home with my tail between my legs. I knew, too, that there was no way I'd be able to get any other job without a decent reference from my first-ever job. So I was stuck with Shanko, and Shanko with me, at least until I could find a way out. I wasn't alone, either, I knew that much. I ran into his wife, Daphne, one day when I was out fetching the boss's lunch. Things were bleak then between Shanko and myself, and she stopped me and asked me how the boss was treating me. I told her how miserable I was and what a hard case he was. I'll never forget her response: 'The way he's treating you,' she said, 'what it's like for you boys down there at the shop, that's what it's like for me at home.'

When I look back at it from his point of view, I have to admit he probably saw me as a cocky little piece of work. From my point of view I was only what I had to be if I was going to make it. Anyway, after working for Shanko for a few months I didn't think I could take it any longer, so I put in an application to work up at Muswell Hill with Keith Hockey. Of course, I didn't breathe a word of it to Shanko, but Keith called him – assuming, quite sensibly, that Shanko knew I'd applied – and asked him if I was a good kid, if I would work hard, etc. I won't ever forget Shanko barking into the phone, 'He's bloody useless!!' slamming the phone down and then turning on me. He blew my hair straight with his yelling. 'What are you doing applying for other jobs? I should sack you right here. You're just an arrogant little bastard!'

He was right, in a way. I was an arrogant little bastard, but really only in one realm, and that's what I don't think Shanko understood. Maybe I didn't fully understand it myself. I just wanted to be a player, that was all. And I *knew* I had it in me. I knew it, even if no one else did. Every time he tried to drag me down, every time he insulted the way I did something, every time he put the needle into me, I resented it because I felt he was not giving me the respect I warranted. He likely would have pointed out, quite properly, that I hadn't earned it yet; fair enough, but I believed I deserved it, and that's the attitude you've got to have. I was intensely convinced I was headed for something great, and this wasn't something I was ever going to apologize for – not to Shanko, not to anybody. It was probably immature of me, but the one symbol I used to think about all the time was Shanko's Austin Westminster sitting out in the car park. 'I'm going to

drive in here in a Rolls-Royce one of these days,' I used to mutter
to myself, 'and I'm going to park it beside his to make it look
like an old piece of crap.'

In 1970 I did just that, and the minute I pulled up beside his
Austin I realized how foolish an idea it had been. In fact, it might
not have been until that moment that I started to think differently about Shanko; I began to understand that in terms of spirit
and fight and heart he'd given me much more than he'd taken
away. He was a wretched old bugger – I'll never change my mind
about that – but when I pulled up in my Rolls, with two Open
trophies in the back seat, I suppose I was finally grown up
enough to see that tearing things apart is sometimes the only
way to make them stronger in their healing. That's what Shanko
did for me. He broke me down so that I could build myself back
up into a stronger version of who I was. I don't recall if I was
ever able to say thank you to him in that way. Probably not. If I
didn't thank him I should have . . . though he'd likely have given
me hell for waiting so long. I sent him a telegram for his nineti-
eth birthday party thanking him for everything, but maybe what
I ought to have done was quoted the philosopher who said,
'That which does not kill me makes me stronger.' Good job I
didn't use that quote; he might have taken it as licence to try and
kill me. If he'd tried, I'd have gone after him, as well.

Shanko aside, I had left home for one reason, and that was to
become a golf professional, a real player. And not just any
player. A great player. There was a run of tournaments through
the season that club professionals and assistants would play in,
and within three months of starting at Potters Bar I managed to
win the Middlesex Assistants Championship. I also finished
third in the overall professional ranks. I could see my game
steadily improving. My mechanics were good, and my game on
the whole was beginning to match my confidence, which showed

when I came second in the Coombe Hill Assistants tournament. (This was a tournament I won again in 1964. The next year, 1965, I won the biggest Assistants tournament in Britain, the Gor-Ray, a victory that nearly didn't happen. I'd been in America, in Boston, playing at the Carling World Open. It was my first trip to America. There'd been a rain delay at the Carling, and so I phoned Major John Bywaters, the head of the British PGA, and asked if he could accommodate me with a late tee time for the start of the Gor-Ray if I was able to make it back. He said yes, and I flew back that night to the UK, made my tee time, birdied the last hole of the second round to make the cut, birdied the final hole of the last round to get in a play-off, and then won it all on the first playoff hole!)

I also played well in quite a few other tournaments through 1963, and was eventually named the Henry Cotton Rookie of the Year, which netted me £100, quite a bit of money to a teenager back then. There was no little symbolism to this award, in that in later years I came to know Henry Cotton and play golf against him; he was a great champion. We eventually became good friends, and I enjoyed his company for the rest of our lives. I also enjoyed his wife Toots, who was quite the package and who went everywhere with Henry, and I mean *everywhere*. She was an heiress to the Argentinian Fray Bentos beef business fortune, and was something of an aristocratic lady. Sadly, her appearance didn't match the quality of her breeding. She was not an attractive woman, to put it mildly; some of the more waggish fellows on tour used to say Henry took her everywhere with him because she was too ugly to kiss goodbye. She was unreal, Toots, poor woman; she had a face that would scare the bloody mice into the traps. I once asked Henry, near the end of his life, why he never went over to America to play. After all, I'd been the first Englishman to win a full four-round tournament in America, but Henry was so gifted that if he'd gone, he'd have done it.

'So how come, Henry?' I said to him. 'How come you never went over to America?'

We were sitting in a chauffeured limo in our tuxes, on our way to the Tour dinner in London. There were just the two of us sitting in the back. He was quite old by then, and Toots had passed away.

'Well, I'll tell you,' he said. 'In England and Europe you get all the lovely room service and what not in the hotels. Lovely. But in America, you've got to go to the "coffee shop" for breakfast. Toots never liked the thought of having to go down to the coffee shop for breakfast and then having to go all the way back up to our room to have a crap.'

He sat back, and that was that. This was why Henry Cotton never made it to America. Toots didn't like to crap in public. I swear on my children's lives I'm not making that up.

In any case, it was an honour to receive the Henry Cotton Award from Henry himself at his Eaton Square flat in London. I was rather nervous, being just eighteen and surrounded by many high-flyers in the game. I confess I enjoyed two or three lagers and helped myself to a pile of cigarettes on a nearby table. Later that week, on Sunday, Henry's weekly golf column appeared, and in it he said that anyone aspiring to become a young golf pro ought not to drink, smoke or get married until the age of twenty-five – all three of which were pieces of advice I didn't come within a million miles of meeting, and which I am quite sure were directed squarely at me. I didn't see Henry for stretches at a time, but I always welcomed his company. I went to visit him in Penina in Spain straight after my US Open win, for a quiet time to get away from the madding crowd. He was still youngish, in his sixties, and we played a few rounds of golf together. I enjoyed them all, despite the eternally amusing and diverting sight of his regular caddie – Pacifico the donkey. Pacifico was the Penina club mascot; his image was even featured on the club tie. He lugged Henry's bag around and occasionally carried Henry, too. There was never a quiet moment with that bloody donkey. I can't say for sure that Henry trained Pacifico to act in certain ways, but it just happened too regularly for it to be coincidence. You'd tee your ball, line up, and then hear a loud pissing noise a few feet from where you were standing, this huge disgusting splashing stream. Right next to the tee! It was disconcerting, to say the least, to have a donkey pissing or farting away in your backswing, fouling the air or creating a huge lake of urine right by the tee marker. Take it from me, donkeys do not piss quietly. Henry always kept his poker face.

However . . . through my first year and a half or so at Potters Bar, as I tried to hone my game, I had various other duties, one of which was teaching. How I hated that. It was such an awful penance to me – for what sins I've no idea – that I'd often take only twelve or fifteen balls out to the range, so that most of the hour had to be spent retrieving them. I once told someone that I'd rather have just given them their fee not to come than have to go through with the actual lesson. Not that I was a bad teacher for certain types of players; I hadn't much patience for beginners, but I had a decent eye with the better players. It was just that it was precious time away from my passion, the single destination I was feverishly heading towards. I never held the teaching against any of the actual members. How could I? It was my job, after all. But they were always very kind to me, and I had a fine relationship with them.

I won't ever forget that, by the way, the support I felt from the club as I tried to find out who I was going to be in the world of golf. I don't mean Shanko, of course, but the membership and club committee. A small but influential group of those very members would later become instrumental in allowing me to move forward in my career. By 1963, I wanted to play as much tournament golf as I could. It was obvious to me. It was part of my trajectory. Shanko, on the other hand, wasn't inclined to pay me a weekly salary to play tournaments. It was Johnnie Rubens and some of the other members who were my salvation. They created an arrangement whereby they would pay my salary while I was away from the shop; if I didn't make my expenses, that is. In other words, if I played well and made some money that was that. But if I played poorly and didn't make my expenses, they would cover them. And all this could take place without Shanko being on the hook for any of my salary while I was away. It was a brilliant arrangement, though it was still a hard go at times; many times I'd finish a tournament in Scotland or some far-off place, then race home at night so I could open the shop on Sunday morning, knowing full well that if I didn't make it Shanko would be waiting, delighted to have an excuse to give me hell.

Nineteen sixty-three was a good year for me in my development as a young professional. It was the first year I competed in the Open, and as luck would have it, it was played at Lytham, where I would win six years later. I managed to finish thirtieth, and won the whopping sum of just over £56. That year I played on the British Professional Circuit in tournaments with names like the Cox Moore Championship, the *News of the World* tournament, the Senior Service Championship. My total earnings for the year were just over £400. Nineteen sixty-four was an even more important year for me as a player, though not necessarily for things that happened on the course. I failed to qualify for the Open at St Andrews, which put me in a bad frame of mind. Then, to make matters much worse, Shanko was short of staff that summer. In fact, for at least two or three months, I think I was the only assistant he had. He worked me like a dray horse, not a day off, making me put in fourteen hours a day. I was doing every bloody thing there was to be done around the course: cleaning clubs, odd repairs, scrubbing the floor, keeping the books, giving lessons. He even had me wash his car. Naturally, none of these tasks were performed quite up to his standards. I somehow managed to do them all badly enough to warrant his abuse, but just well enough to not get fired.

Finally, in September, I cracked. Shanko had pushed me too far. I can't even remember exactly what it was that caused it; probably something small, but big enough to be that proverbial last straw. We had a massive argument, and, with me literally crying my eyes out, I told him that was it. Stuff it! I was done. I'd had enough. I couldn't take another day. I said flat out he could take his bloody assistant's job and stick it, that I would not work for him ever again, even if he paid me a hundred pounds a week.

He stayed calm, stared flatly at me, and said, 'Fine, that's it then. Off you go.'

'Fine,' I said. 'I'm off.'

So I went, although I had no idea where I was going or what I was doing. I had exactly £343 in the bank and no job prospects – in fact, I was certain if I asked Shanko for a reference he'd have told me to go straight to hell, being the bastard he was. I began to almost doubt myself as I stormed off. *What was I doing? Why couldn't I have showed a bit more patience? What the hell was I going to do now?* I walked out of the pro shop door into a gorgeous early autumn day, but it felt like I had a thousand tons of stone on my back. I was eighteen, and though I had begun to achieve quite a bit on the course and had no doubts I was doing the right things as a player, I had just quit in a huff the only real job I'd ever had. I had nowhere to go.

How could I possibly have known that I had just landed at the bottom of the hole and had already started climbing out? At that moment, I can tell you it did not feel as though I'd acted in the service of my career – quite the opposite, in fact – but I had. I did what had to be done. It wasn't about this decision or that plan – I had to get the bloody hell out from under that man's thumb and it had to happen now and I had to go and every single ounce of me knew it. How can you be something other than what you are? You have to listen to what your insides are telling you. So I acted. I did it. And call it what you will – fate, luck, intuition – but leaving Shanko then, fuelled by his fire and his *the hell with you attitude*, was the right thing to do at the right time. Whatever it was that caused it, the end result was this: I was on the fast track, headed for the next level.

Unbeknownst to me, Shanko was on the phone to Johnnie Rubens practically the minute I stormed out of the shop. He told him we'd had a blow-up and that I was threatening to clear off and had given a week's notice. The reason Shanko did this was clear: he was scared of losing his own job. He knew that Johnnie and many of the other members had shown faith in me by supporting my efforts to play more tournaments, and he also saw that those very members were taking no little satisfaction in the fact that I was starting to deliver some results. Shanko knew he'd provoked me to the point that I'd quit, and that such a loss – a talented young player representing a club – could be something that might cost him his job. So he called Johnnie straight away. The next day, Johnnie rang me up and asked if I would go out and play golf with him. This was unusual for two reasons; it was rare for a member to specifically request to play with an assistant, and Johnnie rarely played in mid-week.

Mr Rubens, as I referred to him then, was the wealthiest member at Potters Bar, and was also its President. He made his money with a company he and his partner, Barney Shine, owned called Central & District Properties, which was based in sumptuous offices in Berkeley Square. I know they sold it in 1972 for £22 million, so he was a wealthy man, indeed. He was also a fine man, always supportive from the start, always encouraging, not just to me but to all the assistants and the various amateurs and younger players around the club who were starting out, trying to find their way in the game. He loved golf, and he loved to see people trying to better themselves. He was one of the good ones, simple as that, and he never changed.

During that mid-week round of golf with Johnnie, perhaps four or five holes in, he asked me quite casually how things were going in the shop and how I was getting along with Shanko. I blurted it all out, that I couldn't stand it any longer, that he was driving me crazy, even though I was really only working part-time in the shop by then. I suppose I got a bit passionate, let my emotions spill out, but there was no reason to hold them in. The winter months were rapidly approaching, and though I'd be able to practise and play through the bleak grey days when the sky hung low, the tournament season of the British PGA was done with. Johnnie knew I was hungry, and even though he was no golfer, he knew about being pushed, about being competitive. He knew competitive situations would benefit me the most; not just practice but playing tournament golf against real pros. He asked me what I was planning to do over the winter. I morosely told him I had no idea. I suppose I thought I'd just practise and play, and get ready for the next season on the British tour.

Actually, it isn't quite accurate to say I had no idea. I knew I had to do something after my blow-up with Shanko, and I had already begun to formulate in my mind a plan to play the South African tour. I mentioned this option to Johnnie as we played. His suggestion was that if I put £200 in, he would, too – as a loan – and that he thought Eric Hayes at Dunlop might also put in the same. This amount would let me play the eight-week circuit on the South African Tour.

(It's worth mentioning that later, in the summer of 1965, I went back to Johnnie to repay the £200 he'd loaned me. He asked me what I was planning to do during the upcoming winter, and I mentioned I was thinking of going back to South Africa. Instead of accepting the £200 I had for him, he gave me another £100 and said to use it for expenses in South Africa. It was chalk and cheese between the two years. My first trip to South Africa I'd won £35 in prize money. The second time around I won the Kimberley tournament, finished in the top ten in seven of eight tournaments and made £1,000 total prize money.)

I was stunned by his generosity that day. What a life lesson it was for me, to be around such a man. Not two days before, all I had to look forward to was a winter of folding shirts and catching hell from Shanko. Now I'd quit and was going to play pro golf in the wider world. Even today the memory of it makes me itch and squirm in my seat, recalling how anxious I was for it to start. The world was opening up for me! I thanked Johnnie many, many times over the years for the things he did for me, but I'll do it again here. Life is incredible on so many levels, and though I was always grateful in the moment, as it were, I look back now and can't even begin to express how much he meant to me, to my life. You can't know the impact such actions had on my young mind. I was full of self-belief, but what a boost it was to know that someone else, someone as accomplished and as successful as Johnnie, felt the same way about my prospects as I did.

Some years later I read an interview with Johnnie in a book written shortly after I'd won the US Open. In that interview, he talked a bit about his motivation for helping me out, and showed, I think, what a fine person he was. Even more than that, his words showed he truly understood what I was trying to do, where I was trying to get to. Johnnie had heard from his friend at the British PGA, Lou Freedman, that people like Dai Rees and Michael Bonallack had said 'this youngster Jacklin' had tremendous potential and ought to be encouraged and supported.

'So here's a youngster in the shop with potential,' Johnnie said. 'You encourage him – that's how it started. I sat and talked to him and realized (in hindsight) that he was in a different class, in that he could make scores. I wasn't such a great judge of professional golf, but I realized he had a quality others didn't possess. I found he hated being in the shop, selling golf balls, clubs, and giving lessons – people said he was the worst teacher they ever had. All he wanted to do was play tournament golf. That to me was good, what I liked to hear. He just wanted to be a fine golfer. So we organized an expenses fund for him. Unless you're ambitious, you don't get anywhere. He had ambitions, dreams, drive, talent and intelligence. You need them all. I smelt it in him . . . We gave him the opportunity . . . and it was a gamble that came off.'

He knew about the struggle, about ambition, and he understood my passion, my burning need to make it happen. He respected it and valued it, and I think that was why he was so good to me, why he was so helpful in circumstances where most people might have just said, *Well, he's talented and good luck to him*. He took it a step further and, you might say, invested in me. I hope I repaid the investment, which was not just financial, but moral, even spiritual.

The result of all this was that I remained formally attached to the Potters Bar Golf Club, and I was happy to do so, Shanko or no Shanko. The reduction of sheer stress in my life from not having to live with Shanko's abuse was enormous. I felt I'd been released from a life sentence as a serf to some tyrannical medieval lord. I was ready to set out on my eight-week tour of professional tournaments in South Africa. It was an intensely exciting moment in my life. It felt like I'd been getting ready up to then, preparing myself for my grand entrance on to the larger stage. I was happy, ready, desperate to get out and prove myself.

But I played like a prat.

I was wound up to play, but when I got there, halfway around the world, I found the greens impossible to read. It was my first lesson in the reality of trying to play golf for a living on the global scale. In eight weeks I made two cuts. My grand take in winnings was £35, and I spent the whole £600 bankroll on plane tickets and other expenses. Still, it was worth every penny, because it gave me the first semester of my education as a true travelling professional. I came home after those eight weeks with exactly £143 to my name. I was a bit worried about what Johnnie Rubens might say about such a terrible return on investment ratio, but not a discouraging word was uttered. For this I was appreciative and even humbled.

The support was to continue on into 1965, when I actually began to show Johnnie I was worthy of his faith. But though I played well and continued to improve throughout 1965, something else had an even bigger impact on who I was to become as a golfer and, more important, as a person. My life has been magical in many ways. I've always felt this, and been glad of it. And it has never failed to amaze me how certain things in my life arrived or happened at *exactly* the moment they ought to have, when I was ready, when everything was right. The biggest of them all was about to happen to me in the summer of 1965.

4

Her name was Vivien. I can only state the plain fact – she stopped me dead in my tracks the first time I saw her. It was her beauty. Later on it became clear that her looks were down the list of her endless brilliant qualities, and so of course I only fell further and further in love the better I got to know her. Still, the first time I saw her I think I stopped breathing for a moment or two. When my breathing started again I knew I was going to marry her. In a heartbeat my world changed utterly. I'd found my partner for life. If we're lucky in life we have a few magical moments, those instances where everything is suddenly *right*. This was one of those moments.

Viv was born and raised in Belfast, Northern Ireland. I was over playing in the Jeyes tournament in June of 1965, in Bangor. After the first round, I went to the Queen's Court hall with a couple of pals, and the Witnesses show band were on. Vivien happened to be going out with the lead singer. I had played that day with the manager of the band, Jimmy Adga, and we were sitting around having a drink with a couple of other pros, talking about this or that. I don't even remember. The music was good. The company was fine. The world seemed full enough. Then I happened to glance over toward another table.

Bang! I sat. I looked. I stared. Suddenly, there was no sound in the hall. No music. No talking. Just her.

I knew in my bones what was going to happen. I was going to marry her. Name? Who knew. Already married? Didn't care. Could she speak English? No idea. I knew I'd found myself in her. It was that simple. I'm a sentimental fool, a hopeless romantic, and I simply knew right then I was going to end up marrying that girl. I leaned over and pointed her out to Jimmy.

'That girl,' I croaked. 'That one over there. I'm . . . I'm going to marry that girl.'

I'm sure Jimmy laughed, especially since as manager of the band he knew she was spoken for. 'Relax,' he said. 'You'll be all right in a minute.'

But I couldn't take my eyes off her. Eventually, I got up and went over to where she was sitting. I asked if I could buy her a drink.

She looked at me and said, 'No, thank you.'

For some reason, this made her even more attractive. She was always loyal to those around her, and I'm sure she said no not because she was in love with the singer, but because it would have just been bad manners to have a drink with another fellow right in front of your boyfriend. But she must have felt something similar to what I was feeling, because the next day she agreed to meet me in the afternoon. I practically waltzed around the streets during those moments we weren't together over the next few days. One day, I was a young man chasing a golf ball, and the next I was in love with an amazing woman; and nothing ever happened in our years together that made me consider changing my first opinion, my gut feeling.

There were, however, things I had to take care of back in Potters Bar. I'd been seeing a girl named Linda, and it had begun to become fairly clear she wanted to get permanent. I was very careful with things, if you catch my drift, because I was sure she was doing her best to get in the family way. That was never my intention with her at all. I knew that staying there, with her, was not going to be what was best for me or for my career. Don't get me wrong. She was a nice girl, and we had a great time together. In fact, for the spell I was at Potters Bar prior to meeting Viv, it was an unbelievable situation. I was an eighteen-year-old lad going out with this Linda, and because I could hardly take her back to the Bakers for a little hanky-panky, we usually ended up at her house, rolling around on the floor of the sitting room after her parents had gone to bed. Then she'd get up and go to bed in her room. Most nights I'd fall asleep on the couch. One day, her dad woke me up at five in the morning. He was fit little fellow and a nice chap, and he said, 'Here, Tony, you don't want to be messing about sleeping on the couch like that when you've got to get up in the morning and go to work. If you're staying over anyway because it's late, just sleep in the spare room.'

So I did. I slept in the spare room if I was late getting home after a night out with Linda. But of course Linda would sneak into the room once the coast was clear and spend the night with me, and then near morning she'd slip back into her room before her dad got up. This all went on for a few weeks, until gradually she stopped slipping out to her room and stayed in the spare room with me. Nobody blinked. Her dad would show up at the door of the spare room at seven in the morning, 'Here you are, Tony. A cup of tea.' Her dad! Jesus, I thought I'd died and gone to heaven, everything laid on for me like that. I used to lie there at night thinking, *How great is this?* Talk about a result. I'd get up and go back to Mrs Baker's for breakfast and she knew very well I hadn't touched my own bedsheets. She never said a word.

In any case, I had to talk to Linda when I got back from Northern Ireland. I'd met the woman I wanted to spend forever with . . . and it wasn't her. Well, you should have heard the wailing and weeping. Awful. But what else could I tell Linda? What other way was there to say it? I was only being honest. It wasn't anything against her specifically. She was a nice enough girl and we had a good time while we were together.

Viv and I were married less than a year later after a romantic courtship, though the decision wasn't finalized until I'd taken a November trip to Belfast to ask her father if we could have his blessing. I took Viv and her parents out to the pub for a drink, and while Viv and her mum went to the ladies room, I asked her father (who worked in a local store) if it would be all right if Viv and I got married. I've been nervous over putts to help me win Opens, but I don't think I was ever more nervous than sitting there waiting for her father to say Yes or No. I had nothing to worry about in the end. He was always a delightful man, from start to finish, and he thought it was an excellent idea, though looking back on it, I can't imagine on what objective basis he thought this was such a wonderful match for his daughter – an uneducated, aspiring golf professional, barely out of his teens, who had every intention of traipsing all over the world with nothing but some golf clubs and a few shirts to his name. Hardly the kind of catch you'd break out the champagne for (though I myself had no doubts I was right on track with where I was going). But I suppose his daughter must have told him that she was simply in love with me, and vice versa, and that was all that mattered. He was a true gent about it, and it was such a good family all around. They were quite sporty (Vivien played netball for Northern Ireland as a teenager), and she had already shown how much she could offer to the people she loved around her; she left school at fifteen so she could work as an accounting machine operator just to earn some extra money for the family so that her two brothers – who were quite gifted academically – could stay in school. And so with her dad's blessing we set off with such goodwill behind us it was as if a fresh wind was always filling our sails; we always felt happy to have found each other, and life was always about moving forward and finding out what was going to happen next. It never stopped being exciting.

It's also worth mentioning that this was a fantastic time to be in Northern Ireland. It was well before the Troubles started. I was good pals with a fellow named Hugh Jackson. He was assistant to the former Open champ Fred Daly at Balmoral, and Hugh, Fred and I spent many happy Sundays playing golf at Balmoral just outside Belfast with the church bells chiming out.

Marriage – even though it came young, with me being twenty-one and Viv being twenty-two – was the best thing that ever happened to me. I knew I could play golf and I was burning to succeed; that wasn't an issue. I knew I was not just someone who played golf, but that I was a *golfer*, a player. I was already making it as a pro by then, and though I could hardly have said I was expecting to win the Open, I did feel I was hitting my stride. Every year was better than the one before. Every year I was feeling closer to my goal of being one of the best players in the game. The week immediately prior to getting married I won my first tournament, the Blaxnit at Malone; that weekend we married, on 30 May 1966, at the Cooks Centenary Presbyterian Church in Belfast. My whole family and quite a few friends flew over for the ceremony. It was the first time either of my parents had been on a plane.

There's something about marriage that seems to suit young professional golfers. Actually, let me say that a different way; there must be something of great value in the institution of marriage which young pros are attracted to. The fact is that many professional golfers get married quite young in life. Not that they all stay married to the same woman, mind you. And not that they all choose the best partners. But simply that there must be elements to the state of being married that suit the lifestyle and the temperaments involved. It was certainly the case back in my heyday that players married young. Jack Nicklaus, Arnold Palmer, Tom Weiskopf, Gary Player all married early to fine women (particularly Barbara Nicklaus – if there is one woman deserving of sainthood on this earth, it's Barbara). In this day and age, of course, women, due to career freedom and, let's face it, birth control, are choosing to marry later and later (and more power to 'em, I say, for whatever they decide, though my own feelings tend to be quite traditional on such matters). Also, society is generally more and more open to couples being together and raising children without even being married. Yet given all these changes in society, it's still the case that a great many young professional golfers choose to get married early in their lives. Why? I think it must have something to do with the solitary nature of professional golf. You're so isolated out there on the golf course. Your success is so very dependent on you and you alone. Typically, you have spent hours, days, months, years doing nothing but being by yourself listening to the voices in your head urging you on, convincing yourself you have what it takes. Then, at some point, you reach a certain level, a high level, and you find your game is good, but that your personal life feels narrow, that you perhaps lack a stable base since you've spent so much time cultivating this one solitary aspect of your person. A young man may, as I did, gaze into the future of this journey and see it as exciting but lonely if taken alone. My life has been an astonishing voyage, really, but it wouldn't have been half the fun if taken alone – in fact, I'm convinced it wouldn't have happened at all like it did if Viv hadn't been there.

I remember playing a tournament in Jersey in 1964. After one round, we were at the bar and I met this girl. We had a few beers and next thing I knew I woke up on the beach about four in the morning with this bird beside me. It was just getting light, and I sat up and I swear my first thoughts were, 'What the bloody hell are you doing? You've got to tee off in a few hours. How the hell can you expect to play well? Is this the way to get the best out of yourself?'

Meeting Viv and falling in love with her was something I just instinctively knew would be good for me. Knowing this was the woman I wanted to spend every minute of my life with was something I knew was going to help me, force me, to get serious. I needed to make a commitment to real life. I mean, it would have been easy enough to jog along the way I was for ever; I was young, talented, had a car, enough money for a few pints and a packet of fags. But even then, even before meeting Viv, I knew somewhere inside me I needed to get serious. *Really* serious. I was determined to get better, make no mistake. But I needed to be responsible. I needed the focus, particularly the focus of having to provide for two, not one.

Golf, above every other sport and perhaps even above pursuits of any other kind, requires a quiet mind to excel, and free of clawing fingers, a mind that is not so much simple, as able to find simplicity when needed. I think this is why golfers seek out the stability of marriage at such an early age. You get your romantic life sorted out, and then it's one less thing to worry about. Simple as that. Tiger Woods won the Masters and the Open in 2005, shortly after getting married, and also finished second in the US Open, and though it feels as if he's been around for ever, he was only twenty-eight when he married, which is still relatively young. But he'd been dating Elin for some time, and there was hardly ever the sense that he was out there playing the field. I think it's entirely possible that he'll go on a massive Majors tear-up over the next few years as his emotional life becomes richer. That need for stability, for putting in place an emotional base from which to operate your career, is also, I think, why so many golfers marry women who don't even play the game. When I met Vivien she didn't know a golf club from a hockey stick. But that didn't matter a bit. She came to enjoy watching the game, and even learned to play, but it was always as a way of showing her support for me. She was *always* there. I could always feel her presence walking along in the gallery. I often didn't know exactly where she was, but I knew she was there. It meant everything. We were a team, a unit. It was about *us* succeeding, not just me. And when things weren't quite right on the course, what a gift it was to know Viv was there walking along with me. I was alone as a player, but never alone as a person.

It's impossible to overstate how crucial Viv was to my success. I can't say loudly or often enough that I'd never have accomplished what I accomplished without her support, her sense of stability and calm, the way she handled everything else in our lives so that I could focus on golf. I got the trophies. I was the one interviewed. I was the one made 'famous'. But you can't ever truly know how much those achievements were due to her, and to our ability to be one person, working together, as opposed to two.

It's hard, being the wife of a professional golfer. Ask any of them and they'll tell you. The cruel irony of young golfers seeking this emotional base, this stable platform from which they can then go forward and chase the prize, is that it's often the emotional base which comes to suffer the most with success. It's sad but true. The list of successful pro golfers whose various marriages lie in tatters is long (Monty, Seve, Sandy Lyle, John Daly, Weiskopf, Hal Sutton, Faldo, Tom Watson, and on and on). And the very reason we seek that relationship – to stave off the loneliness, the solitude – ends up being the selfsame thing that kills it. Golfers are solitary beings, selfish in some deep and fundamental way. They have to be, or they won't rise to the top. We're impossible, is what I'm saying. We don't want to be lonely, because we're so often alone, but the minute we're surrounded by support and affection, we have to go out and seek that solitude again. It's like some sort of prima donna act, and would even be a bit comical if it weren't also often so sad.

But I was lucky. I found a person who understood what I was trying to say when I told her, before I married her, that golf had to be Number One, not for ever, but during the time I was trying to reach the top, because otherwise I wasn't going to be able to achieve what I wanted to achieve. She understood, as hard as it must have been to hear it. I remember telling her that I loved her, and that I would always love her, but that golf was first for now. She knew what I meant. And she was secure enough to know that it was never going to be any other person that would get between us. She was okay with it, and that's why we didn't have the troubles so many other marriages had. I'd lose track if I tried to count the number of wives of professional golfers I've known who have come to resent the game, because they stopped seeing it as the vocation of the person they loved, but as the thing that kept them apart. Vivien always understood it was my way of proving who I was. She knew I was a work in progress when she married me, and because she was more mature than I was (she was older, after all!), I think she saw that our journey was simply going to have to be centred on golf. The day after our wedding we flew to London and stayed at a hotel near the airport so that I could play in a tournament at Wentworth. I finished third in that tournament and went on to finish third three weeks in a row; a pretty fair start to my career as a young married pro.

It was an exciting time, those early years, and more than anything else it was a hell of an adventure. We travelled the world and had nothing but fun, just the two of us with a set of golf clubs and a couple of suitcases. I would always tell her that we were going to make it, that one day we'd have a fabulous house, we'd have the things we dreamed about, we'd be able to take our children all over the world and stay in the best places. She would just smile and laugh at me. I'm sure part of her thought I was a bit of a nutter, but we used to go for a drink in the pub or at the bar in whichever hotel in whatever country and I would tell her these crazy wonderful things that we were going to experience and we would laugh until we cried . . . but then most of them ended up happening to us. I never really had much doubt all these things were going to happen for us. Never. The beautiful thing about Viv, though, was that she enjoyed it all and we had a hell of a good time, but she would have loved me just as much if none of it had happened. If I'd gone back to folding sweaters for Shanko, she'd have been just as wonderful, just as loyal, and we still would have had tons of laughs, and great times, and a great family.

She used to say that I would have made it with or without her, but I can tell you I would not have. Don't get me wrong, I believe I'd have had some success as a pro golfer, but I just can't imagine being as ready and as confident and as secure in those early years had she not been around. Two Opens? I don't think so. In any case, having such a wonderful person along on the ride only made it as it was supposed to be. You want to share these things with the people you love. It's about creating a closeness over a lifetime, and I know that Vivien's family was that way when she was growing up. They were a close, loving, easygoing family. I envied her that, and was so thankful she was around to help us recreate something of the same when we started having children. She knew and sometimes commented on the fact that I was ambitious and that part of that ambition was a kind of self-focus, but she was okay with it. She once said she even enjoyed this ambitious streak and that she wished she'd had a bit more of it in herself. The funniest part, as I mentioned earlier, was that she really didn't even care for golf. In fact, she wasn't even certain I was going to make it work. Far from it. But she loved the fact that I was so into pushing myself to reach higher and higher. It was a fantastic journey we were on together, and the fun we had every single day – the challenge, the travel, the people, the things shared – well, it's just impossible to categorize the thrill of it all.

And it didn't hurt that I was really starting to hit the mark as a player. Viv told me some time after we got married, years later, that it wasn't even until we'd been married about a year that she started to think, *Hmm, he just might make a living at this after all*. That was in 1967, and she was right.

5

I finished fifth on the 1966 Order of Merit on the British PGA circuit, but more important, I'd played with Peter Alliss (as the youngest-ever British professional to do so) in the Canada Cup, which is now known as the World Cup. It was held in Japan, and if ever there was an eye-opener for me about the kinds of things that were going to be in store for me if I wanted to make it on the world stage, it was there. Peter and I found ourselves up against Jack Nicklaus and Arnold Palmer. I had a good bit of experience by then, but this was a new league, a different class. To be fair, I had actually finished ahead of Arnie in the 1963 Open (I was thirtieth, he was thirty-third). But now I was playing with them, the two biggest names in the game. It was where I wanted to be, where I felt I *belonged*. It was all part of my learning experience, what I needed to be doing to become the best golfer in the world. I shot a pretty fair 69 the first day, and was on a high. I felt it in my blood that England could win the Cup. We didn't, but that was okay with me. I'd played with Jack and Arnie, and had shown them, and myself, that I belonged.

Of course, I'd already played in the 1963 and 1965 Opens and had got decent results, but in those instances I was, to use the phrase, flying under the radar. Nobody was sitting around with intense curiosity in the Press tent in 1963 or 1965 waiting for news of what Jacklin was up to out on the course. But in Japan I was in the limelight with Jack and Arnie, and I had produced a score. No one but me may have cared, but that didn't matter. It was important in my scheme of things. It was another brick in the wall. Arnold was a god to me, the epitome of everything a golfer was meant to be, everything I was aiming for. Jack was there, too, but he didn't yet have the sheer star power that Arnold Palmer possessed in his prime.

I remember playing with Arnie that day and being acutely aware that not a single person on the golf course – except Vivien and Peter Alliss – cared what I was doing. I even caught myself putting more quickly than I normally would have, just because both Arnie and Jack had such presence. I was feeling my way. I wasn't intimidated by them – not at all – but I was nervous, and I knew right away that I had to get over this kind of nervousness, I had to feel equal to the task. I reminded myself that I had as much right to be there as they did, to make sure I didn't rush. It wasn't the fault of either Jack or Arnie that I initially felt this slight nervousness. I just had to assert myself inside, that was all. It was an important lesson in finding the strength and self-belief to feel you belong, because if you get to a place you've always wanted to go and then hear a voice saying, *Oh my God, am I really here? Do I really belong here? Maybe I was just too much of a dreamer after all*, then you'll bale out of that place pretty soon.

It took me a few holes to acclimatize, as it were, to the rarefied air of Palmer and Nicklaus, but soon enough I was grinding away, pleased as punch to finally be playing in the same group with the men I hoped soon to consider my peers. Once I got the nerves out of the way, I got on with it and played well.

Vivien was with me in Japan, and right after that tournament we decided to combine our idea of a grand trip with another step in my journey as a player. Moving up from the South African tour the winter before, we decided to try the Asian and Australian tournament circuit. At the end of 1966, I had £2,000 in the bank, and so we spent £1,200 of that on two round-trip tickets and used the rest for expenses. What a time! You can't imagine the fun we had, though it's the kind of trip people might not even make nowadays. There we were, the young golf pro and his wife, wandering all over Asia and Australia. Viv caddied for me, and though we did everything we could to minimize expenses, it was still a comfortable and even sophisticated trip at times. We had so many people help us out between tournaments, giving us lifts from one city to the next, arranging for places to stay. It was a once-in-a-lifetime trip, a five-month journey we never forgot, no matter where we travelled over the next couple of decades. One brilliant part was the three weeks we spent at Mount Manganui in New Zealand. A fellow who would eventually become mayor of the town showed us unbelievable hospitality by giving us the use of a bungalow he owned by the beach. On top of that he set up a free account for us at the local grocery store! All the goodwill must have inspired me; I won the New Zealand PGA Championship at the Mount Manganui course, beating the Dutchman Martin Roesink (and I also managed to tie with Bob Charles in another event, during the Australian leg of our tour).

It was just after Christmas during this trip that I received my first Masters invitation, to be played in April in Augusta. I don't remember if I shouted out, 'Viv! The Masters!' when I opened the envelope, but I felt like it. Neil Coles, the great old British pro, had held the spot, but he didn't like flying and so he declined the invitation. I was next in line. I remember telling the legendary Peter Thomson, the gifted Australian who won five Opens, that I'd received an invitation. He told me not to go. I was stunned.

'You won't like it,' he told me. 'You probably won't do well on the course. It doesn't suit your type of game.'

I couldn't believe my ears. Of course, Peter – who is hands down the smartest man I have ever met, and is perhaps the only person I've ever known who could truly *think* his way around a golf course – was probably only expressing his own feelings about the differences between the manicured greenness of Augusta, where he never performed that well, and the bumpy, brown raw state of links courses, on which he was a true genius. Needless to say, I ignored Peter's advice and replied with a Yes straight away. He was a great man, Thomson, class through and through. After I won the US Open he shook my hand and said *I wish it had been me*.

But before Augusta, Viv and I had to finish off our grand adventure. After Australia we moved on to Manila, Singapore, Kuala Lumpur, Bangkok and Hong Kong. What an education. Everywhere we went we were astounded by the number of people, the lights, the pace, the exhilarating differentness of it all. It wasn't all perfect. More than a few times we looked at one another over our dinner plates and said, *Do you have any idea what we're about to eat?* Many a hotel room was hot, steamy, and downright dodgy. But there was no downside to it all. Not a one. We were young, had energy to burn, were hungry for the experience, and we just bloody well loved being together and sharing such a great time. It's easy to romanticize such things, but I'm not doing that – it *was* incredible and we were in it together.

I can't overstate how vital it was for me in life and in golf to have Viv beside me. We were a complete unit, a team, together every minute of every day. It wasn't like someone going off to the office and saying, 'Okay, see you later, love.' She was coming to my office with me every day. She knew I needed her support. What a gift that was, to have that support, that ally. She *wanted* to be there and I *wanted* her there. It was vital to my success. I sure as hell never wanted to do it on my own. I am not one of those tough-guy loners, and never have been. I was determined, yes. Tough as nails, sure. But I wanted her there. It was a very unusual commitment, yet it felt like the most natural thing in the world.

In any case, whatever the circumstances or experiences of our Far East travel, the golf lay beneath it all. And I was learning something every single day, either about the game or myself. I remember at one tournament – it might have been the Hong Kong Open or the Singapore Open – I watched with intense fascination as the Chinese players managed to play exquisite bunker shots while taking almost no sand, just the thinnest slice of it. I practised that very technique after watching them, and it proved to be a pretty useful little shot when playing some links courses back home with the sand either blown out of the bunkers or compacted over time. There was always something to learn.

I don't think it would be possible for two people to have had a more meaningful experience than we had that winter. It was a never-ending, day-after-day whirlwind of excitement, newness, strangeness, fascinating people, odd foods, terrific times. We had to think on our feet. Anything that was going to happen, we had to make happen. It was just us, two young people, out in the world, taking it all in. We saw the world, spent every minute of every day together, learned so much about ourselves and one another, and by the end of it we felt there wasn't anything on this earth we couldn't handle or take pleasure in.

Eventually we reached the end. The Far East tour had come to a close, as had the Australian and New Zealand tournaments. It was early April in 1967, and we were in Hong Kong. Since I'd finished well in one or two of the Asian tournaments (second in the Thailand Open, fifth in the Malaysian Open) we decided to chuck out all our old clothes and junk, and kit ourselves out in new things: shoes, shirts, a suit, a few dresses and a new handbag for Viv. We spent £200 on new clothing. British Hong Kong was the place to do that, a place where you could get a pair of custom-made alligator golf shoes for five pounds. It was a treat, since we had decided we wanted to look good after months of living out of suitcases. After all, we were headed for America. The Masters was on the horizon.

If you've never been to Augusta National, never actually seen the golf course with your own eyes, it will be hard to convey to you just what a shock to the system it is. Of course, this is coming from a Lincolnshire lad who grew up in a landscape where the two dominant colours – grey sky, brown turf – weren't even really colours but shades. These kinds of things are in your DNA, the things you're used to, and even though I'd done my share of travelling before arriving at Augusta, I was simply not prepared for the shock to the five senses that is one's entrance to Augusta National. The intense palette of colours (pink, yellow, green, purple, blue), the entrancing smells (pine, honeysuckle, lilac), the feel of perfectly manicured turf under your feet, the special silence of an early-morning practice round at the far turn of Amen Corner. It's a quite overwhelming experience, and there is a certain Garden of Eden quality to Augusta.

Also difficult to convey in words, or even in pictures, is the sheer scope of the landscape. To call it hilly is like saying Everest plays uphill. The 10th hole drops 150 feet from tee to green. That's ten storeys! In one hole. And then returning to the clubhouse, playing the 18th, TV just cannot do justice to the difficulty of this uphill hole, where the first time I played it I thought I'd have to bring back a rope and pitons to make it up the following day. Perhaps I was still a bit jet-lagged, but bloody hell I was tired after playing that golf course the first couple of times.

We used to have to hit a drive and a solid long iron on the 18th hole – some pros even hit fairway woods for their second shots – and so it just goes to show you how much technology has changed the game, when Tiger, who admittedly is long anyway, managed to hit driver, sand wedge when he won in 2002. I knew some pros who used to hit sand wedge for their *third* shots at 18.

But I digress.

I was chuffed to be in the Masters and hugely looking forward to the week. I was a cocky lad of twenty-two, yet I figured I was going to be in with a shout. I didn't win, obviously, but I played well. I was paired with Palmer the first two rounds, and didn't sleep at all the night before, I was so nervous. Arnie was a god at Augusta, the King. He'd already won four Masters, and as soon as I saw the draw I felt like I'd been thrown into the lion's den. Nobody even knew who I was! They all thought I was some anonymous English amateur. I'm serious. I had Press people asking me if I'd qualified by some obscure amateur tournament they hadn't heard about. The thrust of it all was, 'Who are you, anyway, and how in the hell did you end up here?'

Thankfully, once out on the course with Arnold, I was able to look back at my experience of being paired with him in the Canada Cup in Japan. If I hadn't had that to draw on, I might have been overwhelmed by the sheer adulation and support bestowed upon Arnie by the Augusta crowd, though it has to be said the fans were also generous towards me. Somehow I managed to post a 71 to Arnold's 73 that first round and then a 70 to his 73 on the second day. I was in a good position after the first two rounds, and at one point during the third round I was even briefly leading the tournament (I was paired with Bobby Nichols for the third round and he told me later on he was sure I was going to win after watching the way I struck the ball). Sadly, the enormity of the moment got to me the next day, and I closed with a 77 to finish sixteenth. I was disappointed at the time, but I can look back on it now and see that my game and my temperament weren't yet in place to win a Major. Technically, there were still things I needed to work on (such as bringing my lower body more into my golf swing), and emotionally I was close but not seasoned enough. You'll often hear commentators remark on TV that players need to get in big-time positions a few times before they break through, just so they can gauge how their bodies and heart rates and nerves react to the pressure. They learn to execute mechanically within that pressure. There is some truth to this, but although you will also hear these same commentators say things like, *Well, the first thing to go under pressure is your short game*, or, *Yes, when he starts losing it left you can tell his swing is breaking down under pressure*, or whatever, the fact of the matter is that the first thing to go when you are under pressure, severe pressure, is your decision-making. It is this element of your game that requires seasoning, testing, pressure-proofing. To illustrate my point perfectly, I only need to offer you four words: Jean Van de Velde.

And so this was part of my seasoning – to find myself in the hunt in a Major, to play with and beat Arnold, to be spoken of as someone who was there or thereabouts. At the start of that week not a soul in Augusta knew who I was. But I left Augusta with a better game, a better head, and, significantly, the feeling – which Viv shared – that America was where we could someday end up, that it might ultimately be my proving ground.

I returned to Britain from the Masters as a sort of conquering hero – with accolades in the Press and from the public wherever I went – which I found slightly odd given I'd finished sixteenth. But this response, the adulation of the young Jacklin, the man who dared challenge the titans, seemed to me to betray something less than healthy about the British psyche, both in relation to its sporting figures and in general. When the Press hailed me in this way for a finish that I personally considered acceptable but hardly a dream fulfilled, it was as if that was good enough, that such a finish was in itself the kind of achievement one ought to strive for. That was all we could expect. *Mustn't get above ourselves. Mustn't grumble.*

It was this attitude that helped fuel what are still divided feelings towards my home. I love Britain, but I get frustrated by it, too. Whenever I travelled abroad, I was forever dreaming of England, of a lovely cup of properly steeped tea and a nice biscuit beside it, sitting in front of a good warm hearth. In other words, I missed home. But then when I returned and sat down with that cup of tea, and read the papers or listened to the public voice, I began to wish I was back in America, where dreaming big and wanting to be successful and not being afraid to say, *This is what I want and I'm damn well going to get it*, isn't considered an offence to good taste, to decorum, to all things proper. Of course, I'm simplifying things to some degree. But when you are under the public eye, and more to the point, under the eye of the British Press, matters are inevitably reduced to easily digestible points of view for Harry Overcoat who buys his tabloid to be told what's going on outside his purview. It does sadden me to say this, but Britain has what a friend of mine calls the Tall Poppy Syndrome: if you stick your head above the rest of the field, you'll be cut down. Peter Thomson said a similar thing once about high achievement when he remarked that he also had that 'super ego that you need to stick your head up above the mob, and unless you have that you don't do it, no matter how talented you are'.

I don't think I was ever really able to phrase it in this way, or even understand it fully, when I was a young up-and-comer in my early twenties, but I always felt it, that sense that it was going to be difficult for me to be entirely comfortable in one place or the other. Simply put, in the late 1960s (because Britain has changed a lot since then) America suited my ambition, but Britain fulfilled my sense of home. It's a shame that home and ambition could never exist in the same place for me. If only I could have found a place where I could properly pursue my ambition and then come home for dinner!

It didn't help matters that I played below my potential when I got back, finishing twentieth at the Penfold, thirty-third at the Agfa-Gevaert and forty-second at the Schweppes (for which I won the hardly life-changing sum of £19!). Just a month after returning as the man who challenged the American golfing supermen, I was now cast in the media as a golfing Icarus, the poor sod who'd flown too high, who'd let his ego outstrip his ability, and who was now back to earth, where he was assuming his rightful rank. It was all such silliness, because the truth was in the middle: I *wasn't* quite ready to challenge the supremacy of Arnold and Jack and Gary, and it had showed in my final round 77 at Augusta, but neither was I the one-hit wonder I was now made out to be. All this to deal with in a 22-year-old head made for a sometimes frustrated lad. Luckily, I never lost a shred of the confidence I had in the ever-increasing soundness of my technique. I never doubted the value of tempering my resolve by tossing myself into the cauldron, whatever the result. I wanted to pit myself against the very best. It didn't matter who or where or when – all that mattered was that the best were there and I was in the mix. Otherwise, what was the point? I was on a mission, and I knew where I was going. If no one else saw it, that was hardly my problem.

Finally, things turned my way at the Pringle Championship, then one of the bigger tournaments on the British circuit. It was held at Royal Lytham, where I'd played my first Open in 1963, and which would of course become a central place in my life a couple years later. I began poorly at the Pringle, shooting 75, but recovered to shoot a 70 in the second round to make the cut. A third-round 68 got me within a stroke of the lead heading into the last round. Again, as at Augusta, I struggled early in the final round and took a 7 at the 6th hole. But somehow I managed to reverse the flow of momentum. I birdied the 8th, the 10th, the 15th. In the end I won by four shots after coming home in 32 well-struck blows. I don't recall making a bad swing that final nine. And though I couldn't possibly have known it at the time (since I didn't even know then that the Open was scheduled to be played back at Lytham in two years), the experience of righting the ship, hitting one solid shot after another, getting in position to win and then winning, all at the same course I'd be standing on two years later with the lead, was invaluable. Without even realizing it, I'd banked the knowledge, the experience, and it was there when I needed it trying to bring home the Open.

But there was still that year's Open to be played, at Royal Liverpool, otherwise known as Hoylake, a terrific golf course on the Wirral which I'm delighted to see return to the Open rota for 2006. I played very well that year – 1967, that is – finishing fifth, a finish I was proud of then (because it showed I was in good form and nearing my goals), and which I remain proud of today (because it brought me close for the first time to Roberto de Vicenzo, the Argentinian gentleman who won it). Roberto was one of the game's classiest people, a truly gentle soul, and a wise one, too. He would always be remembered for his signing of an incorrect scorecard at the Masters, which cost him a place in a playoff and handed the title to Bob Goalby. What a sickening tragedy that was. The rules are the rules sadly, and a player is ultimately responsible for his own score. We saw something similar at the Open in 2003 when Mark Roe shot himself into contention with a stunning round at Royal St George's only to discover he'd actually turned in his scores on the card of his partner Jesper Parnevik. Both were disqualified, which was hard for both, though particularly for Mark, as he'd played so well and also since he was and is a somewhat emotional fellow. I'm sure he took it hard, but not anywhere like what Roberto must have felt. It was maybe the saddest, most poignant sight in golf, watching that ceremony as Goalby slipped on the Green Jacket while Roberto sat to the side, his head down, his face a mask. The poor man.

Still, this incident is not what Roberto ought to be remembered for. He was a first-rate player, and an even better human being, and I admired and respected him from the start. I was delighted when he won at Hoylake, especially since he'd come close to the Open Championship many times previous. He'd remarked before the start of the week's play that he'd come back to Britain for the Open, despite getting older, because he had so many friends he wanted to see. The golfing fans of Britain embraced Roberto, as well they should have, and when he emerged through the crowd on the 18th hole, as he marched to victory, a huge smile broke out on his face. The throng roared for him. It was a wonderful moment, and I was happy to be there to see it. Jack came second that year, Clive Clark and Gary Player shared third, and I was fifth. At the presentation ceremony, Roberto told the crowd how proud he was to be champion, and that if he was unable to defend his crown next year, he'd be only too delighted to pass it over to a young British player. I doubt he was thinking *Tony Jacklin* when he said it, but I was! It is my good fortune to have had a friendship with Roberto in the years that followed. He was there when I won the Open at Lytham, and at first he congratulated me, but then he told me he was happy not to be me.

'But why?' I asked him, perplexed.

'British,' he said, dropping himself into a prize fighter's stance. 'And now all your life you will be like a boxer.' He feinted left, then right, bobbed. 'Drop your guard and someone will hit you on the nose!' He faked driving a fist into my face.

It was Roberto who also uttered to me a phrase I've never forgotten, regarding the nature of trying to make a living, and a life, as a golf pro. 'Tony,' he said to me, in his thick and irresistible Spanish-tinged accent. 'This golfing, playing, big tournaments, year after year. Yoost remember. It's a longa dance, a longa musica.'

So, hearing the music, I kept dancing as fast as I could. Immediately after the 1967 Open, I went back to America, to play in the Westchester Classic in New York. While there I received a call from Mark McCormack, the famed founder of IMG (who has sadly passed away recently), a call that was to shape so much of what I did with my life over the next two decades, for better and for worse. George Bloomberg, who was well known then on the British Tour, had approached me at the Open and said I was at a point in my life where I needed representation, and would I like to talk to somebody? It turned out that somebody was Mark McCormack. I confess I was flattered to be thought of as an asset in the same vein as Palmer, Nicklaus, Player, Sanders, Charles, and so many others. After this trip to America, I came back and in early September McCormack held a Press conference at the Carlton Towers Hotel in London, where he grandly announced to the world that he was going to be my manager. I can't remember the world's response, but I think it managed to carry on without too much of a ripple. That day marked the moment I turned into a kind of hamster, stepping into a cage and getting on a bloody treadmill, running my ass off for the next fifteen years. The animal I least associate myself with is a hamster, so you'll correctly guess there was unhappiness to come in my association with IMG.

I'd quite literally stopped off at this Press conference on my way to Sandwich to play in the Dunlop Masters, which was being held at Royal St George's, another course on the Open rota. I think this tournament was my send-off to a life as a professional golfer based purely out of Britain. I'm sure I hadn't stated it formally at that point, possibly not even to myself or Vivien, but I was thinking inside that the time to make the move was coming. My play at the Dunlop seemed only to confirm to me that I was ready. I opened with a nicely controlled 69, which I proceeded to waste the next day by shooting 74. However, my game was feeling strong, despite the rocky second round, and the Saturday proved it (remembering for all those younger readers that tournaments used to finish with 36 holes on the Saturday). I was 67 in the third round, and then shot a course record 64 in the last to canter in with a three-shot victory. This win was significant to me for many reasons. First, a win was a win and it was crucial to my confidence to back up the Pringle win earlier in the year. Second, it cemented in my own mind the correctness of my appearing in the Ryder Cup, to be played a month later in Houston (I'd just made the roster, finishing tenth on the Order of Merit). Next, it put yet another asterisk beside my name that attached me to good old Henry Cotton (whose name was on my Henry Cotton Rookie of the Year Award). This was because my 64 was the new course record; Henry held the old record at 65, a score from his 1934 Open victory, which Dunlop memorialized in naming their number one selling ball the Dunlop 65 (for decades, the world's top-selling ball). Lastly, the Dunlop win was memorable because in the course of my final round 64 I managed to hole in one at the 16th, the first ace ever to be shown live on television.

Sometimes you hear players say they were meant to win; I was meant to win that week. It just happens. I could have played with a cricket bat and still probably have won. Things went right. So right that it felt like a sign to me. After that win, I knew we'd be going to America anyway for the Ryder Cup. I talked it over with Viv and she was right behind me the whole way, as I knew she would be. She loved the travel and loved America. Not to mention, she was thrilled by the thought of me, of us, chasing the prize, stepping it up a notch. The biggest and best were in America. That was where we had to go. It was our assignment, together.

I knew the PGA Qualifying Tournament was being held later that fall at West Palm Beach in Florida. The Ryder Cup – a challenge to be sure, though not what it is today – couldn't help but be a fantastic way to prepare for trying to gain privileges on the US tour. We made the decision. America it was. We packed up for the Ryder Cup, but we also knew we were packing up to try and make the US Tour. My game was starting to approach world-class level, and I knew the best competition was there. The one place left to prove myself was in America, and I was practically jangling with passion and energy. I was on the verge of stepping out in front of the larger world, and I couldn't wait for the curtain to lift for me on the biggest stage of all, the PGA Tour.

6

I suppose most people would look at what I've achieved in the game of golf, and roughly split it along two lines: the two Opens and the Ryder Cup. I would have to agree with that assessment. There was much more, obviously, because of the incredible ride my life has been, but those two areas – the individual winning of national championships and the team play under one's flag or flags – have always stood out. A simplification, but a fair one. For me, the Ryder Cup has been a lifelong presence. It has quite possibly even defined me more as a golfer, and as a person, than has victory in those two Opens.

It would also be fair to guess that my lifelong passion for the Ryder Cup began in 1967 at the Champions Club in Houston, Texas, when I first played in the event. After all, it was the international stage. I played well. I met Ben Hogan. It ignited my love of team competition. But in fact my passion for the Ryder Cup was something that evolved rather slowly, over time. The seed was planted, certainly, in 1957, during the Cup held at Lindrick, but at the time I was less aware of it as 'the Ryder Cup' than of it being a superb chance to see great American players close up. And then, ten years later, in 1967, through some magical mix of hard work and determination, there I was, *playing* in the Ryder

Cup. In one of those lovely ironic quirks of fate, who was captain of the British team in 1967 but Dai Rees? Incredible. Even so, I viewed it all then as an obligation. I was playing for my country, which I valued highly, but the Ryder Cup was not yet on any kind of pedestal for me.

In those days, the captain generally put players together for the week. Dai paired me with the Welshman Dave Thomas. Dave was a fine player, someone who might have had more success in today's modern game of smashing it miles. He was a huge fellow with a great kind manner to him (much like Dai; perhaps it's a Welsh thing to be good-hearted), and he could hit the ball so far sometimes I wondered if I wasn't using substandard equipment when playing alongside him. He'd not won a Major, but had come close in 1958, losing the Open in a playoff to Peter Thomson (I hadn't seen that playoff but I can scarcely imagine the contrast in styles; the titanic belts of Dave beside the patient, safety-first play of Thomson, who often refused to use a driver on even the widest of fairways because he simply wanted to ensure he'd be playing into the green from the correct side and from a distance he could perfectly gauge).

In any event, it was a joy for me to be paired with Dave, and I learned a thing or two from Dai about the strategic sense required for a Ryder Cup captain (though, again, I know I absorbed it without really categorizing it; I was hardly in a position to sit around and think, *Hmm, I'd better pay attention to that, because I'll be captain some day*). Dave could hit the ball absurd distances, but his wedge play and chipping were famously suspect. He and I did the maths and deduced that I should tee off at all the odd holes in the foursomes (in which each team plays alternate shots with one ball) since the par-fives were all odd holes. This meant that if Dave, in hitting his second shot off my drive, was unable to reach the green, then it would be up to me, with my superior short game, to hit the third shot, thereby sparing Dave from having to do it on holes we'd be expected to birdie. And luckily, all the par threes were even holes, which meant Dave would hit the tee ball; again, if he missed the green I'd be there to do the chipping. It all made eminent good sense, the kind of common sense I've seen many a Ryder Cup captain fail to employ in the decades since. (Hal Sutton putting Tiger and Phil as partners? Mark James putting our weakest players in the opening spots in the singles lineup at Brookline? Enough said . . . for now.)

Our plan worked. Dave and I played well as a duo, though I didn't get off to the sharpest of starts. We stood around for some time before the beginning of play watching the flag-raising ceremony and listening to the national anthems. My heart rate kept rising, especially with no outlet for it; I couldn't play, couldn't walk around, couldn't even really talk to the person beside me. The pressure was building. Then, suddenly, my name was being called to tee off, my first shot ever in Ryder Cup competition. I promptly snap-hooked the bloody thing. It might have been the fastest, most ill-tempoed golf swing of my entire career. Anyway, I managed to settle down after that, helped no doubt by Dave's easygoing nature. We ended up playing three matches against the team of Al Geiberger and Gene Littler, winning one, losing one and halving one; entirely respectable. We also beat Doug Sanders and Gay Brewer in our fourth match. I was less successful in my singles play, losing to Arnold and then again to Gardner Dickinson, who was a mean-spirited fellow, at least to me.

It's funny, America in general was so unbelievably welcoming to Viv and me, but it wasn't always like that on the golf course. Dickinson, for instance, was one of a group of American players in the Sixties who deeply resented the presence of foreign players on the US Tour – men like Dave Hill, Bob Goalby and Dan Sykes. It was no fun to be paired with these guys, since they went well out of their way to make life difficult for us foreigners, and for me in particular, seeing as I was the most successful of the imports. I remember many rounds with players like Goalby or Dickinson in which they would not utter a single word to me. Not a word! Imagine that, going through an entire round of golf without saying a single *word* to your playing partner. It's a shame, really, because though I was always cordial, they never made the slightest attempt to get to know me, or to even acknowledge that I existed. And after making an initial effort I certainly wasn't going to change in any way to accommodate them or curry their favour. To hell with that.

I found in my early years in America that most of them hadn't travelled much, and had no idea what the world was like or what it was about. Half the guys on tour back in the late Sixties and early Seventies were farm boys, raised in Texas or Oklahoma or some such place. They were guys who wouldn't take their hat off in a restaurant or after a round of golf, and worse, wouldn't even *know* to take it off. My education, derived from having been around the world, having seen every situation, meant I was educated about the world in a way these boys weren't. When I first went over, I think a lot of the US pros were intimidated by the fact that I was so young but had already seen the world a few times over. Maybe they thought I was arrogant or too self-assured. But that wasn't it. Well, I *was* self-assured. No sense denying that. But these guys simply had never done anything. They'd never been anywhere, had never been abroad. And I'm certainly not saying that this made me any better or any worse a person. That's not the point. It was all just part of what I'd done with my life, the opportunities and amazing adventures and experiences Viv and I had shared. It was an education I was grateful for, but I certainly never tried to act like someone I wasn't. I've never tried to pull the wool over anyone's eyes, then or now.

In the end, the 1967 Ryder Cup was an extremely positive

experience for me. I played well. I felt as though I'd established myself in some way with the American players, and that I'd proven myself to my own countrymen. And, of course, it was of immense value just to watch the way Dai handled the team. I was a young man at the time, after all, still just twenty-three, and Dai was good with me, checking in to see how I was feeling. He kept things so simple, which isn't only good advice for a captain, but which helps the players immensely. They feel well led, as if their captain is a man they can approach, that there are no hidden agendas, no murky realms of favouritism. It was all about who was playing well, how the course suited them, finding them the best partners, then making sure that everyone felt looked after. As I said, simple and productive. I absorbed that, you can be sure. Dai was also very much like me in that he was a person who loved life. He was not a man to walk around with his head down. To him his glass wasn't just half full – it simply had room available for the inevitable moment when it would be filled to the brim with whatever he happened to want in it.

Not everything about that Ryder Cup, however, was steeped in positive energy and enthusiasm. Meeting Ben Hogan, for instance, was an experience that left me with my mouth ajar more than once. Here was the legendary Hogan, in his home state, captain of the Americans. The man who I used to hear inside my head as I practised as a young lad in Scunthorpe. I could even mimic his Texan accent. *You can do better*, my imaginary Hogan would say to me over my shoulder. *No, that's not precise enough. That last one was good, but they've all got to be like that.* And now here he was, standing in front of me. Perhaps it was grossly unfair of me to use him as my inspiration in this way, but I did so because of his ball-striking, his tenacity, his courage in returning after his near-fatal accident. I had no idea what kind of man he was.

Hogan was famous for being a difficult man, but I didn't

really know that in Houston. My first sense that he was out of the ordinary, and was treated as such, came when both teams happened to be sitting around the locker room early in the week. Hogan entered the locker room, silently, and in a snap, like that, the entire American team stood up. I stayed in my chair and might have even glanced behind Hogan to see who was following him. The President? The Queen? The Beatles? There was no one behind him. I was quite perplexed, because it was just Ben Hogan. This was how he was treated in America, however.

I've said in other places that Hogan was not a particularly nice man, and I have to stand by that with the clarity of hindsight. I simply never understood why he had to treat people the way he did (though he was always decent enough to me). My primary impression of the great man was that he used to casually insult other players and the people around him, usually dismissively, and then a brief tight smile would form on his lips. Just as quickly it would disappear. He was complicated, to say the least, and I believe he was an insecure person, or at any rate a sad one inside. How could you blame him, what with having seen his dad commit suicide when he was such a young boy and then with his accident and all? Still, I do believe there was an insecurity in there somewhere. Why else would someone of such supreme gifts feel the need to belittle others? One need only compare the manner of Jack Nicklaus, an even greater talent, who always, and I mean *always*, managed to find a way to offer small kindnesses to the people around him. I can't ever forget Arnold Palmer asking Hogan in Houston, in a room where other players from both sides were well within hearing distance, if the larger ball or the smaller ball was going to be in play the following day. Hogan stopped and stared at Palmer for a second or two. 'Who said you were playing tomorrow?' was his response. It was said with coldness, with not a shred of humour. Arnold said nothing else, though he probably wanted to.

A Hogan anecdote that often gets told to illustrate his personality is that of Gary Player phoning Hogan to ask him a question of mechanics. I know Gary and I know Gary would have prefaced such a question with a show of respect and homage to Hogan's accomplishments. Gary would have had considerable time to practise how he planned to ask Mr Hogan this question because it took him six hours to get a line through (this was in the Sixties, don't forget). After finally getting through, Gary posed his question. He waited a second. 'What clubs do you play?' Hogan asked Gary sharply, only because he probably already knew the answer, given that Gary was by then one of the world's top half-dozen golfers. 'Dunlop,' replied Gary. 'Right,' Hogan said flatly. 'Why don't you just phone up Mr Dunlop and ask him what you should do.' Then he hung up. Hogan in a nutshell.

That Ryder Cup was also one to remember because of what it taught me about the personality of Arnold Palmer. Arnold has been revered by golf fans for five decades now, and there is good reason for it. In his prime, say from the mid-1950s to the early 1970s, he was a captivating figure for his golf, but not just for his golf. He was a muscular, handsome fellow, a man who one member of the Press once labelled as the James Bond of golf. You could see it. What they said about the fictional Bond (the men wanted to be him, and the ladies wanted to sleep with him) was true about Arnold, too. Call it magnetism, star power, sex appeal – whatever it was, Arnold had it in spades. He was a fantastic player, but the truth is that he was never in the same category as Jack. The golf was almost secondary, however, in the same sort of way that today millions of people around the world who have never touched a golf club know who Tiger Woods is, but they may not even know he's chasing Jack's records, or that he went two and a half years without a Major. My point is that Arnold in many ways transcended golf, simply because he had that magnetism. Double-O-Seven-iron, we ought to have called him.

Even the other players were drawn to him, to see what he'd say or do. He seemed an outsize character to many of us, and I had my first real insight into that character at the 1967 Cup. I was standing on the practice range hitting balls with George Will (who was the pro for decades at Sundridge Park). We were quietly minding our own business when Arnold came up to us with that characteristic grin on his face, strutting about, pleased as punch with himself about something. He said Hi and we stopped hitting balls to say hello in response. It turned out that he had just that morning taken possession of his new jet, and he was curious to know if we wanted a ride in it with him. Why he chose us I'll never know – likely because we were the only suckers he could find hanging about. Whatever the reason, we said yes immediately and went with him to a nearby private airstrip, all despite the fact that George was quite well known to be a nervous flier at the best of times. Arnold was his own pilot, of course, and has since gone on to become a pilot of some note, flying around the world and so on. The issue was not whether we were in trained hands; we knew Arnold could fly the thing. But we soon came to doubt, severely, that we were in *safe* hands. We got strapped in and he shot that thing down the runway and straight up into the sky. He gunned it this way and that, twisting and turning it, running it into what I considered gravitational impossibilities just to show us what it could do. I was scared half to death, but when I looked over at poor George he'd gone ashen-coloured and was deathly quiet, the way someone might just before they have a severe panic attack. I think I mentioned to Arnold, who was cackling with glee over his new toy, that George might not be feeling too well. To which Arnold responded that in that case we had better get this thing closer to the ground. He banked it into a 90-degree turn and then dropped it straight down to the ground, the nose pointed at the rapidly approaching earth. A couple of hundred feet from doom, he hauled on the steering wheel (or whatever the hell it's called) and pulled the jet screaming into a 400-mile-an-hour fly-by just feet over the ground, scattering bystanders like a flock of pigeons in Trafalgar Square. At least, that's how my memory pictures it (and I can laugh about it now . . . sort of). He landed the thing and we came to a stop. I was now the ashen colour George had been, but when I looked over at George he was queasy green. There was a dark damp patch on the front of his trousers. I didn't give him a hard time about it, because I'd come close to pissing myself, too. It was a flight that didn't cure his fear of flying, I'm guessing.

Arnold paid a price, too, though in his typical way he managed to charm himself clear. When we returned to the clubhouse, he was told that there had already been numerous complaints both to the police and the Federal Aviation Authority about a Lear jet coming dangerously close to pedestrians and onlookers, and it had been rather easy to put the pieces together after that. Some member from the club informed Arnold that an official from the FAA was waiting to speak to him on the phone, and that the guy was hopping mad and planned to revoke Arnold's pilot's licence, which would have been devastating to Arnold. He picked up the phone, and calmly listened to the man on the other end give him hell. Then Arnold apologized profusely, using his best manners, saying it had been a terrible bit of judgement on his part, that it would never ever happen again, that he couldn't even explain what he'd been thinking. He was ingratiating to the extreme, and said that he would accept any penalty imposed and that he would take full responsibility, and that it was the kind of mistake that he would only ever make once, he could promise that, and his word was everything. While speaking Arnold looked at me and smiled. He kept his licence.

A few days later, I was drawn to face Arnold in my first-ever Ryder Cup singles match. He holed a 50-footer for birdie on the first hole and I was five down at the turn. I was soundly thrashed by the unassailable 007-iron. Arnold had a way about him. You couldn't ignore the star power. It was just there.

After the successes of that Ryder Cup (in which, as a rookie on a team that got rather soundly beaten, I managed to record two wins and one half), I felt quite ready to take on the PGA qualifying school at West Palm Beach. I shot a pair of 68s in the last two rounds to secure my Tour card, and we were set, though it wasn't half as routine as I'm making it sound. It was an eight-round qualifying event back then, not the six rounds of today. And there was a large crop of American Walker Cup heroes – men like Bob Murphy and Ron Cerruto – who had decided to try and turn pro. Those 68s were gutsy tests of nerve, and it was a real achievement just to *get* a Tour card that year. I was hugely proud of passing that test.

Vivien and I agreed that playing in America was the kind of life-changing decision we had to commit to wholeheartedly for it to work. It has to be remembered that such things were much less common in the late Sixties. Nowadays, itinerant workers, I suppose you could call them, are pretty common. Among golfers it's regular. The game is so global now – you've got Americans living in Japan, Swedes in Florida, Englishmen going to university in Arizona, subcontinental Indians with PGA Tour cards. The world is open and accessible, and the living standards are easier to regulate, if you will. But it wasn't like that then. It felt like, and was, a huge thing to change tours. It was a move reported on in micro-detail in every British paper. The question was always, *Why? Why go to America?*

When I responded, as I inevitably did, that it was because I wanted to be one of the best and I wanted to be challenged by the best and so that meant going to America, well, that provoked a wide range of responses, some admiring, many of a more snipy quality. More than once I was labelled big-headed, since it was just bad form to so baldly state one's ambition.

But I was determined and Viv was behind me, and so off we went. It was yet another great learning period in our lives. The American way of life – no longer there as a stopover visitor, but as a regular touring professional – always struck us as so open, so big, so loud, so colourful. It was no wonder the country produced heroes like Arnold – they had to be bigger than life just to fill the available space. Also, the general standard of living was so much higher there. The food was fine, and we were always amazed that everything *worked*. The phones, the switches, the power, the water. It was just a newer country, I suppose, and it hadn't had the centuries to fall apart yet, like dear old Britannia. It was always a bit disconcerting to pick up a phone line and have it work so clearly and so immediately! Nor did it hurt that the conditioning of the golf courses and the practice grounds, and just the set-up for pros in general, was noticeably superior to that in Europe at the time. It was no wonder that when Sam Snead came over to Britain for the Open and the Ryder Cup, he referred to it as 'camping out'.

Not that it was a completely free-and-easy and wonderful transition going to America. Hardly. After a while the food did seem to lack a certain something. And in areas like Florida and California and Arizona, places where the Tour played a lot of golf, the overall feel of the place was that it was not yet fully formed. The whole society felt so new, so thrown together, so young. Of course, that's because it was, speaking from the standpoint of a European. This is what both attracts and repels so many about America, particularly forty years ago: anything was possible, since the place was a bit of a blank slate, but then once you were on your way and got going, got established, then you started to notice that it *was* a blank slate in many ways (I'm talking in historical and physical terms, of course – temperamentally, it was a place that always felt welcoming to me, a warm, friendly place). This was something a person from America wouldn't know or feel, since it would be what they grew up with. But growing up in a different, older and somewhat more mature (or do I mean fogeyish?) culture, America had a brash, unscrubbed enthusiasm to it that I loved. My Scunthorpe upbringing undoubtedly made it easier for me to make the transition to living in America because we had moved around so much when I was young; we had so little, and really had no established pattern of living. The constant variety and newness of our experience in America was a gift to me, and to Vivien, too. I suppose in some ways I viewed it as a gift because in America there was just so much *room*. It wasn't that way back home. There was no space, there were few other sporting figures of international note. The media focused in on so many fewer people than in America. It was all becoming so intensely claustrophobic back home, and that pressure was blissfully absent on American soil.

Also, looking back on it now, I believe one of the reasons I was so attracted to America was because of my relationship with money, or at least how money represented success. If an American wanted to be rich and successful, he said so and got on with business, and that was fine. There were no class barriers, at least not barriers of birth. The downside of immersing myself in this attitude was that I did rather get caught in the chasing of the prize. Money has always been a very complicated thing for me, and these complications are certainly rooted in my upbringing. There are probably a million different ways to express it, but I think the simplest would be to just say that in my younger days I was insecure about money, about how much I needed, how much I was making, how much I was going to make, what amount would define me as someone who was wealthy and successful and *secure*. The problem – and here is where I feel the Press and public got it wrong for so many years – wasn't that I was desperate to be wealthy, exactly. It was more of a negative than a positive thing; I was trying to avoid something, rather than build something. I suppose in my private self I was always a bit worried I'd end up back where I started, in a terrace house, broke, hardly an extra penny for anything good in life. In other words, the way I grew up. My father was obsessed with money, too, was always talking about it, always scheming with that car-fixing and house-moving.

It would be fair to say that after my early success (and this was particularly the case after winning the two Opens) I charged too hard after the almighty dollar. I don't disagree with that take on things. But I did it because I thought I had to, because I wanted 'the good things' in life and didn't want to revisit my youthful way of living, and the only way I knew to achieve that was to say Yes when people offered to pay me for my golf or my name. Part of me could never get comfortable with having 'this much'. I had to have 'that much'. Not that I ever had a sense of how much was enough. The irony, of course (and I'll talk about this a bit later on), is that I ended up losing it all, making it again, losing it all, and then making it again. The final twist is that I've now, *circa* 2006, at last achieved that balance of not worrying or caring too much about money at exactly the time when I've got a good comfort level financially. I'm not unwilling to admit there have been some unfortunate decisions along the way, but I made them because I wanted to be sure to step out from what I'd known as a youngster. Now that I live in Florida year round it's easy for me to look back and analyse things. It only took me a few decades to understand that having money isn't what cures that insecurity; it's always there, but it's just a matter of trying to put it away, to compartmentalize it, as one of my mates says, and be thankful for the living you've been allowed to make. The chase was, in so many ways, always about going after that feeling of being secure, of not having to worry any more about money, about living decently. That was the key: security. It's a search that has never quite ended, a presence I have always felt behind me, pushing me, motivating me and, yes, at times haunting me too.

But it was more than just the openness about money that attracted me to America. I think I also fell in love with the country so quickly after arriving because I happened to play well and because I also happened to fall in with fellows who were not just great players, but wonderful people, Tom Weiskopf and Bert Yancey. They became my closest chums, and like me, they weren't always that crazy about the lifestyle on the US Tour, which back then anyway was quite the social swirl. Nowadays, pros tend to be more self-contained travelling units. Not then. Within weeks of arriving Viv and I ended up at some glitzy party in Palm Springs where we were fascinated by the dazzle and swank. There seemed to be a lot of those parties, but we were just as happy to go out for dinner with the Weiskopfs and Yanceys, and have a nice night out just the six of us.

In making that move to the US Tour, I need to emphasize, again, that in aspiring to be the best you have to be around them, *have* to go where the best are. I simply cannot stress enough how gripped I was with this belief when I decided to go to America. I *had* to go. I'm not sure people will ever really fully understand my decision. It wasn't just about, *Oh, there's more money there.* Or, *Well, it's a bit more glamorous.* No. The best players in the world lived and played in America. I wanted to beat the best. I wanted to be the best! That meant leaving Britain to play in America because Nicklaus and Palmer weren't making regular trips over to play the British Tour. This is crucial to you, the reader, understanding why I felt I had to leave Britain. Yes, America offered many different things – money, opportunity, a kind of freedom – but all that was ultimately secondary to the one single most important factor. I was driven to be at the top, and I was the one *doing* the chasing, which meant going where my prey were. A big game hunter doesn't sit in his library in Surrey sipping Glenmorangie waiting for a rhino to show up at his front door saying, *Shoot me*! He goes to their habitat, to where they live. That's the way it works.

The pace of life increased substantially once we were in America, and I think this might also have had something to do with my recent signing with Mr McCormack, who wasted no time in sending me all over the world at headlong speed. I remember playing in Palm Springs early during our first year in America, when I got a call from Mark informing me that I had been booked for a TV match in Nairobi, of all places. It was to be myself, Roberto de Vicenzo and Bert Yancey in a challenge match, a match that seemed to take ten minutes compared to the days of journeying just to get there and back. It was pure craziness, is what it was. In a whirlwind I was back in Phoenix, missing a cut, and then skipping over to Florida to play Doral.

I paid for my mother and father to travel over from Scunthorpe to spend a good chunk of time with us in Florida during that first year on the PGA Tour, and it was the start of a wonderful stretch for me, both on and off the golf course. The trip really was a dream come true for my parents. Viv and I were having a great time, and we wanted to share that. I had the use of a car for a year, and we drove throughout Florida with my parents. I made the cut at Doral, and then the next week finished fourth in Orlando at the Florida Citrus Open. My game was finding its watermark. The next stop was Pensacola and I was second there. My mother betrayed her upbringing when she began to learn about the size of the purses on offer. I won $7,800 at Pensacola, and I can still remember the look of astonishment and disbelief on her face when she found out how much

I'd made. It would have been a lot more had I not made a meal of a little wedge shot into the 71st hole that put George Archer into the winner's circle. The next stop after that was Jacksonville.

Over a golfing life spanning so many decades, there have naturally been numerous moments when things changed for me, when I became something different than I'd been the day before. Winning at Jacksonville was one of these. Although I'd finished fourth and second the previous two weeks in PGA events, I think it would be fair to say I did not require a Tiger-esque crowd of handlers and bodyguards to safely walk down main street Jacksonville. In the PGA Tour's media interview request list at the start of that week's play some guy named Nobody was more in demand than me. But winning at Jacksonville changed things, in a hurry.

Obviously, given my form the two weeks before I was feeling good about my game and my chances. I've always been a fairly streaky player (and a *very* streaky putter), and when I was on song it all just seemed to flow so well. I've also always been what you might call an 'inspirational' player. In other words, when the mood was on me, I could raise my game. So much depended on my mood, which wasn't always the best way to be frankly. Jack Nicklaus could be having a great week emotionally or a difficult week emotionally, but he always managed to grind it out no matter what. He could play great under any circumstances. You could say the same of Tiger now. I wasn't always able to do this; some days my mental or emotional state just wasn't ready for golf, and my game suffered for it. One could always wish to be slightly different this or that way, and I suppose I could have wished for (or even worked myself into possessing) the kind of temperament that was steadier, less prone to mood swings. But who knows what that would have made me? Perhaps I'd have made a lot more cheques and had a lot more Top Tens, but then

I might not have won two Opens. And without my emotional temperament I might not have had it in me to captain four Ryder Cup teams (and I will return to this inspirational aspect of being a Ryder Cup captain later on). Anyway, I never *wanted* to change who I was. Why would I? I like being me, and it strikes me as foolishness to try and be anything other than who you are.

I was 'on' in Jacksonville. After the first two days I was tied with the flamboyant party animal otherwise known as Doug Sanders (who would, sadly, miss that famous 3-footer at St Andrews two years later to lose to Nicklaus by a stroke for the Open). In the last round I was paired with Arnold Palmer and Don January. It would have been impossible to be paired with players so unlike. Arnold took a vicious swipe at every ball (it sometimes even seemed as if he hitched his pants and cocked his head for tap-in putts), whereas January's swing was so slow and languid it seemed to take him until February. Arnold would grin, wink, stare, glare, and no matter what he scored would always seem to be on the verge of disaster or greatness. January, on the other hand, always seemed on the verge of a nap. By this point in my career I'd been lucky enough to have played with Arnold a few times, and so his 'Army' didn't really affect me too much (I don't think January was even roused from his sleepwalk by the raucous crowds). Typical of Arnold, he stormed out of the gate, birdieing the first hole of the final round, as if trying to throw a scare into me. Somehow I held it together, and shot a steady 71 to win the tournament by two strokes. No doubt, having the imperturbable January in our group helped me; if I needed to calm down and collect myself I only needed to look at January to slow my heart rate, though staring at him too long might have induced a coma.

Both during and after the round Arnold and Don were delightful towards me, and both seemed as happy for me to have won as I was for myself. Arnold even went so far, early the next week, to send a telegram to the offices of the British PGA congratulating them on having produced a British winner on the PGA Tour. I had no clue at the time, but it emerged shortly thereafter that I had in fact become the first-ever British winner of a four-round event on the PGA Tour. For a few days afterwards, it felt like I was interviewed by every possible media outlet in Britain, from the BBC in London to the Scunthorpe Poodle Club Monthly. It was all a bit much, but I revelled in it. Here was proof, vindication, of the rightness of my decision to go to America.

One of the most gratifying elements of winning at Jacksonville was the fact that good old Johnnie Rubens from Potters Bar was there watching, the man who'd done so much to help me out when I was a struggling teenager trying desperately to find the best within me while also trying not to murder Bill Shankland. You can't know how fulfilling it was to be able to hole out and then thank him for his generosity. And he remained so generous. After the win at Jacksonville, he hosted a quite amazing dinner at the Dorchester Hotel back in London in honour of my victory. I have a picture of the two of us standing near the fireplace mantel in the Deerwood Club holding the Jacksonville trophy together. It remains one of my favourite pictures and is perfectly symbolic of what he helped me achieve.

In many ways, it was magical that he was able to be there at all. He just happened to be in America for business, and he decided to come down for the tournament. He called the pro at Ponte Vedra, found out where I was staying, came to the course, picked up the tickets I'd arranged for him, and then walked inside the ropes, a true front-row seat. It was a gift, really; here was the man who'd helped me more than anyone in the early days, the single most important person in my career to that date, except for Viv, and now here he was walking the course, watching me win my first US tournament. His generosity never wavered, either. After I won the Open the following year, he again hosted a huge victory party, this time at the Savoy. Even in later years, he didn't stop trying to help. In 1975, when I moved to Jersey for tax reasons, he rang me up and said, 'Are you okay? You know what I mean?' I said, 'Yes, Johnnie, I'm fine. I'm all right.' Even so, a letter from him arrived the next day saying that he knew I was okay, he understood that, but that if at some point it was required I simply had to call his bank and there would be fifty thousand pounds waiting for me to use if I happened to need it. He was a generous soul, and I used to love his company. We even shared a house together with our wives for years down at Augusta when I played there. I've lived a life full of meeting the most spectacular and inspiring people, but he will always occupy one of the upper shelves of my memory.

Despite the massively successful nature of the whole year, 1968 did end on a rather negative note for me, at least in terms of golf. Ironically, it happened when I returned to Britain to play in the Piccadilly World Match Play at Wentworth, a real top-flight tournament. One of my great hobbies in life has been studying human nature. That might be too fancy a way of saying that I'm fascinated by people, by trying to understand why they do what they do. This is certainly true of myself, as well; I've spent sixty years thinking about my life and what it means, how I can best use it, what it all amounts to.

I've come to believe over the decades that so much of what we do is really about legacy; in other words, how people are going to remember us. My life – anyone's life – has to be defined by how you treated other people, especially those close to you. I like to hope that that's what my legacy will be for the people I've loved and who have loved me; that I cared, that I meant well, that I did my best by them. And that I always lived with passion and tried to share my passion with the people around me. I'll be the first to tell you that faults were not unheard of in the Jacklin decision machine. But the mistakes produced were never ones of intent. In other words, sometimes it may have looked as if I did the wrong thing but it was always because I was *trying* to do the right thing.

In any case, I have also always felt that the small things are often the telling things, and it's when the pressure is on that people reveal themselves for who they are. Which was why my last tournament in 1968 felt like a bit of a sour note to end the year on. I had won my first match at the Piccadilly, beating Lee Trevino 4&3 (if only that trend had continued). Next up was Gary Player, the fit, tightly wound South African (who to this day insists on playing competitively, as if he wants to be the world's greatest living ninety-year-old golfing professional; to which my response is, Why? Who cares?). It was a dour, damp week at Wentworth, but there were still pretty fair crowds out on the West Course. It was a seesaw match the whole way. I was two up at one point, then went through a bad spell of five holes to go two down with three to play. I then birdied the 16th and 17th to square the match. On the 18th, the 36th hole of the match, Gary missed a 4-footer that I had already conceded him in my mind, and so we were all square. We had to stop the match at that point because it was just too dark to continue, at which point Gary complained to the referee that we never should have played the last hole, it was so dark.

We tried to start the next day, but it was a total washout, and we returned the day after for our playoff. There was a good crowd out to watch a match that might not go more than one hole. Gary hooked his tee shot into the heavy rough, hacked it back out on to the fairway, and then hit a decent iron shot to about 12 feet. I nailed a drive and hit a solid 1-iron up onto the green, leaving myself 30 feet for eagle, a putt I left 5 feet short. My dad happened to be following us around, and he was standing in the gallery just as Gary lined up his 12-footer for a birdie.

As the ball neared the hole, it looked to be heading wide and a fellow standing right beside my dad half-shouted, 'He's missed it!' He didn't miss it, though. The ball dived into the hole for a birdie, meaning I now needed my 5-footer to continue the match. But almost before his ball hit the bottom of the cup, Gary swung round on the crowd.

'You said "Miss it, miss it" didn't you?' he said accusingly to the crowd, his voice rising. 'Why would you do that? What is the reason for that? I'm a visitor here in your country. I'm a professional and I'm just here trying to do my job. I understand you're cheering for your home boy, but that's just poor. You should have better sportsmanship than that.'

He went on in this vein for at least a couple of minutes, utterly berating the poor crowd, and I spent the whole time torn between thinking about my 5-footer to halve the hole, getting engaged in the dispute, or calling a referee to settle it, so that we could continue. Two minutes may not sound like much, but when you've got a 5-foot putt to keep a match going, it's a long time I can tell you. There were even some in the crowd who began to chastise Gary for his oratory, saying, *Come on, give Jacko a chance. Let him putt his five-footer.* Naturally, once Gary felt he'd made his point – which I have to say he could just as easily have made once I'd putted out – I turned my attention to my own effort and promptly missed. Of course, there's no way to know if I'd have made my putt had I been allowed to concentrate properly. I blamed myself for not being of a strong enough mind to banish Gary's antics from my head. But I also felt that even though it might not have been out-and-out gamesmanship from Gary, it was at the least very bad manners. The Press asked me afterwards if Gary's outburst had been the reason I'd missed. I said, *No, I couldn't say it was the reason, but it certainly didn't help.*

As I said – small things.

Nineteen sixty-eight was also a significant year for me in a rather ominous sense, even if it was just a niggle at the time. It was about putting. It was at the Bob Hope Classic, in Palm Springs, where I first felt an involuntary movement in my wrists while putting. Something went off while stroking a 20-footer. My hands and wrists did something without my mind directing them to. I thought to myself, 'What the hell was *that*?'

The Match Play brought 1968 to a close. It was the last year of my life I could call anything like normal. The first twenty-five years had been full of resolve, high emotion, true love, and my emergence as a golfer to be seriously reckoned with. All these things were soon to be a blur behind a rush of event, of attention, of achievement. The foot was about to find the accelerator.

7

If you were to ask me what the number one thing is that ought to guide a person's life, from start to finish, there are so many examples I could think of which I've always tried to make part of my everyday life: a sense of honesty and treating people right; to persevere; to be honest with yourself above all else, so that you can fall asleep at night and be okay with who you are; the importance of family; not being afraid of hard work. All these things are central to who I am. But if I had to choose one thing above all else that I've tried to make a factor in my life, I know what it would be. Actually, let me change the wording on that – it's not something I've consciously had to try to make part of my life; it's something that is simply *inside* me. It's there, and I've always known it, and the key for me has always been to let it express itself.

That thing is passion. *Passion.*

You *must* live your life with passion and intensity and commitment. This is what I have always believed, and what I've forever tried to make part of my life at every moment. Have I made mistakes? Too many to count. Have I possibly offended people here or there? I'm sure I have. With the benefit of hindsight, are there things I'd have done differently? Of course. Not making mistakes means you never took a risk, you never put it out there. You can't win if you don't tee it up.

But no matter the circumstance, what I know is that for better or worse everything I've ever done has had my full commitment. If something didn't work out in my life, it was never because of a lack of passion and enthusiasm. That's why I'm okay with the mistakes. You make the best decision you can at the time, and commit fully to the course of action you've chosen. If it doesn't work out, at least you can sleep at night. I have never once in my life put my head on the pillow at night and thought, *I ought to have tried harder today*. That's not to say there haven't been many nights when I've lain in bed and wondered how I could do things better. It's like I tell my young son Sean nowadays, 'Weed your own garden.' It's all about being honest with yourself, accepting your faults and mistakes, trying to be a better person, and going about things the right way. It's not rocket science! It's just about commitment, about passion, about caring. I had a friend say to me once, *You know, your problem is that you're an open book. You tell too much. You're too open in talking about how you feel*. Well, that's something I simply cannot apologize for. Ever. To me, the opposite is a far worse crime. I'd rather say what I honestly think and believe, and live with the consequences, than keep everything bottled up inside merely because I'm afraid of being wrong or of what people think. Sod that. I am what I am, and I don't have a problem with it. The respect I need most is Tony Jacklin's; if I can't respect myself, why should anyone else?

I have always, *always*, done things with a full-bore intensity. I have always put my whole self into whatever I do. I don't think we get a second chance at this thing called life. It's once round the park, my friends, and that's it. And I don't want to get to the end of it and think I left something on the table. So I've always gone into what I've done with maximum enthusiasm and complete intensity. That's who I am, and there can be no apologies for this. When things haven't gone according to the best plans and intentions, well, then maybe it looks bad. But when things go right, the results in my life have been spectacular, not just on the golf course, but in every area of my life. Meeting Vivien and marrying her the way I did is a perfect example. A person different from me might have been too shy or too quiet or not confident enough to go up and ask her out, but I plunged in because that's who I am.

This passion and intensity has always found expression on the golf course, and the years I came into my peak were the best example of it. Even so, as far as what was happening on the golf course, there was no reason in particular to imagine that 1969 would be the start of a three-year period of my life that would carry me to a stunning fulfilment of my dreams, and then dash me down to the kind of lows one can only fully feel through having reached the pinnacle. To say that I was about to enter a time where I would feel the full spectrum of emotions an athlete can feel is to underplay the drama of the time. As Dickens wrote (about a rather different set of circumstances), *It was the best of times, it was the worst of times.*

Nineteen sixty-nine was the best of times, at least the way it turned out in the end. The truth is that the year began in less than spectacular fashion, which was disconcerting to me at the time, considering the 1960s had been a decade in which every single year had been better than the one before, one year of progress after another; every year I felt stronger, a better player, closer to my goal of becoming the best in the world.

Even though I'd missed a few cuts in America early in the year, my form was acceptable. I had begun working on a new leg action in America, one that I hoped would give me some added power, but more importantly a much greater degree of control when the pressure was on. I had become fascinated by, and impressed with, the swings of some of my friends on the US Tour, particularly Tom Weiskopf, Bert Yancey and the great Tommy Bolt. But it was hard to integrate these changes into my game, and it showed. I had just one top ten heading into the Masters, where I'd had such a fine experience the year before. Then I played even worse at Augusta and missed the cut. I was so upset about the whole drift of things that Viv and I went home shortly after the Masters, just to regroup. God, it felt wonderful to be home. I remember landing in London and heading north to Scunthorpe, looking out the window all the while, saying to Vivien, *Look, that's English grass, those are English trees, this is the English countryside!* It sounds crazy, but that's how simply delighted I was to be back home. It was particularly fine to be back in the north, my true home. It was so easy and right-feeling to just slip back into a way of talking, of thinking, of joking, of being.

Visiting home rejuvenated us, and after a ten-day break we returned to America. The break seemed to do wonders for my golf. I was fifth at both the Kemper Open and the Western Open, and played well for long stretches at the US Open in Houston in June (won by Orville Moody), though I ended up twenty-fifth.

Things were now looking up. My new leg action was feeling more natural and more powerful. I was getting into a very good frame of mind with my tempo. It was feeling slow and syrupy, under control. My form wasn't yet peaking, but I was feeling much better than I had been after missing the cut at Augusta. Part of it was simply learning to pace myself, to start to understand that desire and inspiration are elements to be used slowly and in moderation throughout a tournament, a year, a career, rather than balloons to be popped in one great explosion. I was also starting to get it that rest really was important to me, that to play at my best I needed to feel fresh. (This had been a problem

of mine, and would worsen over the years. Nerves and the struggle to sleep were ever present.)

In any case, it was in a positive frame of mind that I returned
to the UK for the Open at Lytham. I was anxious to play well in
the Open, for any number of reasons. First off, it was the one
tournament I'd always focused on. That had been the case since
day one. Second, Lytham was a great track, fast, firm and very
difficult. It's a true test of links golf, though at the time I may not
have held it in the same esteem I do today. I recently played it
with my son Sean, and found it to be a great golf course, everything a golf course should be. Third, I wanted to put in a good
performance after the frustrations of the 1968 Open at
Carnoustie, where a final round of 79 had ruined the good work
of the first couple of rounds, and where I'd ended up eighteenth.
Next, I was looking forward to Lytham because it had been the
site of some of my best and earliest memories as a pro; the thir-
tieth-place finish in the 1963 Open, my first Open, as well as my
victory in the 1967 Pringle, when I had played so flawlessly
down the stretch.

Last, I was greatly looking forward to the Open that year
because the swing changes had begun to feel reliable. This was
an exciting time for me because I felt I was just getting better and
better, and that I was truly on the cusp of great things. I can't
explain it, other than to say that I was feeling ready, rounding
towards what I was meant to be.

Bear with me while I spend a moment talking about the
changes I was trying to make to my golf swing that spring,
because they really were fundamental to my success. I won't
spend too much time on it – I don't want any eyes glazing over –
but essentially it was all about swing speed, and even more to
the point, the swing speeds of the two halves of one's action –
upper body and lower body. What always seemed to happen to
me when I got a bit nervous, or in a spot on the course where I

really *wanted* it, was that I would sometimes get too quick with the upper body. Basically, my arms and hands and shoulders wanted to overtake my legs and hips. They got out of synch.

What I felt I needed was a more stable base. Simple. The left knee had to be through the impact area and stabilized before the club got there, otherwise there was no telling what was going to happen. I knew I had to let the big muscles of the legs dictate the tempo and speed of my swing, a tempo I could repeat under pressure. Speed was the enemy in those days, and slowness of tempo the goal.

It was a revelation to me. I had such control, such confidence in it. This may sound simple enough, letting the big muscles do the work, but remember there wasn't an army of gurus on the practice tee back then like there are now. It's hard to pick the actual players out on the practice tee nowadays, there are so many people on their 'teams'. No, I did this work on my own, through thinking about my swing and through watching, virtually every day, the majesty of Tom Weiskopf's swing, for instance. I watched Jack a lot, too, and he had the best, the strongest, foundation out there.

This work paid enormous dividends for my confidence, because eventually I knew, I *knew*, that I could count on it. There's just no way you can get up there on a golf course, under the gun, and say, *Right, I need to swing my upper body slowly*. It won't work unless you've got your lower body under control and working at the right speed. The adrenalin will play havoc with the arms, the wrists, the hands.

One of the keys for me in this learning process was the 7-iron. I hit hundreds of thousands of 7-irons. I wanted to work on tempo, tempo, tempo. The 7-iron was perfect because it was a full swing yet it was exactly between the power swing of the 6-iron (on down) and the touch swing of the 8-iron (and up). It was a club I could just swing. I was there to concentrate on the motion, not on the hit. It wasn't always easy, either, to restrict myself to 7-irons. I often wanted to hit other clubs, to smash some drivers, to lace some long irons out there. But this is where the discipline comes in. I knew where I wanted to go. And I knew what it would take to get there. It took focus and dedication and enormous discipline. I think the discipline is what most fine players lack when they don't meet their potential. You ask twenty superb young amateurs if they want to win a Major and they will say, 'Of course! I'd love it. It's what I want.' But how many have the discipline to do it?

How wonderful was it to return home to play the 1969 Open? It's impossible to describe the joy. It was like being in exile from one's family and friends, from your creature comforts, from everything you know and trust and love – so much so that you almost begin to lose your memory of what all those things are like. And then suddenly you have them all again. And it's glorious. You revel in it. Don't get me wrong. Viv and I loved America, and we had a fantastic time there. But it wasn't home. It never was. Home was a cup of tea. Home was the north's sense of humour. Home was the green English countryside. England was our home, because nowhere else could ever be.

I felt such support coming back to the UK to play in the Open in 1969. I'd been playing primarily in America, of course, and there was no doubt in my mind that this was what had taken my game to the next level, but that didn't change the fact that I was still largely unknown in America. I didn't have galleries of any size there, and outside of my wife and myself no one really cared what I was up to on the course. It was just a question of playing well and making a cheque. There wasn't a lot of involvement from fans or the media, which wasn't too much of a bother for me since I was so intensely focused on continuing to elevate the quality of my game. I was engaged in a passionate and committed quest in America, but in a rather peculiar way it was a private quest.

When I came back for the Open, it felt so much different. It was an onslaught! I could literally *feel* the support. It was a palpable, physical presence, and made me feel valued. I felt lifted, positive, back in my own environment, among my own. I also believed, wrongly in many cases, that people in the UK understood what I was trying to do by playing in America, and that it was appreciated, this sense I was trying to be the best by playing against the best. My game was very much in the ascendancy, and I went into the week feeling confident, full of a kind of youthful vigour. I felt I had the game to win, I had a track record of solid wins under my belt, I felt like I knew and understood the golf course. My thinking was, *Right, here we go.* I was just ready for it. That's not being cocky or arrogant. It was the truth, and saying it is only stating what I knew and felt.

A steady start was what was needed, nothing fancy, just a solid, classy beginning. Lytham needs respect, after all. The front nine is the scoring nine – you had to shoot 33 or 32 going out – because the back nine was tough and wasn't going to give up anything. You aren't going to win the Open on the first day, but you can lose it. Starting well was important to me. I had always been the kind of player that needed to be in contention in order to maintain my full concentration. Being buried deep in the field early on tended to make me lose focus. One knew, of course, that one had to always keep fighting, but this wasn't always the easiest thing to do. It would have been particularly hard to do at Lytham, which is probably the most difficult of Open courses, save Carnoustie. It's a rather quirky links course, in that you never even really come near the sea. The great Harry Colt laid out most of the course in the 1920s, and it's been considered Open-worthy almost from the start. It's also been considered bloody difficult right from the start. A lot of people tend to refer to Lytham as 'just a beast', quoting the esteemed golf writer Bernard Darwin, but in fact what Darwin said was that Lytham was 'a beast, but a just beast'. He meant it was brutal but fair.

Lytham has a fantastic history I'm proud to be part of. It hosted its first Open in 1926, and this was the Open in which the great Bobby Jones, in the course of winning, retired to his hotel for lunch between the third and fourth rounds (both being played on the Saturday at the time). He went back to the course after lunch to play the final round. An entrance man stopped him at the gate and said he'd have to pay a fee to get back in! 'But I'm leading the tournament!' said Jones. The entrance man was unmoved and Jones had to come up with his two and six-pence just for the privilege of going back in to win the tournament. Luckily, I was allowed entrance without having to open up my wallet.

The early part of the 1969 Open (which was the first-ever colour telecast of a golf event on the BBC, incidentally) went well from the start. I opened with a solid 68. Bob Charles shot 66 to take the early lead; it was a record score for Lytham Opens, and it signalled that he was likely to be there all week. Afterwards he told the Press it was one of the best rounds he'd ever played. A Yorkshireman named Hedley Muscroft had recorded a 68. Shockingly, Jack Nicklaus had fumbled his way around to 75. Typical of Nicklaus, however, he would still be around by the end of the week. Shooting 69 that opening round was Miller Barber, the man known as Mr X, for reasons I confess always escaped me. Peter Thomson and Christy O'Connor opened with 71s, Roberto de Vicenzo a 72. It felt like everybody was there. I read in the papers later that week that it was, in fact, considered the strongest field to date to have contested the Open. I began the tournament as if I was going to have wrapped it up by nightfall. I birdied the 1st, the 4th, the 5th, the 6th. The frantic pace didn't last, of course; I bogeyed the 9th and the 14th. But it was a solid start, and I remember feeling I was right where I wanted to be; well in the mix and feeling great about my game. The second and third rounds, both scores of 70, were but a continuation of this feeling of control, of focus, and left me with a two-stroke lead heading into the final round. It's funny, my mental and emotional state was almost a replica of my golf swing – steady, even, a nice smooth tempo.

The other thing I was feeling confident with was my putting and short game. Simply put, it was one of the best putting weeks I've ever had (the other might have been the US Open at Hazeltine, but we'll come to that). I had twenty-five one-putts that week, and just one three-putt. This superb putting display was not due simply to great reads and pure strokes, but to the fact that my short game so frequently left me with makeable putts if I happened to miss a green in regulation. There were many, many moments during the two middle rounds when things could so easily have gone pear-shaped. My bunker play in particular seemed magical that third round. Four times that day – at the 8th, 15th, 17th, and 18th – I was bunkered green-side. Each time I got up and down, and the longest of the putts my bunker play left me was 4 feet, the others being virtual tap-ins. I have said elsewhere that if there was one club that truly won me the Open, it was my sand wedge.

The final day was one of great tension, but also a strange, even eerie sort of detachment. I think I even once described myself as being in a kind of mental vacuum. Actually, it had started the night before, after the third round, which was played on a Friday then. That night we had a nice relaxing dinner at the house Viv and I were sharing with the Yanceys, but even in spite of this I knew I was going to have a hard time sleeping. I was being honest with myself, and knew I'd need some help in that regard, and so Viv gave me a sleeping tablet. I wasn't worried about being groggy or sleeping in, or anything like that, since, as the leader, I'd be teeing off last, well into the afternoon, at 2 p.m. in fact. I took the pill, and we sat down to watch a movie on television. Before I knew it (and I had to be told later, of course) I was snoring away, long before the end of the film. Viv had already gone off to bed, and Bert, ever the gentle soul, picked me up in his arms and carried me upstairs, where he laid me down beside Viv. I'm sure I felt like a sack of hammers to him, but I don't remember a bit of it. For all I know, he read me a bedtime story and tucked me in. He was a lovely man, Bert, when he was healthy, but his mind left him as the years went on. It devastated me to see him deteriorate so badly in later years.

The next morning, Saturday, I woke at 9 a.m. feeling refreshed, and then remembered what was going on. Part of me screamed inside – *The Open, shit, this is for real, this isn't make-believe!!* I knew there was no way out. There wasn't going to be any rain delay; it was a decent Lancashire day. After a breakfast of steak and eggs – and a quick peek at the paper just to confirm that a fellow named Tony Jacklin was indeed holding a two-stroke lead in the Open heading into the final round that day – I spent some time hanging around with my dad, who'd come by from where he and my mum were staying. It was sweet, and even a bit comical, too, in hindsight. He was just there to help me kill time. We pottered about the house. He picked at a piece of toast, had a cup of coffee, talked about not much in particular. I'm sure he just wanted to help me take my mind off things.

Time seemed to be dragging severely by that point. Everybody knew what was at stake, but we certainly weren't going to start talking about it. In fact, as we hung around the house talking about nothing of much importance, I was all the while talking rather urgently with myself. I was reminding myself, mantra-like, that over the course of the next six hours or so I was not for one minute, *for one second*, going to allow my mind to stray toward the meaning of it all. I repeated it over and over on the inside, that I had to keep my focus, that I couldn't let my mind wander, that it was now all about concentration, that it was, as the sports psychologists say nowadays, about process not outcome. I have always had quite an imagination, and don't feel too badly if my mind pictures the way something might turn out – and I don't mean just with golf; I love thinking about life, golf, business, people, and imagining what this means or that means or what might happen if so and so does such and such. But this was not the time for that. I bore down. This is one area separating the talented underachiever from the champion golfer – the ability to shut out the distractions, the noise, the outer and the inner voices, and focus the mind on the moment.

By the time I got to the golf course, most of the early groups were well into their rounds. I wished it had been me, frankly; not in their position in the tournament, of course, but just already out playing, because I have always disliked the late afternoon start for the leaders. I suppose it was done because we were entering the television era, I don't know. But hanging about all morning and half the afternoon waiting to tee off was never my idea of a good time. Someone like Jack Nicklaus always seemed to be able to sleep in a bit longer, occupy himself, and generally not get too bothered by when he started, early or late. I envied him that gift, but we are who we are, and I was certainly learning to deal with every emotion I was feeling. It was part of getting to the big stage, of being counted amongst the greats, which had been my goal all along. You either learned how to cope or you failed, simple as that; like Shanko, who'd come close a few times to the Open, near enough to touch the Claret Jug, but had, as he put it, crapped himself when the pressure built.

Not that I was thinking of Shanko, I can tell you. Once we got to the club, I changed slowly into my clothes for the round, and went out to the practice ground to warm up. This was where I began to truly focus. All week I'd been starting my practice sessions with a few easy 8- and 9-irons, then switching over to do the majority of my warming up with a 7-iron. I didn't even hit every club in my bag during that day's warm-up. It all felt good, and maybe this contributed to the strange sense of focus and calm I felt. It was almost as if I wasn't even there. It felt like a state of limbo, of being present and not present at the same time, of having a certain detachment while simultaneously experiencing a full focus on my task. You could almost see this eerie calmness in me when I was interviewed by the BBC before the start of the round. I was asked how I was going to approach it, and I think I was even speaking slower than normal, though the reply was sensible enough. 'I've just got to keep my head,' I answered. 'I'm going to play the course, and do my best, and if someone comes out and plays better, so be it. But I'll do my best and we'll see what happens.' The interviewer then wanted to know if I'd taken that little sleeping pill that I said I might in an interview the day before. I smiled when I answered. 'Yes,' I said. 'I took it about eleven-thirty and didn't know much about anything until nine-fifteen this morning.'

'Feeling a bit sleepy, then?' he asked.

'No,' I said in a slow voice, smiling. 'I'm feeling a bit jumpy at the moment.' I may have been feeling jumpy, but I looked as if I were about to nip down to the grocer's for a pint of milk and some biscuits instead of embarking on a four-hour journey towards that thing I'd been chasing with every bloody ounce of my being for half my life.

And so we set off. I was on 208, five under par, holding a two-shot lead over Bob Charles, with whom I was paired, and Christy O'Connor. One stroke behind them were Peter Thomson and Roberto de Vicenzo. Nicklaus was lurking five back. It was a nice breezy day, but certainly not windy in the way it can be at the Open. In any event, with Bob Charles, Peter Thomson, Christy O'Connor and Roberto de Vicenzo as my closest pursuers, it was clear I was being chased by a group of players who could handle any conditions.

I got the start I wanted. A couple of pars, then a 4-iron second shot to the third green that left me a 16-foot putt that I holed for a birdie. Charles had dropped a shot at the first and parred the next two. My lead was four. At that point, I remember noticing that my caddie, Willie Hilton, had hardly uttered a word in the first few holes. My suspicion was that he'd administered his own sleeping aid the night before in the form of whisky and a few pints of lager, and that he was feeling a bit haggard. Still, I needed him right there with me. This was the Open, for Christ's sake, and I didn't want him lurching around all day like a sick dog. I nailed a driver up the fourth fairway, but even this didn't provoke a response from him. Walking up the fairway, I said, 'For God's sake, Willie, say something. It doesn't even have to be about golf or what's happening. Just say something.' My mini-outburst seemed to wake him up, and he managed to chat about this and that for the rest of the day.

Things went steadily on through the front nine, though I remember Bob playing one of the finest wedge shots I've ever seen on the 553-yard par-five 7th. He was facing a third shot from the long grass left of the green to a pin just over the lip of a greenside bunker. There couldn't have been more than four paces between pin and bunker, but he lofted a sand wedge up into the air and watched as it landed literally on the lip of the bunker, from where it trundled down and stopped beside the hole. It was the kind of shot you could stand there all day trying to hit – with ten buckets of balls, no pressure and no one watching – and never pull off, yet he'd managed it with one chance during the final round of the Open. It was one of the most astonishing shots I'd ever seen, but I also told myself that it was up to me to respond, to not let it rattle me. I managed this, matching his birdie to keep my lead intact.

By the time we got to the 10th tee, I had four shots to play with to bring home the Open. I knew what my lead was, and I understood the enormity of the situation, but there was so much danger still out there, and the closing nine of Lytham is a stretch of golf that will expose physical or mental weakness, and has done to many. Maybe Bernard Darwin meant the front nine was 'just' and the back nine a 'beast'. Who knows. But I knew I'd need my resolve and concentration over the final nine holes. This knowledge was fully brought home when Bob knocked his approach to 8 feet on the 10th green and made the putt. My lead was three.

It was also around the 10th hole that I began to notice the crowds. They were swelling as the early groups finished, and as it began to grow evident that it was boiling down to match play between Bob and myself. Christy O'Connor was not having a sterling day, and neither were Thomson or de Vicenzo. The only player who posted a great score that whole day, in fact, was Peter Alliss, who blitzed the course with a 66 to finish at a two-over 286. Jack wasn't doing much, either, and so it was down to two.

Prior to the third round Bob had told the media that it was always going to be the final six holes of the last day that would be decisive. And with six holes to play, I had some time to think about his prediction, though I hardly wanted the break. Bob went to use his driver on the 13th tee, but the whipping had come loose (back in the days, of course, when a driver's persimmon head was bound to the club with glue and nylon whipping a couple of inches up the shaft). It was the kind of thing that happened every now and then on the course, but one hardly expected it to happen in the middle of the final round of the Open Championship! Bob spent a moment or two trying to do the repairs himself, but couldn't seem to make it work. At that point, he was about to send his caddy scampering back to the pro shop to see if they could fix it up and get it back out to him. This clearly would have taken a while, and really without even thinking of it I told Bob to let me have the thing and I'd fix it on the spot. I'd spent so many days and weeks doing just this very thing in Shanko's back shop that I could do it with my eyes closed. I threaded the whipping through, tied it tight, asked someone in the crowd for a pocket knife, and cut off the bit left hanging. Quick as that I had it repaired and we were able to keep the round going without too much of a delay. The last thing I wanted to go through at that moment was a stoppage in play that could disrupt what you might call the mental and emotional equilibrium I had found. I don't know if it would have been within the rules for him to have sent the club off to have it fixed in mid-round. I'm not sure it was even legal for *me* to fix it. Anyway, I do recall thinking Bob might take note of, and be affected by, the calm and cool of my ability to just say, *Give me that thing, I'll fix it for you and then we'll get to it, shall we?* Perhaps I ought to have asked him for a couple of pounds on the spot for the repair.

I can't say if it affected Bob or not, but the golfing gods clearly didn't think much of my act of camaraderie, since I proceeded to bogey the damn hole. Some thanks. My lead was down to two, though it went back to three after Bob bogeyed the next. I managed to three-putt the 17th hole, missing from 6 feet, and so the two of us stood on the final tee, with a massive swarm of people milling around the hole at every compass point. I had a two-shot lead and my fate in my hands. It was a brilliant, intense moment on the stage I'd always sought, and it's no exaggeration to say that as exciting and as nerve-racking as it was, I also felt utterly in my element, that this moment and this place and this situation was where I *belonged*. It was where I had become my best self. There was no fear, only concentration.

Bob played first, since I'd just bogeyed 17. He pulled his drive which, as a lefthander, meant he was heading for the right-hand fairway trap. He blurted out that it had gone in the bunker, but I thought it hadn't. Willie confirmed it had gone over the trap and was probably in a spot where he could have a good swing at the green. Bob was always a good fellow to play with, and I don't know if he was employing a little gamesmanship or not by implying his ball had gone in, but it didn't matter. It was about what I did from here on in.

This was where I had always wanted to find myself – in a position to decide my own fate, to perform, to win the biggest trophy of them all. But, you see, it was also about much more than that; this was the position I'd always wanted to be in so that I could test *who I was*. It wasn't just about making a good swing, or performing technically, or even anything necessarily to do with the final result, though all these were the immediate goal, the direct thought processes. But deep down I had always wanted to be here, precisely in this spot, because I *wanted* to feel the pressure and see if I would respond. I wanted to test the person inside, that passionate and intense young man, to see if he could stand up to the ultimate test, to see if he had the steel. I had to ask the question and I wasn't afraid of the answer.

I pulled my driver from the bag. I suppose I could have played it safe and used a three-wood or a 1-iron. The 18th at Lytham had been the graveyard of more than one player. I knew that both Eric Brown and Christy O'Connor had lost Opens by taking sixes on that last hole. It's such a demanding tee shot, principally because there really isn't a safe play. There are bunkers left and right, as well as big whin bushes and rough down the right. Still, it would have been safe enough to hit a smaller club, and there would have been nothing wrong in it, but to me that might have told my subconscious doubt was present in my mind.

Doubt, you see, was *not* present in my mind. I had been

hitting my driver beautifully all day and I simply knew, I *knew*, I would make a good swing. How? I don't know, I just did. *You've done this a thousand times*, I told myself. *Just keep it wide and smooth, wide and smooth.* In fact, I was a bit wrong about knowing it would be a good swing – it was a *great* swing. The tempo and speed were perfect. My swing had held up. But even more than that, it had held up in exactly the manner I wished it to, the way I had meant it to. My tempo was exquisite the whole week, with that slowness of rhythm I'd been seeking. It felt like I owned it, like it was mine and mine alone, and even if I hadn't won it was still a sensational feeling right the whole way through. But when the pressure was at its greatest, standing on the last tee with Bob already down the fairway, I made a perfect swing. I was in balance. The ball went dead solid off the middle of the face. I kept my tempo and then watched as the ball sailed for miles straight down the centre of the fairway. It was one of those moments when the planets align in every single way. Under pressure there is no substitute for that practice and time you put in learning your own swing. That last tee shot was one of the best of my life because I knew in my heart and bones my fundamentals were pure, and my mind was free enough to let those mechanics soar through.

Of course, I couldn't hear it at the time, but watching the BBC telecast of the tournament some time later, I think Henry Longhurst echoed my own thoughts when, after I'd hit my tee shot, he told the television viewers, 'What a corker! My word, that was a fine drive. Look at it! Miles up the middle. One of the finest I've seen in my life. Oh, what a tremendous drive!'

The ultimate twist was that when I found my ball in the middle of the fairway and calculated my yardage it was precisely 145 yards; a nice comfortable 7-iron! Exactly the shot I'd hit hundreds of thousands of times working on my tempo. It was the one shot I would have picked if you'd given me the choice.

That perfect little control shot I'd done all my swing work with – same club, same yardage. I couldn't believe it. It was the sort of distance I could have easily covered with an 8-iron, but I had been hitting easy tempo half 7-irons all week during my warm-ups and the shot was as comfortable as slipping on an old sweater. I knew a control shot was the right shot. Bob had laid his second shot tight, perhaps 15 feet to the right of the hole, as I knew he would. I was already assuming he was going to make it, given his way with the putter. So I stood over that ball, holding my trusted 7-iron, and proceeded to produce the shot exactly, and I mean *exactly*, as I had pictured it in my mind's eye. Good speed, pure contact, the correct flight and trajectory. It felt perfect, but I only had a half-second to see that it had landed a few paces to the right of the hole before the crowd exploded through the ropes like a reservoir through a burst dam, engulfing Bob and me. In the mad crush, someone stepped on my heel and my shoe came off. Luckily I found it, but I had to carry it as two burly police officers helped Willie and me to negotiate our way through the horde. It was mad but, hell, it was fun. Once out of the crowd, I slipped my shoe on. I neglected to tie it until just before we got to the green, when it occurred to me that if I was going to be Open champion it would hardly do to stand there with my shoelace untied.

It's funny how the mind works. Even as I was thinking that I'd better tie my shoe up if I was going to be handed the Claret Jug, I was also suddenly caught up with the strangest of thoughts, that something totally unheard-of might still happen. What if I stood over my putt and lost control of my putter, given the way my hands were shaking, and it fell and knocked my ball for a penalty stroke? What if I bobbled and touched the ball as I addressed it? It was crazy, but if we could predict the workings of the human mind, life would be boring, wouldn't it? That whole time – from the moment I struck my 7-iron until Bob stroked his putt for birdie – I was not quite able to enjoy the moment, because to my mind there was nothing to enjoy yet. I was still going about my business. It would not have been impossible for me to three-putt from where I was – a surge of adrenalin, a failure of nerve – and as mentioned I certainly expected Bob to make his. I knew, of course, that I was on the verge, but I never did allow myself to think, *Okay, you've got it won, you can relax.*

In any case, Bob's putt stayed out, to my surprise. Only then did I allow myself the luxury of enjoying the moment, since I knew I could take three from there and still win. I made a nice putt at a birdie, wanting to finish with a flourish, and thought I'd made it, but it stayed just fractionally right. I had a tap-in to finish it off. I didn't have the same kind of casual panache that Peter Thomson had in 1954 when he won the Open at Birkdale by just strolling up and backhanding the ball into the hole from 8 inches or so to win by one stroke! I used the correct side of the club, and when the ball went in I picked it out of the hole, dropped my putter, hurled the ball into the crowd and then started to realize what I'd just accomplished.

I was Open champion.

When that final putt dropped it was hard to say exactly what I felt. I've been asked over and over again what that moment felt like, what was going through my head and my heart when that last short putt went in and I knew at last that I was the Open champion. I could almost cry right now, thinking back to the moment. So much work, so much of my soul, such a huge part of *me* was in that moment. It was so moving it was almost emotionally paralysing for a moment or two. *Oh my God*, I thought. *Oh. My. God.*

I had won something every professional golfer longs to win, particularly British and European golfers, of course: Americans tend to focus on either the US Open or the Masters. But I think that was one of the strongest sensations of all – that so many golfers had wanted to be standing in this exact place at this exact moment, as had I all my life, and now it was me, Tony, that kid at the end of the range down at Scunthorpe. It was.

A Briton had finally won the Open again, after eighteen years. Viv ran across the final green and gave me a big hug and a kiss and said, simply, 'Well done, darling.' There wasn't much to say, really, that's how astounding it was. I had enjoyed the whole week, but I was also so glad it was over, the pressure of the thing. One of the very first people I spoke to afterwards – I can't even remember if it was before or after I'd signed my card – was Jack Nicklaus, who, as always, was gracious enough to be there to congratulate the winner if it wasn't to be him. I blurted out to him, 'God almighty, Jack, I never knew anybody could be so scared, so frightened.' He put his arm around me in a warm and genuine way, and said, 'Don't worry, Tony. It happens to everyone in the big ones. They say it even happened to Hogan.' (It was great of Jack to say that, and it was in keeping with the kind of sportsmanship he would show later that year in the Ryder Cup.) 'It's fun, isn't it?' he concluded. No, it bloody well wasn't! Gratifying to the extreme, and surely the greatest experience of my playing life, but fun? This was typical of Jack. Pressure was fun to him, which certainly was not the case for most players on tour. It put me in mind of what Arnold Palmer told me after my dear pal Bert Yancey had lost the 1968 US Open to Lee Trevino. 'I didn't think Yancey would win,' said Arnold. 'He was talking too much.' I asked him what he meant. 'He's trying to get rid of the pressure,' Arnold replied. 'But you can't talk. You've got to take it inside your gut.' Arnold was right. That's why there are so few people who win at the highest level – because they can't come to terms with the pressure.

My mum and dad were there, too, as were dozens of friends from Lincolnshire and Potters Bar, but I was almost too damn tired to celebrate with them straight away. Winning a Major takes every single fibre of energy and will you've got within you – it's such hard work. But it was extraordinary to be at the centre of it, and though there was a crush of people and emotions and laughter and tears, I suppose the one thing I felt deep in my core, in the quiet middle of me, was that I had done something that nothing could ever change, that no one could ever take away, and which I would always have as long as I lived. It was mine to keep for ever, and the truth is that I was probably alone in some way at that moment. This goes back to that solitary element of the golfer's life that I alluded to earlier. I know that even as I stood there in front of those tens of thousands of people on that final green, after four days and 280 shots, I was aware that I was in some way alone, isolated, unique and different from every other person there that day. It was a powerful feeling, yet also one of 'Oh shit, what now?'

That week was also a great lesson in, among other things, the kind of play it often takes to win Majors. The truth is that I really didn't do anything spectacular the whole tournament. It was just steady play from start to finish. I was a little bit fortunate, too. Nobody took a big run at me. No one came from behind in a great rush with a birdie run on the last day. There were no 64s or 65s from the challengers.

In some ways, I was both overwhelmed and quite calm as I stepped to the microphone to make my acceptance speech. I was surrounded by goodwill. On the way to the prize-giving, dear Roberto de Vicenzo had been walking beside me, as the previous champion, and he gave my hair a friendly ruffle – perhaps he was merely trying to imagine what his head felt like before he'd gone bald. When the crowd went quiet, and I raised the microphone up, I thanked the Open committee, Lord Derby and the rest, and then offered my congratulations to Bob Charles. He'd been a great playing partner. 'I tried to forget that magic wand of his,' I told the crowd. 'Even if it didn't work as well today as it normally does.' There was a spontaneous and wonderful moment then, when the crowd broke into a giant roaring rendition of 'For He's a Jolly Good Fellow'. Still holding my medal I did a bit of impromptu conducting. There was real joy in the air. I didn't notice at the time, since he was seated behind me, but later on when I watched some of the footage I noticed that a grinning Peter Thomson actually pulled his camera out of his pocket and tried to take a picture of that moment, with me conducting and the crowd singing away! Can you imagine? That tells you so much about Peter right there, that as great a champion as he was, and as much as he surely would have wished to be giving that victory speech himself, he still had it in him to share in the joy of a fellow competitor. Quite the gesture, one that has gone virtually unnoticed.

I spoke to the crowd about my playing in America. It seemed to me that it had been crucial to my success and I told them so. 'Last year,' I said, 'I played in America for five or six months, and I'll do the same this year. I'll be going over right after this for another five or six weeks of play. And I want to say that I believe the main reason I am standing here today is because of that decision to play in America. I think more young players from Britain ought to do so, to get those competitive situations. It's helped me immensely.'

I can't say the response to that statement was rapturous applause, but it was simply the truth. Anyone with a strong competitive streak in them understands what I'm talking about. I don't think I won any friends saying it, but of course it was in no way meant as an insult to Britain or British players or the British Tour. It was just fact. To be a great player, you need to play under the best of conditions against the best players. America had the best players – fact. As for the conditions, well, tournaments in Britain were played largely on links courses in spotty, windy weather. As pure and as fun as links golf undeniably is, it nevertheless is not the best form of golf for one's development as a top-flight professional. There are so many bad breaks, strange lies and high winds that you constantly need to alter your swing to produce a variety of shots. This is fine if you've already got sound mechanics, but it's not so good if you're in a developmental stage. Not to mention that good young players need to get rewarded for good swings. America's more uniform conditions made it easier to become a better shot-maker with a more consistent swing. That's just the truth. I'm sorry if some people felt criticized by it, because I never meant it to be judgmental or critical of anyone. It was simply a fact in my mind, a piece of information that wasn't about blame or accusation. It was just the way it was, as clear as the sun rising every morning, so I said it. I suppose it shocked a few people, but I wasn't trying to shock anyone.

Perhaps it was naive of me to say it so bluntly, and at the Open prize-giving ceremony no less, but it was just what I was feeling and thinking, and my aim was to encourage talented youngsters to consider doing the same. I wanted to be a role model for players, not a spokesman for the R & A, or the British Tour, or the PGA Tour, for that matter, but for other young British players. In some quarters I was branded a traitor, but if I had not gone to America and proved myself there first, I would never have had the strength, the mental fortitude, to be able to win the Open. It simply would never have happened, end of story. The final proof of the correctness of my decision lies in the history books. How many Britons won the Open between Max Faulkner in 1951 and Sandy Lyle in 1985? One. Me.

And so it was over. I had the Open to my name. Part of me still couldn't quite believe it, even as I stood there holding the Claret Jug, my medal and my first-place cheque for £4,250.

What did it mean?

Who was I now?

Yes, I was Open champion. But did that make me a different person?

As my dad had once said of players like Nicklaus and Palmer – said so that I wouldn't be intimidated by them – they had two arms, two legs and a head just like I did. And so it was true of me now. I was still only twenty-five, remember, and just newly twenty-five at that. Only five years before I'd come back from a winter tour in South Africa with £35 in prize money. Now I'd won the Open. Life had changed, and would never again be as it had been in the early days of relative anonymity.

Almost as immediate proof of this, there was a moment immediately afterwards that was deeply unsettling for Viv and me. You could even say it sickened us, and made us wonder just what kind of place we were living in. We left the course after I'd finished up with all my duties, all the pictures, all the interviews. Finally we were able to go (though the time in the Press tent was remarkable, in that when I came in the Press rose as one and gave me an ovation). We were on our way back to the house to change, rest up a bit, have a shower, and then get ready to go out and celebrate at that dinner I mentioned with our family and friends. It was a special moment, just the two of us, me holding the trophy, strolling through the car park as the light was fading. The car park had pretty much emptied out by then, and I could see my car not far away. It was an Aston Martin DB5, a recognizable car, since it was exactly the same one that Sean Connery had driven in the Bond film. I've always had a passion for cars, and this was a fantastic automobile, silver-grey in colour, beautifully finished. (For some crazy reason I traded in the Aston Martin for a Jensen Interceptor FF not long afterwards, and then promptly crashed it – the only car accident I ever had.)

We got to the Aston Martin and when I put the key in the

door to open it, I noticed there was a note stuck in the door. We'd already had hundreds of people congratulate us since I'd holed out the final putt and we naturally assumed it was yet another note of congratulations from someone who either couldn't reach me or who didn't know me, but recognized the car. I unfolded the note and the first sentence began, 'I always knew you were a shit . . .' It had more to say, all of it in a similar sort of vein. It was sickening language, and the sentiments behind the language were so sad, even disturbing. Viv and I tried to convince ourselves it wasn't us specifically this malice was directed towards, but rather what we now represented – a kind of success, a reaching of one's goals. The kind of success this sorry person had not had in his life. We found it so depressing that there was someone out there so hateful. Maybe it even had something to do with my comments about playing the American Tour. Still, it was hard to imagine someone would go to that trouble, write such a hate letter, find my car, surreptitiously stuff it in the door, and then skulk off. It left a bad taste in my mouth, to say the least, but it was I suppose a quick lesson – the short, sharp shock – in the darker side of the fame I now possessed, whether I wanted it or not. I crumpled up the note and threw it away. We drove back to the house, met up with our loved ones, and celebrated the victory that became the dividing line of my life.

We didn't over-celebrate that night; just a quiet meal with family and friends. But the next day I confess I woke up thinking about myself in a slightly but noticeably different way. To date, I'd been a very confident and often a cocky fellow, as Shanko could have attested. I was okay with that. But to that point in my life, this confidence had been based upon self-belief, upon the faith that I could do what I was setting out to do, to win the Open, to become one of the world's premier players. But it was a notion, you see. It was all about the power of the mind setting a goal and going after it with conviction and resolve, but also as an act of faith in oneself. It was belief. Very strongly held, but still a belief.

Now, as I woke the next day, it wasn't about faith, about a notion, about a dream. It was reality. This was not just playing at it. It wasn't make-believe. It was *real*. It had happened. I wanted something, set my sights on it, and now I had it. I could scarcely believe it. Yet part of me was not surprised at all. What a remarkable feeling it was, this sense of incredible events happening to me coupled to an inner belief that I was meant for this, that I had greatness in me. This was now my life.

I was exactly that thing I had set out to become.

8

The lead in to the 1969 Ryder Cup was full of all sorts of talk.
I was now the Open champion and expected to be a stalwart for
the team. Palmer had not been playing that well in America, and
there were serious doubts as to his form. There was also much
discussion about the fact that we had been so soundly thrashed
in 1967, and that this held long-term implications for the competition. What was the point, many argued, of continuing to
play these matches if the result was always going to a lop-sided
walloping? It was worth arguing about, I suppose, although I
personally was feeling quite good about the make-up of our
team.

With Palmer off form, and with me as Open champion, it
seemed that there was no little anticipation heading into the
event. Adding to this was the fact that our captain Eric Brown
(who I never particularly got on with) had made sure that the
Birkdale fairways were tight and the rough high and heavy. It
was an odd approach, I thought, for two reasons; first, I'd seen
plenty of American players drive it straight under pressure, and
second, it seemed to me the case that American courses generally
featured tighter fairways anyhow. This seemed to be the kind of
setup that would suit them. In fact, it's become something of a

trend nowadays for Ryder Cup captains to go out and fit the golf course to the make-up of their team. Fair enough, but the players still have to go out and hit the ball off the middle of the clubface. If you can't handle that pressure, fixing up the course won't make a spot of difference.

Eric Brown must have felt I could handle any amount of pressure, because he told me many times before and during the competition that he was expecting great things from me, and that I was essentially the team leader. Of course, Eric really couldn't say anything but. If I hadn't been Open champion I suspect he'd have been a little less respectful. We'd had our run-ins in the past, even going as far back as 1964, when I was playing him in the old *News of the World* Matchplay at Walton Heath. On one hole I recall being bunkered but not knowing who was to play first, him or me. I looked over to him, and he must have thought I was taking too long, because he was leaning on his club faking an exaggerated yawn, trying to get a laugh from somebody I suppose. It infuriated me and it only made me want to beat him even more, which I did, badly. I was certain he never forgot it.

Not only did Eric go on about the rough and the tight fairways, he also spelled out a variety of team rules we were to follow, but which I thought were bloody ridiculous and even unsporting. Things like not helping opponents look for balls in the rough. I did not follow that or most of his other like-minded rules, and didn't mind him knowing I thought his attitude wrong-headed. Golf is a game that relies on honour, after all, and the only satisfaction you can take in winning is through having done it fairly and sportingly. It's ironic that Eric carried on in such a way at the start of a Ryder Cup that would end up being famous for exactly the opposite reason, namely, for one of the game's greatest gestures of sportmanship.

As always, the matches opened with a variety of events, some for the Press, some for corporate sponsors, all of them involving copious amounts of alcohol. It was Maurice Bembridge who said that in order to survive a Ryder Cup week one had to be a scratch drinker. Naturally, I did my share of drinking, but that was done purely out of team solidarity . . .

In any case, the matches did open on time, despite the socializing, and we immediately showed that this was going to be a far different year from the thrashing of 1967. I was paired with Peter Townsend, and we teamed up for two victories that opening day, beating Tommy Aaron and Billy Casper in the afternoon, after a morning win over Aaron and Dave Hill (which I enjoyed, given Hill's negativity in America towards foreign-born players; it was also a victory that would create some positive memories for me to use in the 1970 US Open, when I would be paired with the ever-controversial Hill). The rest of the team played well in spots, and we held the lead after the first day. The following day I was paired with Neil Coles. We were up against Nicklaus and Sikes in the morning and won the match on the last hole. In the afternoon Neil and I struggled but still managed to halve with Trevino and Mr X, Miller Barber. After that second day, the two teams were all square. It was hardly the thumping some had feared.

The next day it was all singles matches, eight in the morning and eight again in the afternoon. I drew Nicklaus, which I was pleased about, though it hardly came as a shock, since the captains back then used to save their most on-form players for the anchor spot, as a matter of course rather than through any written rule. I always wanted to play against the best, and even though I was the Open champion, I regarded Jack as *the* man to beat under any circumstances. My excitement must have energized my game, because in the morning match I played like a dream, winning 4&3. We had some lunch and then it was back at it again, head to head.

We were the last match out. It was close the whole way through, with neither of us ever holding a lead of any real size. Jack was playing well and making a mile's worth of putts. When we got to the 17th hole, I was one down. I knew that the rest of the matches were either over or close, and that the overall result was likely going to depend on what happened between Jack and myself. He was in fairly tight with his third shot at the par-five, looking at a birdie, and I had a monster 50-footer for eagle. I can't explain how I managed it, but I ran that cross-country putt dead in the hole to square our match. I still think it may have been the most important putt of my life, and it was certainly one of the best, being down to Nicklaus with two holes to play and the Ryder Cup in the balance. When that putt dropped a massive cheer went cascading through those huge Birkdale dunes, and Brian Huggett heard it all the way over on the 18th green. He was in the last of his match with Billy Casper, and when he heard that cheer he thought I'd won my match, which meant he then needed his own 4-footer to beat Casper and for us to win the Cup outright. Of course, that *wasn't* what it meant, but he wouldn't have known that. Somehow he managed to hole his putt, and he broke down, practically weeping on the spot. He must have been gutted a few minutes later when he learned the truth, though what inner pride he must, and should, always have had for making that putt under the circumstances.

But I didn't know any of what had happened with Huggett. Jack and I made our way down the 18th fairway after both having hit good drives. As we walked close to one another, he caught my eye and said, 'Are you nervous?' I told him I bloody well was. Typical of the sportsman he was, he smiled and said, 'If it's any consolation, I feel the same, too.'

I had a 30-footer for birdie and left it about 2 feet short, no gimme by any means, but neither was it a putt I felt anxious about. I was confident I'd make it, but wondered if I'd even have the chance. Jack had a 15-footer for birdie. We knew where all the other matches stood by then, and we knew where things stood with the Cup. If Jack made his putt to win our match, the Americans won the Cup outright by a single point. If he missed and I made, we halved our match but the Americans would still be declared victors in light of the rule stipulating that the Cup holder retains the trophy in the event of a tie.

Jack missed his putt and, shockingly, ran it 5 feet past. Being Jack Nicklaus, however, he firmly made that putt coming back, and my first thought was, 'Right, now it's up to me.' I wanted the half in our match very badly.

But before I could even approach my coin to replace my ball and attempt my putt, Jack simply bent over and picked it up, then handed it to me! He was giving me my putt. A concession. I was stupefied. I didn't expect it. He dropped my coin into my palm, and said, 'I don't think you would have missed that one, but in these circumstances I wasn't going to give you the opportunity to miss.'

It was a stunning, majestic turn of events.

But here's the part I find really incredible. Not just that Jack managed to calmly hole his own 5-footer (when missing it would mean I'd have a putt to win the Ryder Cup). Not even that he then picked up my coin and handed it to me, though it was pretty astonishing. But that he must have been trying desperately to make both his first and second putt – because he was a competitor through and through, after all – while also *simultaneously* processing his incredible gesture in case he missed his first and then in case he made his second. Surely he had decided even before his first putt that he was going to give me my 2-footer. In other words, he was trying to beat me as hard as he could at the exact same moment he was wanting to share the moment. Now *that* is sportsmanship.

It was a half for our match, and a tie for the Ryder Cup. It was a tremendously exciting moment for me and for our team. We'd managed a draw with the mighty Americans. Though a spirit of sportsmanship and goodwill seemed pervasive at that moment, it was not the case in every quarter. Sam Snead, the American captain, was less than thrilled with Jack's gesture. He wanted to win outright. (Though in one of those great life ironies, it was me who got to chaperone Sam around St Andrews thirty-one years later, when we all returned there for a Past Champions dinner in 2000. I met him at Dulles Airport in Washington and we travelled over. We had a good time together and there were no hard feelings at all. Talk about coming full circle.)

I've remarked on it to many people before, but I do wonder if I'd have had the spirit to be as generous and sportsmanlike as Jack was in that moment. I believe I would have. Mind you, it would have been a much different frame of mind, given that we had won the Cup so seldom in the past decades. But all things being equal I feel quite certain I'd have done the same for Jack. I respected him prior to that moment, but his stature was elevated even further after that. It had been a summer when I'd learned a lot about Jack Nicklaus: from his being there to congratulate me at Lytham practically the moment I came off the final green; to walking up the last fairway at Birkdale and having him admit that he was as nervous as I was; down to his concession on the final green. A great champion. Later on I sent Jack a note telling him again how much I was impressed by his gesture, how much it meant to me personally, and how much it would mean to the game of golf. It's the only time in my life I wrote a personal note to another player about something that happened on the course. I think his gesture must have sent waves of positive feeling through everyone, since Lord Derby and the US PGA President Leo Fraser decided afterwards that even though the US had technically 'won' by drawing the match, it would only be fair that each side keep the trophy for one year. The matches ended with Leo Fraser handing Samuel Ryder's hardware to Lord Derby with the promise it be returned one year hence.

The Ryder Cup, in which I'd gone undefeated in six matches, was a significant way to end my breakout year – my first Major, a fantastic swing improvement, a satisfying personal and team performance at the Cup along with being part of what I knew even then was going to become one of the game's most celebrated acts of sportsmanship. Not a bad year for a lad from Scunthorpe who was still only twenty-five, after all. I had been building and building, year after year, and I can honestly say that I rarely wavered in my belief that I was tracking towards this achievement. But I'd done it, and what I realized fairly soon was that I didn't have much of an inkling of what to do next! How can you blame me? I always thought – or at least felt I had it in me – that I'd win an Open, but it came early on. Looking back, I can say that although I was ready as a player to attain these heights – just look at the progression of my results, the state of my game – it would be fair to say I may not have been ready to handle what came afterwards. Or at least that the intensity took me unawares. Don't get me wrong; I wanted it, and Viv and I were having a fantastic time with it all. But it still came as something of a shock.

The treadmill started. Mark McCormack, my IMG man, said I had the potential to become a millionaire based purely on my Open victory. After the Open what probably would have suited me best would have been a break just to absorb what I'd done, to enjoy it, let the batteries recharge, since the effort of winning a Major (the physical effort, sure, but mostly the enormous emotional effort) had drained me absolutely. To play would have been just trying to manufacture it. And you can't manufacture the truth. The real juice, the real me, wasn't there right after the Open.

'But you've got to go to Westchester,' said Mark.

'My God,' I said. 'I've got no beans left in the tin. My try's all gone.'

He said, 'Look, this is a 250,000-dollar tournament, the biggest tournament of the year. Fifty thousand dollars first prize.'

I didn't want to go, but I went. What happened? I missed four cuts in a row. It was the worst month in my life, having just won the Open but unable to enjoy it. This was just the first tiny step in what became something of a theme between Mark and myself, over the next decade anyway. He might have given me advice based more on my long-term career rather than the short-term exploitation of my new fame. I'm not blaming him. I'm just telling you the way things were. I was a young and still very ambitious person, particularly in terms of wanting to guarantee security for my family and myself. Viv was pregnant with our first, and it was absolutely my thinking at the time that I had to take advantage of what was on offer. Who knew how long it would last, after all? I still wasn't that far removed from Scunthorpe, in my mind, and let's face it, it had only been seven years earlier that I'd bought my first set of new clubs!

So when Mark, the manager of Arnold Palmer and Jack Nicklaus, said things like, 'Tony, I think you ought to go to Nigeria to do this exhibition match, and then stop in Paris on your way back to play in the tournament there, and then you can catch the red-eye to make it back in time for that week's PGA stop,' well, you tend to go ahead and do it. Or at least I did. But I shouldn't have. This is something I came to feel even more strongly as the 1970s played out. It was a disastrous thing to do, chasing every dollar, though I could hardly have understood the full effect of it at the time. My relationship with Mark and IMG in general soured as time went on, but I believed at that moment in time that Mark and all agents in general were actually there to better my and their clients' lives, not simply their own. I know . . . naive, wasn't it?

9

As the new decade broke upon us it seemed to me that I was blessed with a piece of every single thing great about living on this planet. What a life it was then! I was Open champion. I had a delightful, attractive, intelligent, supportive wife. We had just had our first child, a boy, Bradley, and we wanted more children. I was informed that I was to be made an Officer of the Order of the British Empire (OBE) and would be meeting Queen Elizabeth to receive the honour.

Because I had the opportunity to play some big tournaments, and win them, I was able to meet and get to know many people outside the game of golf. Many of them were people I enjoyed immensely, people I often respected for their achievement, but more often who I respected for their incredible ability to stay just people, good folk, no matter what. But whether it was Bob Hope, or Bing Crosby, or Frank Sinatra, I was also always left impressed by that awesome combination of talent and fierce determination. You don't make it to the top in any field through luck. It's not done with mirrors, you know. There aren't any magic tablets. It's having talent, yes, but then it's also about bloody hard work. They weren't playing at it, these people. They wanted to be the best, and when they made it big it was never by accident.

Don Rickles, Glen Campbell, Vic Damone, Steve Forrest, Burt Lancaster, George C. Scott. The list is long, and it was terrific fun for Viv and me to meet these people. We'd go to some party in Palm Springs, and end up hobnobbing with Bob Hope and Dean Martin. Incredible! Many of the Hollywood figures were introduced to me by Jim Mahoney, the wonderful fellow who was Frank Sinatra's Press agent for many years. He was a fantastic fellow, Jim, and Viv and I used to stay with him whenever we were in LA. I counted him as a friend.

I played golf with the King of Morocco, the King of Greece, the President of Kenya, not to mention President Ford, of course. Some of the British greats I got to know and like, people such as Harry Secombe, Jimmy Tarbuck, Nigel Mansell. Jimmy and I became good pals. Sean Connery also ended up becoming a lifelong friend, someone I drew much inspiration from, and who ended up being very close by my side when I most needed a friend many years later.

But it was always astonishing to me, this odyssey I'd been on. You couldn't have made it into a movie; they'd have said it was too far-fetched! In 1961 I left home to go to Potters Bar with one suitcase, five pounds in my pocket and a hand-me-down suit. I lived in a semi-detached with no heating and a few years later Frank Sinatra was asking me if I wanted to fly back from Europe with him on his private jet. There were times Viv and I would sit wide-eyed at some celebrity party, trying to figure just how life had brought us to this place.

But what cemented everything together at that time, what made everything else possible, was that I was playing wonderful golf. It's hard to fully convey the sense of confidence one can feel during times like this. Don't misunderstand; I didn't think I was going to win every tournament, or that the Majors were mine for the taking. It's a fool that takes such an approach to a game as famously fickle as golf. The game will hand you your head on a platter the minute you think you've got it beat. It doesn't work like that.

But within that context, still keeping the right dose of humility about yourself, I was playing well enough to feel confident whenever I teed it up (at least, in striking the ball well enough; my putting was suspect early that spring of 1970). I played well at Augusta in April, finishing twelfth, nine adrift of Billy Casper, on a course that never really did suit me (yet another thing, of course, that Peter Thomson was right about). But I was steady and my game was under control. My finishes weren't particularly strong at lead-in tournaments such as Atlanta, Memphis, Kemper and the Western Open, but I wasn't overly concerned. I only needed to rediscover a semblance of the putting stroke I seemed to have misplaced somewhere. I was particularly weak heading into the US Open on holing those key 10-footers, the ones you need to make to cash in on fine iron play.

That year's US Open was being played at the relatively new Hazeltine club in Chaska, Minnesota, in the great, wide open Midwest, *wide open* being the operative phrase. As a fairly new course (Hazeltine had only opened in 1962) the trees and even the landscaping were not that mature, which, combined with its exposed lakeside site and the June date, made for strong winds. It was rather funny at the time to read and hear from American commentators and many of the players (particularly those who'd rarely played in the UK), that the scores could be sky-rocketing. At 7,151 yards, Hazeltine was the second-longest US Open course ever, and Larry Ziegler, who at the time was a long-hitting young player, even went so far after the first round as to predict for the Press that a total score of 300 might win the whole thing.

It wasn't just the wind that was ruffling a few feathers. By the time we arrived for our first practice round the players, or at least some of them, were already in full gripe mode. To say

Hazeltine was proving unpopular with the players is like saying the *Titanic* shipped a bit of water. I personally didn't see the problem. Why was everybody complaining? We were all playing the same course. Dave Hill, who would eventually finish second and who was never a man to send in diplomats when battalions of troops were available, came right out and said it was a terrible golf course, that it should be ploughed up. 'All it needs,' he added, 'is eighty acres of corn and some cows.' For this, a funny but perhaps unwise remark, Dave earned the scorn of the local crowd. I played the third round with him, and up and down the fairways he went with the sound of the crowd mooing after him. You might have thought this would be something of a distraction, even in a humorous sense, that laughing it up might have put me off my focus. But it was never going to happen. I'd been around the world by then. I'd played under virtually every set of conditions you could imagine, from the Australian outback to the heat and humidity of Bangkok, from the cold and wet of Lancashire to the veldt of South Africa. Although still only twenty-five, I'd been through all kinds of playing situations. A bunch of spectators mooing at my playing partner was hardly going to affect me (though part of me did find it pretty amusing). In short, as a professional, and particularly one as intensely focused on winning as me, you either learn to empty your mind of everything but the shot at hand or you don't succeed. In fact, I don't think it even really bothered Dave all that much. He was a curmudgeonly sort of fellow, okay to play with, and throughout the round we chatted about this or that shot; never once did he seem overly affected by the crowd treating him like Bessie the cow.

I felt good about playing Hazeltine, though it wouldn't be accurate to say I fell in love with it. More than anything it was the conditions that suited me. Good strong breezes on a difficult golf course with lots of blind shots. Not that different from links golf when you think about it, although of course it was not linksy at all in terms of its soil and grasses. It was all those blind shots Jack Nicklaus seemed to take exception to; this was one of his primary criticisms of Hazeltine, that he could never see where he was hitting the ball. He opened with an 81. Gary Player shot 80, Arnie a 79. It was carnage everywhere.

Except in the Jacklin camp. I'd come into the week, as mentioned, striking the ball well enough, though rather adrift with my putting. But on the second practice day I was standing on the putting green when Jim Yancey, Bert's brother, came over to say hi. We got talking about the state of my putting. After watching me stroke a few he hit upon a suggestion. Why not line up the putt, he said, set the blade behind the ball, look at the hole and then strike the putt with my eyes still fixed on the hole. His notion was that the actual mechanical stroke I possessed was so ingrained into both my muscle memory and my routine that it would be completely straightforward to make that stroke without having to actually look at the ball. He insisted there was no inherent advantage in keeping your eyes on the ball. I'd never heard such an idea in my life, but there was no reason not to try it.

It was a gold strike! Putts began dropping into the hole from everywhere. Good vibes started oozing out of me. I went out and played an extra nine holes that afternoon, and they kept going in. I did make one slight variation, however, to what Jim had suggested. I followed his method – line up the putt, set the blade, home my gaze in on the hole – but just before drawing back the putter blade I would return my eyes to the ball. GO. Stroke. Ball in hole.

It was miraculous. I had a fully 'felt' picture of where the ball was going to finish – in the hole – with every single putt I lined up. And I made a lot of them that week. I really ought to have given Jim a share of my winner's cheque, because I still think that one chance meeting with him on the putting green carried me to the win, a win all the more remarkable in that it was only the second US Open I'd played in, having been placed twenty-sixth the year before.

It's funny, too, how things just seem to go your way sometimes. There were other things going on that week that normally might have worked against a high finish. At times it wasn't easy to find sleep, since our joy and delight, Bradley, who was seven months old by then, had started to cut his first tooth. What an almighty racket he made! He was a rather precocious young lad, and he'd also discovered what fantastic fun could be had by hoisting himself to a standing position in his cot and rattling the thing as if he were a caged animal screaming to be set free. As babies are wont to do, the middle of the night seemed to him as good a time as any to show off his new tricks and his new tooth. It was such a to-do at times that early in the week we even looked into getting another room at the motel so that I could get some quiet time at night in order to avoid stumbling around Hazeltine like an extra from a zombie movie. The motel was chock-full, though, which forced Viv to cat-nap every night so she could pop out of bed the second Bradley made a peep. She told a golf writer that she 'spent half the week in the bathroom with Bradley at nights', just so I could sleep undisturbed. It seemed to work, and was another example of all the things that go completely unnoticed by most golf fans – the ways in which you still have to find ways to make family life work, and how a significant portion of this burden falls on the spouse.

After managing to get a nice bit of sleep before the first day, thanks to Vivien, I woke up and opened the curtains of our room at the Thunderbird Motel to see that it was lashing with rain and wind. I can't honestly say whether I smiled to myself or not, but I wasn't displeased. Blustery grey skies, a steady drizzle, 40-mile an hour winds . . . it felt like home. I was fourteen again, getting ready for a game at the Scunthorpe Golf Club. Where were those old hickories anyway? The only difference was that it was 70 degrees instead of 60. When we got to the course later that morning, the rain had started to run its course, but the wind had only gathered muscle. It was gusty and strong and unpredictable, and by the time I got to the first tee with my partners Billy Casper and Steve Melnyk – the reigning US Amateur champion – I almost had myself convinced that with this weather and my new putting stroke things were lining up for me and me alone.

Not that I recorded it mentally as an omen of things to come, but I birdied the first hole of the competition, much as I had at Lytham eleven months earlier. Given the fact that scores were already ballooning up all over the place, it meant I was essentially already in the lead, which was just right by me. It really was like the start at Lytham, when I'd gone out on fire. Four birdies in the first six holes here at Hazeltine were a blitzkrieg. I didn't lap the field, at least not that day. A par at the last gave me a 71, one under par. The next-best score in the entire field was the 73 recorded by Bob Charles (a fact that sparked some imaginings about coming down the stretch again with the putting master). Hazeltine hit the field hard that first day. As I mentioned, the Big Three – Arnie, Jack and Gary – recorded 240 blows between them. Half the field was 80 or over, and walking about the golf course, the range, the putting green, the locker room, it was just one tale of woe after another. The pros had been embarrassed, and even to this day (Carnoustie in 1999, Bethpage in 2002, Shinnecock in 2004) you can be sure that if the scores are uniformly high there will be complaints about the setup and the layout (not always unjustified, it has to be said). It's a kneejerk thing, because pros are so schooled in the field of self-belief that it simply can't be *our* fault if the scores are high. It was the course! It was the setup! It was the weather! Funny how rarely you hear somebody say, *I played like crap today, no excuses*. Dan Jenkins, the veteran American sports writer, summed this up in some ways in his regular column the week after attending the US Open: 'The touring pros have been making it increasingly plain in recent years that they object to any track with a tree, a pond or a par five that can't be reached with a drive and a swizzle stick.'

The weather changed for the second round; it was a perfect, calm, warm day. Golf is simply an impossible game to figure out, and on this day, a day much more conducive to scoring, I got off to a ragged start, though in the end some really strong iron play allowed me to up my lead to three shots. The third round was much like the second, save for the weather, which had gone cold and grey, and a new playing partner, Dave Hill, who'd been fined $150 for his comments about the cow pasture (a fine delivered, ironically, on the birthday of Robert Trent Jones, the course's designer). Hill paid the fine practically on the spot, and then let everyone know he was tempted to pay double the amount of the fine just for the privilege of voicing his opinions about the course again.

Perhaps there was something peculiarly American about this penalty-doubling gesture. There was the story about Tommy Bolt – who I played with a lot and learned a great deal from – and his regular visits with the Tour disciplinary panel. Tommy was a man I considered something of a tortured genius, and he could be wicked and profane at times. He was a devil. He once told a couple of ageing ladies near a tee box to please stop chatting while he was trying to tee off. They either didn't hear him or ignored him, so he went over – all of this in the presence of a PGA official – and cussed them out, telling them to be quiet 'while a man's trying to do his job'. He used rather more colourful language than that, and the PGA official was instantly on it. 'That's going to cost you two hundred right there, Bolt.' Tommy swung round to the official. 'Okay,' he spat. 'Then make it four hundred.' He turned back to the ladies, addressing each in turn. 'Fuck you . . . and fuck you, too.' Tiger Woods is the most fined player on the PGA Tour today, but Tommy might have given him a run for his money, so to speak. You could write a book on Tommy's personality alone. I remember once being on the first tee with him at Fort Worth. Homero Blancas was paired with us, and Homero said to Tommy, 'Now, Tommy, don't get pissed off today. Tony and I are just two guys out here to play with you, and we've got a lot to learn. We want to learn from watching you swing the club.'

'Well,' said Tommy. 'We'll see what happens. I'll tell you one thing, though, boys. You can't play this game if you get pissed off. And if that happens I'm getting off this golf course.'

Within two holes a huge thunderstorm came in, and there were a couple of lightning flashes in the distance. Homero was still carrying his 3-iron.

'Goddamn son of a bitch,' Tommy said. 'That's a lightning rod you got in your hand there, son. Let's get out of here.'

With that he was gone, no official cancellation of play. He was just gone. That was Tommy.

He also had a habit of passing gas on the tee, and once he let go with a long and loud fart as a PGA official stood nearby. 'Do that again, Bolt, and I'm going to have to fine you,' said the official. Bolt grumbled and said, 'That's the trouble with you guys, you're taking all the colour out of the game.'

In any case, in the US Open at Hazeltine, Dave Hill was okay to play with, and he didn't pass gas on any of the tee boxes. I went about my business as the crowd mooed him mercilessly. In different circumstances, I might have even tossed in a 'Moo' of my own here or there to stick the needle into him, but I was far too involved in my own game to pay much attention. I followed his score, but that was about it. In fact, in many ways, his actions probably helped me out, in that they took a lot of the attention and heat off me. I remember telling somebody at the time that I was going to let him do all the talking and I was going to do all the playing. I stuck to that, and despite some tension cramps in the middle of the round managed yet again to increase my lead, now up to four strokes. I was putting well. My tempo was slow and pure, my swing speed well under control.

It's still worth emphasizing, however, that all these various planets aligning didn't necessarily translate into feeling relaxed and supremely confident about the whole thing. That night, back at the old Thunderbird, my cramps from earlier that day had persisted and worsened. I knew it was from the tension, from the mental and emotional strain, but it was making itself known as a physical problem, so I spent some time that night resting my legs, massaging them, and doing it all myself. I remember writing once that I'd had Viv do things like this in the past, and though she was ladylike in every respect, she was also a very strong woman; her massages were just too painful to endure. But she was there the whole night, keeping the cot-rattling Bradley at bay. We had dinner on our own, talked about life back home, about any number of other things, except what it would mean to my career were I to win the following day. I'm a dreamer and a romantic, a man not short of imagination, and it's always been easy for me to drift off a bit and say, 'What if . . .?' but Viv, to her credit, would never let me indulge myself with this kind of fantasizing about tournaments I was in. There was nothing to be gained by it, and she knew that. She was always there to serve me a dose of reality, to remind me of where we'd come from and how easy it would be to end up there again (how right she was about so many things).

It all goes back to what I was saying earlier about how absolutely central Viv was to any success I ever had. We were truly a team, a full partnership. People didn't see the things she did, they only saw the result, which was my play. But I can't even imagine what that night and so many others would have been like had she not been there to help get rid of that God-awful tension, the worry, the nervous energy. She helped me focus, helped me stay present. It's simple to me: I would not have won that tournament if she hadn't been there to help me through it.

The final day broke bright and sunny. I started going about my morning routine, though I did one thing that morning that was unusual for me. I'm not a religious man, and I never really have been. I believe in God, and I have the utmost respect for the faith of others, but it's just not a big part of my life. Yet that morning I was so nervous, so absolutely beside myself with not really knowing if I had it in me to take what was coming, that I actually offered up a prayer to God. And it wasn't even a prayer about me winning. I simply asked for the strength to do what I had to do throughout the day, to get through it.

I went into the locker room when I got to the club, and there was a sign inside my locker. It had one word on it, and that word was 'Tempo'. It was from Tom Weiskopf, and I was really touched by this gesture, not to mention that it drilled home exactly what I needed to be thinking throughout. I turned my thoughts to the demands of the day, of controlling my nerves, of playing within myself, of considering it a job to be done.

The course was packed with fans, and though they were cordial to me, as American galleries unfailingly were, I actually felt quite alone. It was a vastly different scene compared with Lytham, where I'd been practically carried along on a wave of goodwill. Here, there was not a word of abuse or badgering or poor sportsmanship from the fans, but neither was there that palpable sense from the crowd that they were hungry for me to win. I was on my own.

Vivien was walking along in the crowd, which was comforting. But to give you a good sense of the relative solitude and anonymity in which I was pursuing this lofty prize, there was but a single journalist from the UK! That was Ben Wright, who was at the time reporting for the *Financial Times*. Can you believe it? One journalist at the US Open. Ben would go on to work as a television commentator for CBS for many years, covering the Masters until having to resign over a political correctness fiasco involving his comments on female anatomy and the golf swing. But that fact, that there was just the one reporter from the Britain, is also evidence of some of the things I talked about earlier – the sense of Britain being perhaps too insular in those days about what was happening in golf around the world. It was as if no one in Britain cared about what was going on anywhere else. I was the first British player to be in America full-time. I'd won the Open. I'd won Jacksonville. I'd contended in the Masters. I'd been part of momentous Ryder Cup moments. And yet there was just one British reporter covering a US Open, a Major in which a Briton held a four-stroke lead going into the final round. It was mind-boggling to me.

The final round began. I was playing with Gay Brewer, but I sensed Hill, who was four behind, would be the one I'd need to watch out for. Luckily, he was playing directly ahead of us, so I could keep an eye on him, as it were. I remember actually feeling rather comfortable about the pairings, just knowing that I would be able to play my own game, and react if the circumstances dictated it, but that I could play safe if need be. My thinking was quite simple: if I could shoot, say, 71, then Hill would have to shoot a 66 to beat me outright, and that kind of score had simply never looked like happening all week.

I played solidly through the early part of the front nine, but missed a 5-footer on the 4th hole, and then managed to miss a 4-footer on the 6th, after one of the most beautiful 4-iron approaches of my life. Suddenly, somehow, I was dying out there. That was the moment, missing that 4-footer, when I knew

I was in trouble. I was feeling the pressure, there's no denying it. My mind was starting to talk back to me. Even though I was one under par for the round and holding a steady lead, doubt began to creep into my mind. I'd missed two relatively easy putts, and could have made a couple of mid-range putts: yes, I was one under, but I could have been, should have been, three or even four under. This was precisely the sort of mindset that bedevils golfers the world over. I lost my momentum. One moment I was cruising along on autopilot, the next I was losing altitude fast. How does it happen? Why on earth can't one stop the doubt? Difficult questions, and if I had easy answers I'd have made tens of millions by now sharing them. It wouldn't be a lie to say I could feel panic rising up in my throat, that queasy sense you get when you can feel it slipping away and there's not a damn thing you can do about it.

It got worse. I hit a tree on the 7th hole, and then somehow contrived to three-putt on the 8th. Now I was going under fast. The pressure was killing me, and though it's not the most insightful thing to share, my exact thought at that moment was, *Oh, shit.* I'd missed three putts under 5 feet in five holes, and my lead over Hill had shrunk to three. You can't know the feeling of that kind of pressure, the pressure you feel when you're sinking and there's not a bloody thing you feel you can do about it. It's *so* public. You're trying so hard. There isn't anything on God's green earth you'd love more than to just go steady for an hour or so, not make mistakes, not look the fool, not hear the whispers of, *Oh, my God, look. He's choking. It's happening. This is getting interesting.* The tension starts to become almost too much to bear.

Hazeltine's difficult par-four 9th hole was hardly the place to regain one's confidence, and matters didn't look like improving when I pulled my tee shot into the heavy rough. But when I got to my ball, a surprising sensation came over me. Though the galleries all week had been polite and mildly supportive – as if they liked me but didn't quite know what to make of me – when I tramped into the rough I felt as if they had somehow taken me into their hearts. I thought to myself, *They want me to win. They know I'm fighting like hell for this and they're pulling for me.* What a powerful feeling that was. I don't mind admitting it was energy and goodwill I was desperately in need of. A 4-iron to the green left me a 30-foot putt up the green. I was quite focused on hitting a solid putt, since I didn't want to leave myself 5 feet short.

It would be safe to say I overcompensated. Maybe it was nerves or some sort of muscle spasm, but I hammered that thing across the green and when the ball was about halfway there, I thought, *Oh Christ what have I done?* I was filled with the most awful vision of my ball sailing past the hole under full steam and coming to rest who knew how many feet past. Five? Ten? Another three-putt was in the works, at best. Everyone on the planet was going to know I was leaking air in the worst way. This goddamn putt was going to sail *miles* by the hole!

But it didn't happen. The ball slammed dead into the back side of the cup, popped a good few inches into the air like some ping-pong ball, and then fell straight into the bottom of the hole. I felt disbelief more than anything, though relief ranks right up there. A huge, almost embarrassed smile came over my face. Like that – snap your fingers – a mammoth of pressure leapt off my shoulders. It was there and then it wasn't. Suddenly, I was hundreds of pounds lighter. I could stand up straight. I felt my head lift. You can't imagine how gigantic that break was. I would have lost the tournament had that ball not caught that sharp back lip and jumped up and into the hole. I can't even envision how I'd have been able to come back and win had that putt done what it ought to have done. It might have been the embarrassment more than anything that would have finished me off.

It was with a grin on my face that I later read what Ben Wright wrote about that moment: 'It was a dreadful putt – it could have gone ten feet past the hole. I shut my eyes and thought he'd knocked it off the green. He was certainly edgy, it was a neurotic stab, but when it went in you knew there was no problem.'

He was right. There was no problem after that. I can still recall the massive shudder of relief I let go after seeing that putt drop. The rest of the round after that, honestly, was just keeping it in play and doing the smart thing. One minute I felt as if I was tossing the whole tournament away, and the next there was no way I could lose. The back nine was actually fun, or at least much fun as you can have under the constraints of Open pressure. I had a big lead by then: neither Hill, nor Brewer, nor any of the other challengers was able to make a sustained charge. It wasn't my nature then or now to play for safety, but there was simply nothing to be gained in being overbold (a strategic mindset which didn't escape my notice at the 2005 Open, won by Tiger at St Andrews; with a five-shot lead on the 72nd hole, he hit an iron off the tee into what is surely the world's widest fairway. Why? Because it was all he needed, that's why). I played it safe, and enjoyed myself once that massive load of pressure disappeared with a Whoosh when that ball flushed itself down the hole on the 9th.

At the final green, I could have taken six putts and still lifted the trophy, but every champion likes to finish with authority. The gallery was wonderfully receptive. I knew I was the winner, but a few different things went through my mind as I lined up that putt on the last green. I wanted to do no worse than two-putt, since that would mean I had been under par all four days, a rarity in the US Open. I stroked the putt, and the second it left my putter blade I knew it was going to drop. It was a certainty. How fitting that in a week transformed by a putting tip from a friend, I should end it by holing a 30-foot putt to cement the win. The shot of me after that putt dropped is one of my favourite visions of victory. My arms are in the air, I'm smiling, and I have a *This is almost too good to be true* look on my face. It was just my way of saying, *Can you believe it? One of the best weeks of my life, and I cap it all off by holing this outrageous thirty-footer. What a world!*

I was the winner, the holder of the Open trophy and the US Open trophy simultaneously. I had become the first Englishman to win the US Open since Ted Ray in 1920. I finished as the only player under par; Dave Hill finished at even-par 288, and it remained the largest winning margin in the tournament since 1921 until some flash in the pan named Woods won by fifteen at Pebble Beach in 2000.

Certainly, it was one of the best stretches of putting in my life. My ball-striking was as reliable and solid as ever, but it was my putting that week that carried me. I made miles and miles of putts. Even more important, I'd handled the pressure. I thought back to that last morning, when I'd offered up my little prayer of hope that I'd be able to handle what the day would bring. You can look back on it now and say, *Yes, it was a seven-shot win, what a stroll in the park*. But it wasn't like that at all inside, I can tell you. I've said before that golf is a game of opposites, and there is a huge reverse psychology that can affect players when they have big leads. This state of mind is essentially about embarrassment. In fact, in 2000, when the USGA decided to inaugurate a celebration dinner for past champions every time the US Open came to Pebble Beach (an idea based on the R&A holding such a dinner every time the Open goes to St Andrews), David Fay, then the Executive Director of the USGA, passed the microphone around and asked each of us, all the past winners, to reflect for a few minutes on what we went through in winning and what the US Open meant to us. When my turn with the microphone came,

I was brutally honest and said that I remembered going into the final round with a four-shot lead terrified that if I lost I would be the joker of all time. It was the truth! I told all these other greats – Nicklaus, Watson, Palmer, Player, Trevino, and so on – that I'd been so proud of myself to lead the first day, increase my lead the second day, do so again the third day . . . and then I had to sit around all day on Sunday, waiting until two-thirty to tee off. I would have changed places with any other person on the planet that morning. *What's going to happen? What time is it? What's going to happen? You've got to get through this. I've got to get going. What's going to happen?* It was nerve-racking beyond belief, and I told my fellow sufferers this.

I'm not sure who among my fellow US Open winners would have sympathized. It's hard to know what each champion is like inside, because we all get so good at hiding the turmoil underneath; we're all the proverbial swans, calm as can be on the surface and paddling like hell underwater. Individual temperaments have so much to do with it, and I have always had trouble just letting things slide off me. I've always gone about my business with the highest level of intensity and passion and emotion I can. I'm glad of this, and wouldn't change it a whit. But having such a nature has always meant I've felt the stress deep down inside me. Some can shut it all out, others can't. I'm one of those who can't. What I could do, though, especially when I was young, was control it. I couldn't be casual about it all, but I could control my body, control my breathing, control the tempo of my swing. This is significant, too, because I believe it has a lot to do with one's longevity in the game. Being able to shrug off the pressure makes for a longer career, obviously. If you are emotional or inspirational (as opposed to mechanical or even a bit analytical) you can make off with some fantastic moments. The problem lies in sustaining that high over the decades; the cost is just too great. Whereas the analytical or 'process-oriented' player is more measured, more consistent, and more likely to have a steady chart, as it were, in the pressure cooker of the Majors, rather than peaks and valleys.

It was certainly peaks and valleys that final day. As I said, I would have changed places with anyone that morning. But finally I teed off, and four and a half hours later I wouldn't have changed places with any other person on the planet. What a total swing of emotion. It all happened on that one putt on the 9th hole. I went from blowing it all, to having a huge release valve open up and expel all the pressure. Unbelievable. To win the Open Championship had always been my dream, because I was British and because it was the oldest championship and because I loved links golf. But to win the US Open was to capture a truly different beast. It was harder to win. Plain fact. I don't mean this as any insult to the Open Championship, or to the Masters, or the PGA. But the US Open is the hardest to win. And I had it.

Try to fully understand the utter and total transformation my life had undergone in just eleven months. Less than a year before I was on the ascendant. My game was strong. I was full of confidence. I was young but felt as if I'd done the right things to forge my will and resolve by coming to America to play against the best. And then, in an eleven-month blur of event and emotion and execution, I'd been transformed from a state of *becoming* into a state of *being*. It was no longer about potential. No longer was I one to watch out for in the future. No longer did I think, 'I'm going to get there. I will get there. I know I am going to be there.' I *was* there. It wasn't a movie. It wasn't some daydream. It was actual. It was real. At that moment, as the holder of the Open and the US Open trophies, I was one of the best golfers on the planet, if not the very best. And I embraced it. It was what I had aimed for, and I'd hit the mark, despite the incredible improbability of it all.

But was it a final destination? Of course not. Which only began to raise other questions. A friend once gave me a poem that I found compelling, and though I'm never going to win the Nobel Prize for my own poetry, I think I recognized this poem said a lot about what I was experiencing then. It's called 'Ithaka', the spiritual home of Greek legend, and it's by the Egyptian poet, long dead, C. P. Cavafy. Part of it reads:

> As you set out for Ithaka
> hope your road is a long one,
> full of adventure, full of discovery . . .
>
> May there be many summer mornings when,
> with what pleasure, what joy,
> you enter harbours you're seeing for the first time . . .
>
> Keep Ithaka always in your mind.
> Arriving there is what you're destined for.
> But don't hurry the journey at all.
> Better if it lasts for years,
> so you're old by the time you reach the island,
> wealthy with all you've gained on the way,
> not expecting Ithaka to make you rich.
> Ithaka gave you the marvellous journey.
> Without her you wouldn't have set out.
> She has nothing left to give you now.
>
> And if you find her poor, Ithaka won't have fooled you.
> Wise as you will have become, so full of experience,
> you'll have understood by then what these Ithakas mean.

I may not have finished school, but that doesn't mean I can't understand the point of what he's trying to say. The true meaning of it all lies in the experience of the journey, the savouring of the experience, not in what's waiting for you at the end, wherever or whatever that may be. When I won the US Open I was still only twenty-five. I was young, and had a young wife, a newborn child. The world, my unbelievable voyage, felt as if it still stretched out in front of me. The previous eight years had been perfect in every way, so full, so fulfilling. And yet it all still felt like a beginning to me, as if we'd only just got going, found the right gear. I couldn't wait for each day to begin, and show me what it was going to bring. Excitement and adventure and newness were always on the menu. You can't imagine how gratifying and thrilling it all was, and Vivien and I were loving every single minute of it. But even though our voyage seemed only just under way, heavy seas were waiting for us.

10

When Vivien and I made our way to St Andrews for the Open Championship in the summer of 1970, it was with a spring in our step and a lightness in our hearts. How could life be better? It was unimprovable. We were young, healthy, had a lovely little boy in our arms, not to mention a couple of trophies; namely, the Claret Jug from the previous year as well as the US Open trophy from earlier that summer. I was the holder of both, one in each hand – I suppose that means Viv was carrying the eight-month-old Bradley in her arms. She always did make it easy for me, by doing so much with the family. It was something I never had to worry about throughout my years of tournament golf – what a superb mother she was – and when I wasn't golfing it was the easiest thing in the world to be at home, playing with the kids, being a father, a husband.

It was in this comfortable frame of mind that we waltzed into St Andrews. I felt inspired and ready to play. This was in contrast to what the papers had been saying about some sad fellow named Jacklin, who apparently had shown up for the Open exhausted and burnt out after the drama and excitement of winning the US Open earlier that summer. The tabloids reported this Jacklin fellow had been far too busy jetting all over the world for matches and tournaments and endorsement opportunities, and there was no possible way this poor empty bag of a man could be ready to defend his title.

Vivien and I read these stories, as we always did, with a combination of amusement and irritation. How the bloody hell could they have any idea how I was feeling, or how ready my game was? These newspapers! Where do they get this stuff? This is a question, incidentally, that has occupied me from time to time for the better part of four decades, and I still don't have a satisfying answer for it. I'll talk more about this later on, in the years when my experiences with the Press bottomed out. But I do remember commenting at the time, tongue firmly in cheek, that I was almost so convinced of my own state of unreadiness to defend my title at St Andrews that perhaps I ought to just send my dear old dad, Arthur Jacklin, and his seven handicap, to tee off in my stead, since I was so clearly unfit for the challenge.

In any case, it *was* true that I'd been busy leading up to the Open. But it has always been that way with the most visible and successful golfers, and it always will be. Even today, one can listen to newly crowned Major champions talk about the demands on their time, and it's easy to hear in their words the balance they are trying to achieve between, on the one hand, making the most of this new, wonderful fame and earning power they carry, and, on the other, maintaining that sense of self and focus and drive. It's a difficult position (though one we all seek, of course), and it was no different thirty-five years ago. Nor did it make things easier that I was under the management of Mark McCormack in 1970. The man was an out-and-out workaholic, and he expected everyone around him to be the same. I sometimes wondered if he ever gave his drive and compulsive ambition any real thought, or if it was just his operating assumption that the rest of the world worked the way he did . . . or if it didn't, then it ought to. There were only two types of people in the world to Mark: those like him, and those who needed to be more like him.

Consequently, I was here, there and everywhere in the weeks between the US Open and the Open Championship. There were all kinds of appearances and television shoots and interviews, and it did feel like a bit of a Keystone Cops film at times. *Where am I and what am I doing here?* were questions I sometimes asked myself during these hectic times. I have friends who are still excited by the thought of stepping on a plane and going somewhere, but the romance wears off fast. I'd be delighted to never step on another commercial flight for as long as I live.

But all this travel and activity receded deep into the background as the week's play began. I'll come to the start of the week in a moment, but one of my most significant memories of that tournament was at its conclusion, after I'd finished and signed my card, knowing I was destined for a fifth-place finish. Jack Nicklaus and I were sitting in the scorer's caravan after holing out on the 72nd hole. We were seated practically within touching distance of the Royal and Ancient, the very nerve centre of the game around the world, and Jack was bemoaning the fact that he thought he'd blown his best chance to win at St Andrews. Bobby Jones, Nicklaus's hero, had famously said that a man's bid for true greatness could not be considered valid unless he won the Open at St Andrews. These were words Jack had taken to heart early in his career, and as we sat there watching Doug Sanders on the television, lining up a 3-foot putt to win the Open and relegate Jack to second place, Jack was chastising himself. 'If you want to be one of the greats,' he was saying, half to me and half to himself, 'you've got to win at St Andrews. I blew it. Doug's not going to miss that putt. There's no way. Who wants to be second here? No one, that's who.'

It's one of the oldest saws in golf that you don't root against someone else, that you do not hope to win through the misfortune of another player. I believe it myself, and there is no one who has ever personified this spirit of sportsmanship better than Jack. But Sanders's putt was easily missable. I told Jack this. You have to have stood at that exact spot on the 18th green of the Old Course, with the pin in that precise location, to know just how sharply it breaks, to fully realize how hard a putt it is, and to understand how so short a putt can play with your head. Not to mention that there was the small matter of the Claret Jug on the line.

'That's an awful putt for Doug to have right now,' I said. 'You know he's got to hit it hard or it'll turn right at the hole, but will he hit it hard enough, since he's probably thinking a miss at the speed he has to hit it will give him a bad one back.'

I wasn't rooting against Doug, not at all, but I told Jack right then I'd have bet ten thousand pounds on his eventually winning the trophy. He tried to smile. Our eyes turned to the television again as we watched Sanders bend over to pick some imaginary bug or pebble off his line. He returned to his putt, but failed to go through his full routine over again. I knew then he would miss. It was a fatal mistake not to start over. It was almost as if he was suddenly worried that he was taking too much time, that people were impatient for him to get on with it. Well, who the hell cares what anyone else thinks? It's the Open. Take all the time you want.

And so Doug missed. When the ball stayed out – the putt diving straight right at the end and not even touching the hole – everybody in the scoring trailer yelled, 'He's missed it!' Jack was astounded, but I wasn't surprised. Jack went on to win the next day, of course, but for myself, it was a tournament of no little heartache. I was defending champion, my desire to win at the Old Course was as strong as Jack's, or anyone's, and I was so completely on form to begin the week it just wasn't true. In many ways, it was a tournament I felt destined to win, and perhaps that was why the disappointment was so sharp. I had nothing to be ashamed of, certainly. By the end of play I'd finished fifth, no humiliation as the trophy holder. Yet my start to the tournament was so magical I felt it was mine to be had. Only the fickle Scottish weather conspired against me. There was nothing to be done about it. Golf is a game played under the elements, which is one of its great charms, but it's a curse, too.

The playing conditions were perfect when I was warming up that first day. I'd been hearing reports back from the course that Sanders had come home with 68, Tommy Horton a 66, and that Neil Coles had gone round in 65. The old lady was quite defenceless that day. Links courses need wind to make them difficult, and this is particularly true of the Old Course. It's not the most popular thing to say, but when the weather is warm and there is no wind to play havoc with your ball and your thought processes, the Old Course is easy. There are so many places to miss without penalty, and the greens are huge. There's just not that much to worry about on a nice day. If one is keeping the ball in play and is putting well enough, it's almost impossible for any decent pro to shoot worse than par on a calm day around the historic links.

There had been a light haar that morning (a slow-moving fog that comes in off the coast), but it had cleared away soon enough. It meant the course was soft – there was little wind, the greens were receptive, and their speed was not intimidating. It was a day for pros on song to get busy. As I went to the tee I felt ready to be up there with Coles and the rest by the end of the day. I was primed for attack, anxious to start my defence.

Attack I did. I began by birdieing the first after a drive and a wedge to 12 feet. I did the same at the second and third, drives and pitches followed by short putts. Three birdies to start. The fourth is not a drive and a wedge under any circumstances, but I hit a drive and a 5-iron, and then narrowly missed the putt, which would have given me four threes to start. I birdied the par-five 5th, after getting home in two, parred the 6th, made another short putt for birdie at the 7th, and then parred the 8th to find myself standing on the 9th tee five under par after eight holes. Somebody back on one of the earlier holes – I think it was the 3rd – had shouted out that it was 'Ridiculous!' what I was doing to the Old Course, though I was only three or four under at the time. But if he thought it back then, he ought to have kept following me around. I hit a 1-iron off the tee on the short par-four 9th, since I didn't think I could reach the green with a driver. Then I took a pitching wedge, played it back in my stance a bit, knocked a tight little runner up on to the hard flat green, and watched as the ball ran straight into the bottom of the cup. It wasn't ridiculous, it was fantastic! I had taken twenty-nine shots on the front, seven under par. It was a rush and blind thrill. I think it was the best nine holes of golf I've ever played. Seven under par on the front nine of the Old Course in the Open. Hard to top that, wouldn't you say?

Walking from the 9th green to the 10th tee, my caddie Willie Hilton said he'd never thought there could be such a commemoration for the birth of his fifth child. He and his wife had just had a girl the day before, and though I'm sure they'd already named her, Willie told me they were going to name her Antonia just so that he would never forget the day he was on my bag when I shot 29 on the front nine at the Open. I never did double-check on that. Maybe there's an Antonia Hilton walking around out there, and I've never known it.

Incredibly, after this delirious front nine, I also managed to birdie the 10th. Eight under par for ten holes. I was in the zone, that shorthand term for those rare and special times when we simply can't do anything wrong – but it's more than just that; it's a deep, almost hypnotic kind of space. You're present, but also distant. You can see what's going on around you, but the level of concentration is so deep you almost come out the other side and appear even a bit lackadaisical. It just happens, and it's almost as if you aren't even in control, as if some part of you gives in to a greater force and just goes along for the ride. You're almost hypnotized by your brilliance.

Though I wasn't really keeping close track of the numbers (since you don't want to focus too much on scores in that situation), I knew I was on to something special. I was defending champ, and given the way I was hitting the ball (with the short 12th, the par-five 14th and the short 18th ahead of me), there was no reason to think I wasn't going to be signing a card with a 61 or 60 on it a couple hours further on.

It was not to be. If there's a golfing power out there somewhere he (or she!) must have decided I'd had too much of my own way with the venerable course. I parred the next three holes, and then on the 14th it all fell apart. I'd hit a good drive, but couldn't help casting an eye skyward. The East Neuk of Fife has some of the fastest-moving weather in all of Scotland, and it was with a scowl that I looked at the darkening skies. Thunder rumbled over the hills and out to sea. Something ugly was coming, and it sure as hell didn't look like it was going to help me shoot 61. I wasn't completely aware of it at the time, but upon reflection I know my mindset changed when I saw that weather grumbling angrily as it came our way. Without even knowing it, I'd left the zone. The switch had gone off. I got to my drive in the middle of the 14th fairway, a perfect spot to play my second from. I pulled my three-wood from the bag, and just as I was waggling – though not yet swinging, to be fair – someone from the crowd yelled 'Fore!' with all the volume he could muster. What the hell?

I stopped and tried to refocus, wondering all the while why someone needed to shout that. We were miles from any other group, behind or ahead of us. Perhaps I let these thoughts stay with me as I prepared to hit my shot. My concentration was off just that much – that's all it takes in championship golf – and I made my only really bad swing of the day, pushing the ball into a gorse bush down the right-hand side of the fairway, near the old railway stone wall that now serves as a course boundary. Then all hell broke loose. The sky ripped open like some paper bag piñata. The grim weather arrived with the kind of ferocity you only seem to get at the Open. By the time I got to my ball up near the green, there were quite literally tiny lakes forming all over the course, in the bunkers, on the greens. For some reason, pure hope I suppose, we stayed on the course, standing under umbrellas. It felt like we stood there for ever, but even though we stayed out, there was no doubt golf was no longer on the agenda for the day. It was a typhoon, and all of a sudden cold to boot. The committee decided play had to be halted, a rather obvious decision, it has to be said. I was scheduled to restart at seven-thirty the next day.

To say I was disappointed is like saying Custer had a spot of bother at the Little Big Horn. I was on my way to something truly magical, something unique. But pure bad luck had halted it. What was to be done? Nothing, that's what. The game will drive you to the madhouse if you sit around and question why this happened or why that happened. It's simply golf, a game played in the elements, in front of spectators very close at hand, a game in which the athlete's level of control over the circumstances of play has to be lower than in just about any other sport I can think of. Why had that person shouted 'Fore!'? I'll never know. Why did I continue to think about it? Why didn't the weather hold off? Why hadn't the committee given me a starting time just an hour earlier? Why had there been a haar that morning? You'll drive yourself nuts with the questions, since there aren't any answers. Luckily, I managed to spend a decent night back at our place in Dundee (a gorgeous house owned by the

American NCR company, which they had generously placed at the disposal of my family, not to mention Bert Yancey and Tom Weiskopf and their families, too). I was disappointed about not being able to cruise on with such an otherworldly round of golf, but when I sat relaxing in a warm bath, I had to allow objectively that I'd made one hell of a start to my title defence. I was eight under par for the tournament (even if my ball was sitting in a bush on the 14th hole).

Early the next morning the rain was just hammering down, but the committee decided play would go on. I arrived at that horrible spot where I'd left my ball the day before, took the only sensible move – which was a drop and one-stroke penalty – and got my ball on the green in four. My putt for par was from some distance, and though I nearly holed it, it was a bogey in the end, my first of the round. After two more bogeys coming in, I trudged into the scorer's tent, went through my round hole by hole, and then signed a card for what had to be one of the most disappointing 67s of my entire career. You could hardly call an opening round of 67 in a Major disastrous. I was only a couple of shots off the lead. There were still three rounds to be played, and I was in the thick of it. So, yes, it was a respectable start. But I'm a human being, too, and I suppose my disappointment was only the measure of the distance between what was and what I had hoped would be. Not only had I wanted to shoot a really low number to start my title defence, but halfway through the round it began to seem inevitable to me that I *would* shoot such a number, would make a statement to the assembled field, that it was simply a given I was going to be the player to beat if anyone had designs on the Claret Jug. And when events turned around to such a shocking degree – at least shocking to me – that air of inevitability dissipated just enough to let doubt in through the side door.

Many's the time I went out on the golf course not completely into it. This is normal and natural, especially when you've been doing it half your life. Sometimes the grind seemed never to stop. But I can't recall ever feeling less enthusiastic about playing in the second round of a Major than I did later that day, particularly after shooting what every player in the field would have considered a stellar opening round. But there you go. It just shows the extent to which my subconscious had expected a 62 or lower beside my name on the huge yellow leaderboard after Round 1. But the first round, in sum, had been such a swing, such a shock to my system on both sides of the coin – going eight under par after ten holes is hardly the stuff of everyday life on tour. And then having to paddle home on a bloody life raft from the 14th hole with nothing but three bogeys to show for it. All after that twit had shouted 'Fore!' to no one. Well, perhaps it was just a bit much. I remember telling Willie, as we stood on the first tee waiting to start the second round, that from that very second on we were no longer going to discuss what had happened in the five holes that morning. It was history.

And, essentially, so was I for the tournament. My scores got successively higher as the tournament went on, although it's only fair to note that everyone else's did, too. The weather deteriorated throughout the week. I had a 70 for that second round – quite respectable given the psychological Carnival Hall of Mirrors I'd gone through in the first – and then a 73 in the third round, followed by a 76 the last day. The final day was a cold hard application of the putting woes that were now truly beginning to plague me, and which would strangle both my effectiveness and my love for the game so dramatically in the decades that followed. The dagger to the heart on that final day was a missed 2-footer for par on the 15th hole. It's worth noting, given the toxic effect my putting would eventually have on my tournament play and even on my simple enjoyment of the game, that it was at that Open I first saw someone use what is now called the left-hand low putting grip, the kind employed so regularly today. Players such as Jim Furyk have even used this grip since they started playing the game, that's how accepted it has become. But it was there, in 1970, that it first came to my attention, and it was through Gary Player, who was nothing if not obsessive about finding any way to become a better player. It was at a pro-am just prior to the Open that he used the old cack-handed grip while putting. True to Player form, he declared with some certainty that this grip would be widely used by the end of the Seventies. Gary says a lot of things, but in this case he deserves some credit; he wasn't all wrong. Still, at that time, I could never have envisioned using such a grip, no matter how distressing my putting became. But then, I never could have imagined using the long putter either. Desperation is the mother of invention, isn't that what they say?

Incredibly, given everything that had happened at the Old Course, I still managed to finish just three strokes out of the epic playoff between Sanders and Nicklaus, at 286 to their 283. At the time, though I was certainly supportive of Jack while sitting with him in the scoring caravan after the fourth round, I was also ruing my own fate. Three shots! I'd tossed away three shots in the space of five minutes on the 14th hole in that heartbreaking first round. If I'd dreamed of one day winning the Open, I'd scarcely ever allowed myself to dream of repeating the victory on the Old Course, which was and remains the true gravitational centre of golf on the planet. Of course, St Andrews was criticized even then for a variety of reasons: too short; inadequate practice facilities; not the best of courses for spectators; a difficult town to get in and out of in the crush of an Open. Some of these problems have been fixed, though, as I mentioned earlier, if there is no wind and a bit of moisture on the greens it can still be rather defenceless against today's bombers. But it is simply a magical place, a place unlike any other in the world of golf. The buildings ooze history from every window, every door, every cobblestone, and when you stand on that last tee, looking at the R & A and Hamilton Hall, across that vast field of the shared 1st and 18th fairways, you know you are in a very special place.

How dearly I would have loved to have won at the Old Course, especially after such an electrifying start. It simply wasn't meant for me, that's all. But deep as this disappointment was, there was worse to come – much worse – in my Open experience. In fact, I would look back at the St Andrews Open as a time of sweetness and light relative to the damage in store. The following summer I was to finish third at Birkdale, behind Mr Lu of Formosa and the winner Lee Trevino. I played well in that tournament, but never felt quite destined for it, the way I had at St Andrews.

The real trauma was two years removed from that 1970 Open at St Andrews (two years, incidentally, during which I played very well, and won my share of tournaments, including a second Jacksonville Open on the US Tour). In the memory of my golfing brain, the missed opportunity of St Andrews is the start of a line that began in the East Neuk of Fife and moved across the Firth of Forth, to the 1972 Open at Muirfield, to the tournament that was to become another fulcrum point in my still-young life.

11

Life was certainly not all about golf in this heady time. Vivien and I were enjoying family life immensely. She had such wonderful steadiness and control of our household and our children, and in fact, pretty much everything about our lives. All I had to do was worry about playing golf. I would come home at night, and it was like returning to a sanctuary, a place of safety, where no one judged me, no one berated me for missing a putt, no one slagged me off for wanting to prove myself in America, no one criticized me for not practising as much as people thought I ought to. It was just home, with my wife and children, and we had a wonderful togetherness to our lives.

One of the issues we did face, though – an issue that actually became something of a theme even up to recent years – was that of deciding where to live. It was becoming increasingly clear as the 1970s got under way that living in Britain was going to be very difficult from a financial point of view. Money, as I wrote earlier, has always been complicated for me. I was always less than comfortable with the way Americans treated money, or at least their attitude towards it – covetous of it, yet also strangely cavalier towards it. I never was able to be as relaxed about money as my American peers. I remember once telling the story of how shocked I was when I first went to America to see pros I played with order a sandwich and a Coke in the locker room, put down a large bill to pay for it, and then leave the room without finishing the drink or even picking up their change beyond a healthy tip. I was always a bit flabbergasted by this, even when I was holding a couple of Open trophies and making a significant annual income. No doubt it jarred with my upbringing, and from the start I had an insecurity about money, about having enough, making enough, wanting more, feeling guilty about wanting more, about decisions designed to produce more, but which – made in relative haste – perhaps did the opposite. That anxious search for security was never far from my mind.

I was at the height of my golfing powers during the early Seventies, and I should have been at the height of my earning powers, too. But I don't think it happened the way it ought to have. Certainly, this was partly about my own decision-making. After all, I was a level-headed young man, in possession of my faculties, with an intelligent wife to help me make decisions. But on the other hand, in the maelstrom of new fame and fortune, and caught up in the obsessive resolve and focus you must have in order to achieve the kind of sporting heights I was seeking, most athletes require managerial and financial advice they can trust. It's something you don't want to have be up at night worrying over.

I was an IMG man, but, honestly, if I had to do it all over again, I would not sign with IMG. In terms of my business life, my fifteen or so years with them were very much a mixed bag. But you don't know how these things are going to turn out, do you? How can you? All you can do is look at the information in your possession at that moment and make the best decision you can.

There was so much going on for me in the late Sixties. There were other prominent managers floating around the players.

(Such as Fred Cochrane, who managed Sam Snead and had managed Tony Lema. Fred had been in the golf business a long time, but he was a one-man band, and had no real organization behind him to speak of, though he was trustworthy and well respected.) But there were so many stories out there of players getting cheated, losing money, making the wrong decision. It was well known that Lee Trevino had had serious management troubles around this time. So it was always easy for IMG to say, 'See what can happen? You don't want that happening to you.' Mark was very skilled at making IMG seem the only game in town. I was flattered at first to be associated with IMG and Mark McCormack, but as 1970 and 1971 progressed it was becoming clear to me that I wasn't exactly what I thought and hoped I'd be to IMG, nor them to me. I wrote earlier that directly after winning the Open in 1969, McCormack had me on the treadmill. That didn't stop. Round and round and round. I should have just jumped off, but I didn't. I think it was naiveté at first that made me think every single thing McCormack did for me was always going to be in my best interests. Still, there were times even very early on when I doubted it. In hindsight, there should have been more of those times.

I decided to go with IMG because they could boast Arnie and Jack and Gary, and then they also signed Ray Floyd right around the time they were expressing an interest in me. Mark seemed very determined to have Jacklin on the dotted line, and who doesn't want to be wanted? So I signed with Mark, and even though I had been thinking that it was getting to be a time in my life – roughly the stretch from the win at Lytham through to the 1972 Open at Muirfield – that we ought to be moving to the US full-time to live and play, Mark counselled heavily against. Both Vivien and I adored America, and we would have moved there without a doubt. Yes, we also loved Britain, and we always missed it insanely when we were away. For my career, however, we would have set up shop in the US in a heartbeat, but Mark strongly recommended staying in Europe and so we stayed. It was a huge mistake, and you'll never convince me otherwise. America was where we ought to have been, full stop.

It wasn't until some years later that I fully understood why Mark wanted me to remain in Britain, why he counselled against my living in the US full-time. It was because he wanted me as an anchor to help him to develop the European arm of IMG. Simply put, I was to be the catalyst for his European base. He would have had a much more difficult time building it if I'd run off to Florida the minute I struck it big. But with me as his big fish in the little pond of Britain, relatively speaking, he could lure other clients, different businesses, work on a wider variety of deals. This was also indisputably how he eventually managed to work towards controlling the operations of the European Tour to the extent he did. I'm not bitter about this, or at least not bothered about it in the way that I might have been during some of the financially fallow periods of my life, but I suppose if I were to be completely honest about it – and this is hard to say, given one's desire to honour the memory of someone so recently passed away – I would have to admit that I don't think Mark fully did right by me. I was certainly never given anything like his or the agency's full attention. Still, once I realized that was the way things were going to be, that he was there for Arnie first and foremost, and Jack next (although Jack did leave IMG in 1971), I was relatively comfortable with it. I understood his position. He had to protect his Number One investment, as any of us would, and his Number One investment was Arnie. But what I expected after that was to be handled with attention and concern by dedicated staff members of IMG, and more than that, to be handled with some consistency and constancy, so that my finances and business dealings were things I need not worry about.

It didn't happen that way. It seemed like every year I was assigned a new representative. Of course, it was only natural that most of my relationships within IMG were not with Mark, but with whoever represented me within the agency. Yet that was the whole bloody problem I had in the early days. I bonded with an individual, he got to know me, phoned me often, was wheeling and dealing on my behalf, and then McCormack would say to him, 'Hey you're going to go to Australia or Cleveland or South Africa.' I had that happen four times during the early Seventies.

The first person assigned to me who then got shipped off was Andrew Marconi. Then there was Sir Martin Sorrell, now one of the biggest advertising agents on the planet. He's got to be a billionaire by now, and good luck to him, but he didn't do me that much good at the time because McCormack took him off my case to do other things. And then there was James Erskine. James was the one I bonded with the best. He came in there as an office boy, a failed medical student, but he was one of those characters I enjoyed, and he used to say what he meant and do what he said. He was on the ball, so I phoned Mark up and said, 'I want this kid to do all my stuff, he's confident, he's good.' Well, I guess he was *very* good, because after about a year in the London IMG office, which he went through like a dose of salts, Mark cleared him off to Australia to open that office up and run it. He was so good McCormack didn't 'waste' him working for one client. In the end, James didn't stay all that long with IMG. He forged ahead with his own business, and subsequently made his millions.

Our various living situations were indicative of what I would call dubious advice handed out by Mark and IMG. The first real issue in this regard came after I won the Jacksonville Open for the first time. I had agreed to represent the Sea Island Resort on the Georgia coast, a place I have always loved and which is one of the world's most sublimely beautiful spots. It was not a huge amount they were paying me, but I was happy with it. After I won the Open at Lytham, Mark asked that the fee be increased – perfectly within our rights – and Sea Island agreed. Then I won the US Open. Well, this sent Mark off after increases like a starving dog after a buried bone. He demanded that Sea Island, if they wanted the distinction of being associated with me, had to pay me $150,000 a year and provide an apartment for me with the title under my name. Sea Island, probably reasonably, said 'No thank you.' Worse, they didn't renew the earlier contract. I was left with nothing from them. I found this not just financially upsetting, but personally too. Viv and I had made many friends there, and they were so gracious with us. Irv Harned, who was the manager of the place, and Bill Jones III, who now owns it, treated us very well. I used to take Bill out fishing when he was a younger lad. The whole thing essentially fell apart because Mark wanted too much money; even more to the point, he wanted a cash component, a liquidity, because if Sea Island had simply given me a condo to represent them, well, then it would have been more difficult for Mark to figure out how to extract his 20 per cent from me. This was devastating to Viv and me. We adored Sea Island; it was so sublime and gorgeous and comfortable.

Mark continued to advise that we remain in Europe throughout the time I was winning my two Opens. Up to that point we'd lived in a couple of different houses, one at the East Lodge in Elsham and the other a place in Cheltenham (which we put a lot of money into renovating, money not recouped when we sold it). Taking to heart Mark's advice about remaining in Europe, Vivien and I decided that if we were going to stay in the UK, then we were going to live the way we'd always dreamed of living. We bought a fantastic place in Gloucester, a house called Langley, near the village of Winchcombe. We moved there in the late summer of 1972. It was just two hours from Heathrow, and our nearest neighbour was half a mile away. It was a lovely house, made of old stone and with a stunning tiered garden. There were thirty-three rooms, three cottages in the grounds, and in all I employed six people who lived in those cottages.

It was true country sportsman living, but, hell, after a while you start to realize just how much money you have to spend every single month simply to keep the place up and running. Forget about stashing away huge amounts of savings for some far-off rainy day. I was paying out £500 a month in salaries alone to the people employed around the house. Every penny I made, it seemed, went into that house. But make no mistake about it: we loved that place, loved spending money on it, and loved trying to get it just the way we wanted it. There is no complaint from this quarter about what it cost or the way we lived. We had a fantastic spell living in Langley. I had worked so hard to get us to that point, and Vivien had put so much energy and faith into my career, that we felt it was only what we deserved. We'd earned it, and we enjoyed making it into what we thought was going to be our 'forever' home, the place our children and grandchildren were going to gather for the generations that followed. We put in new carpets, velvet curtains. We had hand-made Spanish furniture. We renovated the kitchen. I had an indoor swimming pool built, with a fireplace at one end of the deck. We added a solarium and a sauna. Down in the garden I put in a putting green, a bunker and a short practice fairway. We spent £110,000 getting it just the way we wanted it, though the most spectacular addition of all came four weeks after we moved in, when our second son, Warren, was born in September.

In case you haven't yet picked up on it, Langley was a palace. What a glorious place it was. Life in many ways is about the things you dream of. We all dream, don't we? It's only human nature, and when I was growing up, when I spent all those hours on the range as a young teenager – and particularly when I put up with day after day after day of Shanko chewing me out for one thing or another – then I suppose I was motivated by my dreams, by what I wanted to achieve. That was to win championships, of course, particularly the Open. But it also meant to me that I wanted to achieve a certain kind of lifestyle. I promised Viv when we met that I would make enough of myself to treat her to a lifestyle a cut above, and that's what we went for with Langley. I'll never forget the house. It was supposed to be for ever. That's how we saw it, and that's what we wanted it to be. But, sadly, it wasn't meant to happen that way.

In 1974, the new Labour government of Harold Wilson came into power. All politics aside, timing is everything in life, and it was just my bad luck to be doing some real earning when Wilson got elected. The new taxation levels were preposterous. I don't care if you were Labour, Conservative, or an environmental feminist anarchist, it was utter stupidity. The taxation level for me with the new government was 83 per cent on worldwide income. I spent seven months a year travelling, playing golf, doing what I did, all for the privilege of coming back home for five months to pay income tax at 83 per cent. (It was ironic I had to move away from England because of the massive tax burden, yet someone like Bob Charles, who I competed against regularly, could actually live well in London because he was a foreigner and was paying taxes in New Zealand.)

But just think about that for half a second. Eighty-three per cent. Of *all* my income. If I made a pound in Paraguay or Thailand or Birmingham, it didn't matter. If I made a pound sterling, anywhere in the world, I got to keep 17 per cent of it. It sounds like make-believe, but trust me it wasn't. It was all too real, and was a crippling blow for us, and for so many others in Britain. The brain drain ensued shortly thereafter, but it wasn't just the brains that left, it was most of the talent in virtually

My mother, sister and I, 1946.

With my grandfather in Mablethorpe, Lincolnshire, 1947.

Aged thirteen, with the Holme Hall and Elsham Open Day trophies, 1957.

First Lincolnshire Junior Championship win, 1957.

My father and I winning the Iron & Steel tournament, Hesketh, 1960.

Playing during the 1969 Open, Royal Lytham & St Anne's.

Victory at last – my first Major.

Relaxing with the famous claret jug the day after the Open victory, in my father's back garden in Scunthorpe.

Mum and Dad after my Open win, 1969.

With Nicklaus after the famous 'Concession', 1969 Ryder Cup.

Hitting a ball across the Thames from the top of the Savoy, November 1969.

With Bradley at East
Lodge, Elsham, 1970.

Arnold Palmer, Mark McCormack and my partner Jim Mahoney
at the Bing Crosby pro–am, 1970.

On Pacifico the dreaded donkey, 1970.

Playing in the final round of the 1970 US
Open, 21 June 1970.

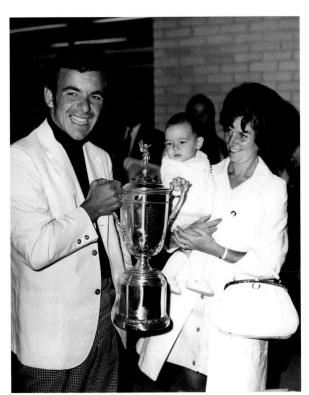

With Bradley, Viv and the US Open trophy, June 1970.

Recording *Tony Jacklin Swings*, October 1970.

With Viv in Hawaii, 1972.

Pointing the way to Lee Trevino during the 1972 Open at Muirfield.

Partying in Paris with Palmer, Player, Floyd and co., 1973.

With Johnny Miller, Bing Crosby, Peter Alliss and Sean Connery, 1976.

With Jack Nicklaus at Palm Beach Gardens, 1983 Ryder Cup.

Warren, number two son, caddying at The Belfry in 1985.

With Samuel Ryder's daughter and Lee Trevino at the 1985 Ryder Cup.

Looking anxious as captain during the 1985 Ryder Cup, The Belfry.

Victory at last – celebrating on the roof with Woosnam, Howard Clark, Seve, Sam Torrance, Paul Way and Bernhard Langer, 15 September 1985.

With Faldo and Woosnam at Muirfield Village during the 1987 Ryder Cup.

With Seve Ballesteros, 1987 Ryder Cup.

With the Ryder Cup
after the 1987 victory.

The first publicity shot with Astrid, 1988.

Marriage to Astrid, 1988.

With Astrid at the 1989
Ryder Cup, The Belfry.

With Torrance, Watson and Ray Floyd at the 1989 Ryder Cup.

With my son Sean at home
in Scotland, 1992.

First Senior Tour victory, Grand Rapids, Michigan, 1994.

Gathering of former Open champions, St Andrews, 2000.

With the family at my induction into the Golf Hall of Fame, 2002. Left to right: Bradley, Anna-May, AJ, Sean, Astrid, TJ, Tina and Warren.

With Sean at the grand opening of The Concession, Florida, 2006.

every field. Actors, sportsmen, everybody. Langley was supposed to be for ever, but that world ended *totally* in an instant with that taxation decision by that government. It was gone. All of it. Was I bitter about it? You're damn right I was.

In any case, Mark's solution to this ridiculous state of affairs was that we ought to move to the Channel Island of Jersey, which is a tax haven but a bloody great pile of rock. By the spring of 1975, eight months after Wilson came in, we were in Jersey. I think the flat tax rate there now is 10 per cent, but back then it was 20 per cent, still a hell of a lot better than 83 per cent. Leaving Langley was purely a financial decision. I have no idea how many tens of thousands of pounds I must have lost on that house when we had to move (well, actually I do know; it was about £110,000). So we packed up and carted off to Jersey, where we lived for the next eight years. But that was very bad advice, going to Jersey, mostly because it never truly felt like home.

It's funny, Mark was once quoted as saying he thought I 'would be bigger'. Well, I was certainly big enough to have deserved more attention from him and his company. He did betray his feelings occasionally. 'Perhaps when [Tony] got to a certain level of success,' Mark once said, 'he wasn't hungry enough to win more and more championships at a time when he could have done so.' Mark also wasn't afraid to offer his opinions on our housing situation. 'As it turned out,' he continued in the same interview, 'Tony bought and sold at the wrong times on the property market.' This was rather hard of him, considering that many of those decisions were made on his advice. He was correct, I suppose, but it certainly would have helped me live with the frustration of it all if he'd even acknowledged somewhere along the way that we made some of our moves by setting great store by his advice. I can't even begin to recall how many hundreds of thousands of pounds I've lost along the way in housing deals; actually, it is certainly well over a million pounds. I'll get into some of the later ones further on in the book, such as my issues with our house in San Roque, Spain, and in Scotland, but the Gloucester and Jersey moves were certainly enough of a headache at the time.

Reading back on some of the things Mark said about me, I at least have to give him credit for seeing fairly clearly the nature of what I had to go through being a British sports hero living in Britain, as opposed to an American or even a Brit living abroad, someone like Jackie Stewart, who lived for decades outside the UK. 'With Tony the British Press overdid it,' Mark once said. 'The man had a cold and the *Daily Express* would say, "Jacko Has Cold" or "Jacko Sneezes at Tucson". Jesus, it's ridiculous. It's the British method indigenous to the British Press, whereas the American Press is more interested in results, not the person. The British Press gets a hero, and then anything he does, they write, because they figure that's what the reader wants to know. The *New York Times* would never have said that Arnold Palmer has a cold.'

Though Mark was sometimes very supportive and sometimes rather distant, sometimes a friend, sometimes busy with others, what he and I were about at the end of the day was business. It was a business relationship, and I'm sure he wouldn't have had it any other way. I respected him as a businessman, but to me that respect didn't always flow both ways.

12

I knew what was what when it came to the world of business, and although I knew a good deal from a bad deal it would still be fair to say that the vast majority of my energy and attention, rightly so, was directed toward golf. *This* was my realm. This was where I knew *precisely* what I was doing. That summer of 1972, I was, as always, aware of a rise in my excitement level and anticipation for the upcoming Open Championship. In 1972 we were called to assemble at Muirfield, the informal name for the club of the Honourable Company of Edinburgh Golfers. There are various squabbles back and forth about which is the oldest club in the golfing universe – whether it be the Royal and Ancient in St Andrews, or Musselburgh, or Royal Burgess in Edinburgh, or the Honourable Company. But these are all just fights over nothing in my view. Who cares? Not me. I couldn't give a toss if this club started in 1754 or that club in 1758. All that matters to me is that a club such as the Honourable Company cares for its remarkable gift to the golfing world, their golf course (which they do, beautifully), and that the R & A continue to administer the game properly and do a good job of running the Open (which they also do).

Though I managed to finish third in the Open in 1971, played at Royal Birkdale, there was no sense of real agony or heart-break. I had a good steady week of play, and if I'd somehow managed to eagle the last hole and Trevino had parred, we would have been in a playoff. I birdied, but so did Trevino, as did the delightful Mr Lu (who managed to do so while hitting a massive hook into the gallery, his ball striking a lady so hard on the head she fell in a heap. Poor Mr Lu was so distraught, and so thankful she survived, that some years later he paid for her to take an all-expenses-paid trip to the Far East as a kind of apol-ogy. It was a wonderful gesture on his part.). But with his birdie Trevino managed to win by a shot over Lu and two shots over myself. It was an astonishing achievement for him, since it capped a five-week run in which he won the US Open, the Canadian Open (then one of the Tour's most prestigious tour-naments) and the Open Championship.

And so it was a third-place finish for me in 1971, to go with my win in 1969 and my fifth in 1970 (a result actually harder to swallow than third at Birkdale, given the heaven-and-hell the-atrics of my first-round performance at St Andrews).

Now it was on to Muirfield in 1972. I was feeling confident about my game, and about life in general. Bradley, who was two and a half, was growing up beautifully right before our eyes and Vivien was pregnant with Warren (he was born a couple of months later, on the 10th of September). It was a delightful time not just for me as a golfer, but as a family man. I had been play-ing quite a bit in America, which suited my desire to test myself continually against the best in preparation for the biggest tourna-ments. As mentioned, I'd won the Jacksonville Open again in the early part of the American season, and felt ready for a return to play at home, though such returns always brought on spasms in the Press, writing all kinds of idiotic rubbish. Really, it was nau-seating sometimes. The fact is that the British tabloids are run by the subhuman. I'm sorry, it's the truth. They are too often vicious and cruel, and pay no attention to simple common decency. I suppose you don't sell newspapers with simple common decency. To this day I feel a sense of distaste for that segment of the British Press, but it would be fair to say that back in the early Seventies and then throughout my struggles later in the Seventies, my feelings towards the tabloid Press verged on hatred. I considered them liars, and almost evil. I left for Jersey in 1975 for two reasons. One was to escape that 83 per cent tax bracket I mentioned before. The other was to escape the tabloid Press.

Although I was feeling quite confident heading into Muirfield, it had been emerging in my mind, over the course of the previous few years, that my putting was a problem. And I don't mean a problem in that I missed the occasional 2-footer, or that I would have days when nothing seemed to go in – every pro has those things happen. But I mean I was starting to understand it was a problem of a much deeper kind, much more psychological and even emotional. I don't think I would have been able to articulate it in this way at that time, but it was something I know I was feeling on an almost intuitive level. It was like some great underground river slowly and steadily eroding the landscape above, a landscape that to the outward eye might look stable and supportable, but that lay on a crumbling foundation. Part of me knew it deep down.

This hidden but felt fear was not aided by a three-putt at Muirfield's first hole. It's a brute, a long par-four into the prevailing wind, with swaying fields of hay on either side; a par to start would have been satisfying. Instead, after two solid shots and three putts, my frustration bubbled up. But I was proud of the way I was able to say, *Tony, this is the Open. You're here to win this thing. This is just the first hole. Don't be a daft bugger. Just move on.* Move on, I did. I played some wonderful golf through the middle of that round, notching five birdies across

Muirfield's astonishing links. Many have spoken of the virtues of Muirfield, and rightly so. Jack Nicklaus said it was the fairest championship golf course in the world, and by that he meant it was a very difficult golf course, but one that presented its difficulty in a direct and straightforward manner. The trouble at Muirfield is always in front of you. The bunkers are almost all visible. The greens are subtle and require superb judgement but they are not outrageous. Basically, the Old Tom Morris course (rebuilt almost wholly by Harry Colt in 1922) is a great, fair test, and it's a testament to Jack's affection for it that he named his course in Ohio Muirfield Village. It has to be said, though, that Muirfield is often a course which inspires respect rather than out-and-out love. I have no quarrel with ranking it one of the world's finest golf courses, though if I were told I could only play one golf course for the rest of my life Muirfield would not be it . . . but perhaps there are personal reasons for that.

Sadly, I compounded the bad feelings of the first hole by making the same mistake at the last – three-putting, this time from about 30 feet. I ran it 4 feet past and missed coming back for another bogey and a round of 69. A 72 the second day put me in a share of the lead with Lee Trevino. The weather was very peculiar for East Lothian at that time of year, in that it was blisteringly hot. You can have some fine weather around the east coast of Scotland in the summer, but it's rare for it to be so hot and so dry for such a prolonged period. The course was so baked it was almost dusty in spots. This made for conditions, ironically, that were a whole lot tougher than had it been cooler and damper. Only one person broke 70 that second day, and it was Johnny Miller with a new course record of five under par 66. That spectacular round put him just a shot back of Lee and myself. Jack had a 72, which put him two shots adrift.

The third day found Lee and me paired together. We both played some wonderful golf through the outward nine, but then we came to the 13th, which is surely one of the world's great par-threes, an uphill shot of about 180 yards to a green guarded by mounds and some pot bunkers. My tee ball found one of those bunkers left of the green. Trying to hit too good a shot, I left it in the bunker. Then, compensating too much, I managed to blast my next clear across the green, deep into another bunker on the right side of the green. After getting out of that trap, I took two putts for a triple bogey six. A triple bogey! I kept my mouth screwed up tight and my emotions reined in, and somehow I managed to steel myself yet again. A furious resolve actually rose up in me that hadn't quite been there to the same degree ten minutes earlier, and it was almost a kind of anger. *You're not going to let this worry you. It's nothing. It's finished, and worrying isn't going to change one thing about the past.*

This began what has to have been one of the great runs of play from a pairing in all of championship golf, though it was also when I began to think Trevino was perhaps from another planet; it wasn't about talent or possessing good timing – though he had both in abundance – but more about being outrageously, audaciously lucky. Of course, it would be silly to not acknowledge that we all get our share of luck, good and bad, but come on! What he did that third round was freakish and supernatural (though it was merely an appetizer for his final-round miracles). I birdied the 14th and so did Lee. I birdied the 15th and so did Lee. I parred the difficult par-three 16th; Lee had hit the ball in a greenside trap and from there he hit the most horrific thinned shot – the stroke of a 15-handicapper, really. It sailed directly at the flagstick, clanged against the iron pole and dropped to the bottom of the cup for his third straight birdie. At the next, the long par-five 17th, I birdied and Lee did, too, nearly eagling it in fact. At the last, the punishingly hard par-four that always directs your eye straight onto the elegant Muirfield clubhouse, Lee striped his drive and I pushed mine into the left rough. His

5-iron ran long off the back of the green and my 6-iron made the green but left me a long approach putt.

I was further away from the hole than Lee, but he almost hurriedly said to me, 'I'll come up,' and I agreed. If I'd had my thinking cap on, I might have said to him that I preferred to putt first, but he had said it as if he was informing me rather than asking me, and so I allowed it. Naturally, given everything that had already happened, Lee casually chipped his bloody ball into the hole, for his fifth straight birdie and a score of 66. The cheek! Now the crowd was abuzz, and I was left to try and get down in two from 60 feet just to stay within a shot of him. My approach putt stopped 6 feet short. It was a moment when some bottle was required, and I managed to hole what to me was an extremely important putt. It kept the momentum and good feelings going, so that I could carry them into the final round. I knew I was going to need momentum and strength and positive feelings, given that Lee was so clearly operating on this strangely intuitive level – he was going along as if it almost didn't matter how he swung or what he did, because he somehow knew he was going to rescue himself from any predicament. It would have been much more fascinating to watch had I not been trying to beat him so badly, or had I been further back. As it was, I remember thinking, *I'm working my arse off playing one quality shot after another and this guy's winning the tournament slapping it all over the park with his eyes closed.*

Well, maybe that's overstating it, but I was incredulous at his performance, and kept reminding myself that a run of luck has to end sometime. I mean, luck is luck; we all get lucky. You play tournaments long enough, and you'll see it even out. But, still! There was no way he could keep it up. Wasn't this what any normal person would have been telling himself? You almost had to laugh, it was so outrageous.

The final day was one of massive anticipation and excitement.

There was something palpable in the air, as if the crowd sensed great events in the offing. It was another hot, dry day, and the greens were starting to go brown and crusty. I was a shot behind Lee, but word was drifting back to the starter's area that Jack, seven behind, had got off to a good start. As we stood on the first tee, Lee said to me, 'Well, Nicklaus might catch one of us but he ain't going to catch us both.' He was wrong. By the time Lee and I got to the 9th green, Jack had reached the 11th tee . . . and he had passed us both. He was six under par for his round through ten holes. The game was well and truly on.

The excitement was only just starting. Both Lee and I reached the par-five 9th in two. Lee ran his 35-footer into the cup for an eagle. The crowd erupted, and I saw later on the film of the tournament that Jack had to back away from his tee shot on the 11th, about 500 yards away, because of the volume of the roar coming from the 9th green. He must have known one of us had made an eagle. Jack began to address his ball again as I stroked up my eagle putt, and from 20 feet I poured mine right into the hole. This time the crowd nearly broke into a riot. The howling and roaring was massive, and Jack again had to back away from his tee shot. Undoubtedly, he now knew that both Lee and I had eagled the hole, and that he no longer had the momentum to himself.

It was tension and anxiety throughout the back nine. Jack bogeyed the 16th, which ultimately cost him any chance at the title, but Lee and I stayed beside one another throughout after the explosives of the 9th hole. By the time we got to the 17th tee, we were both at six under par aggregate. Jack had finished with a 66 and a total of five under par.

The 17th hole, the long dogleg left par-five, is certainly one of golf's great holes, but frankly it's one I wish had never been imagined by Old Tom Morris or Harry Colt. Trevino hooked his tee shot into one of the large bunkers that cover the inside elbow of the hole. Lee hitting such a wild hook meant many things to me beyond the fact that he was now in serious trouble on the hole – those bunkers were hell to get out of, and frequently it took quite an imaginative shot simply to make it back on to the fairway. But what it told me was that he was nervous. Lee didn't hit many hooks, and on those rare occasions when he did it was to veer away from the trouble not towards it. So I knew he was feeling the heat, which boosted my confidence as we left the tee and made our way down to where our drives had finished. I'd made yet another solid swing and was safely in the middle of the fairway. Lee fashioned a fine shot out of the bunker to get more or less even with where I was on the fairway. I played first and hit a three-wood up towards the green, not quite on, but just short and left, within chipping distance. As my ball came to a stop up by the green I was filled with the feeling that I was going to make birdie, and more than that, that *Lee* knew I was going to make birdie. Yet again, I saw the pressure affecting him as he hit another swipe hook short and left of the green into the heavy rough. It was incredible. It was as if he was handing the Open to me. I was just short in two and he was buried in the heavy stuff in three, and I knew he would struggle just to hold the green from that mess.

We walked down the fairway together, Lee chattering away the whole time. I don't remember his exact words, but he more or less told me he'd thrown his chance away, and that it was my tournament. He'd conceded. I knew Lee well enough to know he wasn't trying to psyche me out or employ any radical games-manship through his incessant talking. That wasn't Lee. After all, we'd been through this before and would again, though not quite under this kind of pressure. (In fact, it was just a few weeks later that he was at it again, this time in the World Match Play at Wentworth, when I said to him as we teed off, 'Lee, I really don't feel like talking today, if that's okay, so I'm probably not going to say much.' 'Hey, Tone,' he said, jovial as always, 'you don't need to talk, just listen.')

Of course, everybody on the Tour knew this was just Lee's way of dealing with the pressure. He *had* to talk. That was his release valve, and anybody playing with him was just supposed to absorb it. The truth is that it was more than you had to take from anyone else. Nicklaus never talked much. Bob Charles never talked much. No one talked as much as Trevino. And it was always just that little bit of a distraction. Did it take away something from his opponent's resolve and concentration? Yes, it did. But what's important is that Lee never *used* it that way. It wasn't a conscious thing on his part. He never said inside, *Hmmm, if I really talk a lot today maybe that'll throw Jacklin off his game.* Never. Lee would never do that. But having said that, Lee Trevino was Lee Trevino and he couldn't help himself. To compete against him you just had to learn to deal with it. It wasn't against the rules to talk. But was he harder to play against than Jack or Arnie? Absolutely. Was it fair? Well, it was never about fair or unfair. It just was. It was a factor to playing with Lee and you knew it going in. You either learned to deal with it or your game suffered.

In any case, I arrived at my ball near the front left of the 17th green, and looked back to where Lee was trying to figure out what to do from the deep rough. He didn't waste time, and soon hit a pitch over the large mounds guarding the green like a horse collar. As I thought might be the case, he had a hard time holding the green, since he tried to fly his pitch shot all the way to the back pin placement, which was deep up against the back edge of the long narrow green. His ball landed on the green, but had no action on it whatsoever; it skipped through the wispy rough and about 15 feet up the rise of the mounding at the rear. He was now in serious trouble. I was in front in two, facing a long but relatively straightforward chip to get up and down for a birdie;

he was off the back in four, facing a delicate pitch that would take no little genius merely to leave a putt for a bogey six, a score that seemed his best-case scenario. Jack was in the clubhouse, a stroke adrift. In other words, the Claret Jug was sitting in front of me; Nick Price once said after losing the Open that he had one hand on the trophy and couldn't wait until the day he was holding it with both hands. Well, I am never one to think too far ahead. My concentration has always been one of my strengths, and so I was focusing quite fiercely on the job still at hand. But to any external observer, it must have seemed at the moment – as I lined up my pitch for my third shot – that I not only had both hands on the Jug but both lips, too, preparing to drink champagne from it. Even after I'd left my long pitch-and-run with a wedge from the wispy rough some 16 feet short, there was still an air of inevitability to things for me, since it was a very makeable putt and Lee had yet to try and chip it close enough to have a reasonable putt for par. In fact, there seemed every chance to me that he might still be away after he'd finished chipping.

He dragged his feet as he wandered over to his ball, apparently disinterested, and almost blindly pulled a club from his bag. He was chattering away the whole time. 'My goose is cooked, baby. I'm done like dinner. This is over. Just stick a fork in me and pull me out. I am done.'

What happened next has gone down as a dramatic moment in the history of golf, and though it will always be remembered, I suppose, as a great moment in Lee's career, it was a devastating, crushing moment for me. Really, it ripped out part of my soul, though it wasn't until later that I realized the full extent of the damage.

He chipped in.

Again.

His caddy Willie Aitchison told me, later on, that he too was sure Lee had given up, that he knew he wasn't going to win, and was already preparing his Press conference explaining how he'd lost it on the 71st hole. But Lee took that club, whichever one it was, and though I'm not even sure he was looking at the ball he took a stab at it, sending it toward the hole. It was a good chip, that was clear when it landed, and it seemed he'd be left with a makeable putt for a bogey. But the ball began to turn slightly toward the cup as it ran out. It trundled up to the hole and without so much as a thought of going anywhere else it just ducked its head and settled into the bottom of the cup. There was a millisecond of pure silence, and at first the crowd didn't cheer so much as let out a huge collective gasp. Lee himself couldn't believe it. His body sagged. He flipped his club up in the air and let it drop to the ground near his bag. He didn't smile, didn't talk, didn't wave, didn't make one single gesture of joy or excitement. He just walked around the green shaking his head in a combination of, I'm sure, disbelief and embarrassment.

I have watched the film of this moment time and time again, and every time it makes me wince; it's a body blow even decades later.

I was staggered, stunned, not believing what I had just seen. The man had played only one decent shot on the hole, and he'd escaped with a par. My reaction was not exactly anger, but a kind of aggression flooded into my system, pouring itself into my veins along a flow of pure adrenalin. How dare he?! How dare that son-of-a-bitch come out and butcher the hole, and then just when he had so obviously given up produce a shot that he might not be able to reproduce if he stood there until the next time Muirfield hosted the Open? I still had a birdie putt, and it fitted my eye. Yes, Lee had made a par, but I still had a shot at a birdie, and if it went in, I would be playing the last with a one-shot lead. This was my mindset as I stood over my putt. *Okay, you absolute bastard, you do that to me? Well, I'll do this to you!* I knew I was going to make that putt. I knew I was going to have a one-shot lead on the last. I knew I was still going to win this Open despite Lee's colossal good fortune.

I missed. I had too much adrenalin in me, and hit it too hard. It went 3 feet past. I can say honestly I don't quite remember what I was thinking as I stood over my 3-footer for par, and perhaps that explains why I missed that one, too; because I wasn't thinking about it. At least not the way I should have been.

I knew I'd lost. Three minutes earlier I'd had what looked to be two shots in my pocket. Now we were heading for the final tee and I was a stroke down. I was mad, confused, anxious, stunned. How could this possibly have happened? It wasn't right. It wasn't logical. It simply was . . . not . . . possible.

It was with a quick step that I made my way to that last tee, because I was still so desperate to make something good happen. I could birdie. Lee could bogey. Jack was done, his card signed. He was tied with me, and we were both a shot behind Lee. But rather than accompanying me at my pace to the last tee, Lee slowly made his way to the tee box, ambling along like he was looking for a lost coin in the grass. It was smart of him. He was letting what he'd done sink in. He had gutted me and he knew it; he wanted me to be thinking about it while I waited for him. I don't blame him; I'd have done the same.

There was no birdie to be had for me at the last, where Lee made a solid regulation par. I was so shell-shocked by the whole thing that I bogeyed, which meant I didn't even have the solace of finishing second; that honour belonged to Jack. I ended up two shots behind Lee and a shot behind Jack.

How had this happened? How had I lost an Open that was mine? Was it Trevino's greatness, or had this happened because of something missing in me? I thought long and hard in the days, months and years to come.

My psyche was simply too fragile to escape long-term damage

from what Trevino did to me on the 71st hole, particularly since it seemed he'd given up. As the fine American writer Rick Reilly once wrote, it was as if my Open trophy was being handed to someone who didn't even seem to want it. Perhaps someone else could have shrugged it off. But I couldn't.

When we holed out on the 72nd Lee didn't even really say much in the way of an apology. What could he say? It was golf. He'd hardly been trying to make an absolute mess of the 17th just so he could give himself the opportunity to chip in and turn my life into a living hell. Twenty minutes before we shook hands on the last green, I had been quite reasonably thinking I was in position to be having Lee congratulate me for winning my second Open. It would have been my life's greatest golfing moment. I had played beautiful golf the whole week – certainly much better than when I'd won at Lytham (and, in fact, I'd played wonderfully for four straight Opens, finishing first, fifth, third and third; with some Trevinoesque mojo behind me I might have reeled off four in a row). I had come into the week absolutely stuffed with confidence, in my ball-striking, my mental strength, my powers as a competitor; simply, I saw myself as a winner, as *the* winner. And there was nothing that had taken place the entire week, right up to that moment, that did anything to change this belief. After all, Lee had been chipping in from everywhere all week, usually while I watched, and I'd coped with that, resolutely staying the course, telling myself over and over again that his luck could not continue, that I simply had to keep playing quality shots, keep making quality swings, keep staying focused, and that if I did these things I stood a solid chance of prevailing. This hard mental work paid off, I thought, when the events of the 17th hole began to unfold. Lee had cracked. It was obvious. The pressure had got to him. He was hooking the ball all over the goddamn place. It was his game that had broken down, not mine, and inside I knew I had come out on top because I had stayed patient, had not let his constant miracles upset me, had managed to listen to my inner voice telling me to persevere. And then at the one single moment in time when I was going to be unveiled as the one who'd best resisted the pressure, he produced the only shot capable of cutting me dead in two.

I wasn't the winner. I wasn't the best. And I didn't even have enough jam left in me to finish second.

Complete system failure would probably best describe my state. The rest of the weekend was a blank, and I still wouldn't be able to recall who we had dinner with that night at Greywalls Hotel. I don't think I cracked a smile or tasted my food for at least a week. They say trauma victims often walk around in a sort of disengaged fog for a time afterwards; this is what was happening to me. Something inside me had been wounded, damaged for ever. What Trevino did not only devastated me on that day, it twisted up some deep part of me for the rest of my career. I can say that now. I put on as brave a face as I could at the time. But distance has brought perspective. I was never the same after that. It ruined me for ever as a serious force as a player. I never came close again to challenging in a Major. My inner self-belief was gone; residing in its stead was a three-putt from 16 feet on Muirfield's 17th green.

Before he so cavalierly chipped in, Trevino made his rueful joke about sticking a fork in him because he was cooked, he was done. But he got it wrong. It was me he stuck the fork in. A pitchfork. I was done. Cooked and done.

13

Life seemed a blur, streaks of bright, violent paint stropped across the canvas of who I was. In the autumn of 1972 or even the spring of 1973 most people – myself included, probably, had I been one of those external viewers – would have said, *Jacko's got the world by the tail. He's at the peak of his talents. He's got IMG earning him a fortune. He's got a beautiful wife and lovely children. What more could a man want? What more does a man deserve?*

I suppose it was true, mostly, though there were serious discrepancies to the picture. There was a significant gap between the way it must have looked and the way it was beginning to feel inside. As 1973 began, I was striking the ball as well as I ever had; that wasn't a problem, and even today the least of my worries on the golf course is what happens between the tee and the green. It was also true that I had a beautiful wife and children. Vivien was running a fantastic household, and our children were a constant source of delight to both of us. I had taken to fatherhood very keenly, perhaps even more than I expected to, and it was always a source of both joy and comfort to me to be around our children (a fact that would prove to be helpful to my very survival fifteen years down the road).

But that was where the perfect picture began to deteriorate. To begin with, IMG was hardly earning me a fortune. Yes, there were deals here and there earning me some income, but there were also those problematic housing situations that soon began to bleed a considerable amount of income away. I think it's just being honest, too, to say that perhaps we lived somewhat above our means at the time, especially given that I never would again scale the heights from which I was then looking at the world. The way I figured it, I was going to be in that zip code for a long time to come; there was no reason to not live a certain way, since I felt secure in my earning power. But I must admit in hindsight that perhaps there were a few less than perfect financial decisions made. In short, our situation was a lot more complicated than it may have looked from outside.

As for the golf, given that I was a professional golfer, one of the best in the world at that time, that was what people naturally focused on. I did, too, even if my self-definition was always much more complex than just being a golfer. There's too much out there to simply say *I'm a golfer*, and leave it at that. The world is so full of unbelievable, mind-bending things, and I have such a curious nature, that I've always considered myself a person of the world, and a person *in* the world, someone who wants to experience the strange and wonderful things the world has on offer, but who also happens to have been blessed with a gift to play golf and to compete. That was who Tony Jacklin was to me. Still, golf was the centre of my life, the core around which everything else was constructed, and though this core was not exactly crumbling at my feet, neither was it true that it felt as unshakeable as it once had.

There are so many things to talk about when it comes to analysing the repercussions of Muirfield. There was serious psychological damage, that's clear, although part of me has always wondered if it wasn't actually more emotional than psychological. What I mean is that part of me was dealt a psychological blow, clearly, but in a way this was not all that hard to get over. I still competed, still won tournaments, still hit fantastic golf shots. There was no rift in my psychology that made me unable to think my way round the golf course and produce a fine score. I didn't stand over every shot and every putt, and think to myself, *Okay, now put Muirfield out of your mind. Just do it. Forget about it!* At a conscious level, the level of trying to operate as a professional on a daily round-by-round basis, I got over it soon enough.

But from an emotional standpoint a fire had been extinguished, even if I fought hard to reignite it in the months immediately following Muirfield. Though I missed the cut at the tournament right after the Open – the Benson & Hedges Open – I made a superb charge through the last two rounds the very next week at the Viyella PGA Championship. I'd been nine shots back after 36 holes, but came home with two strong rounds of 68 to take the trophy by three shots over Peter Oosterhuis. Through the rest of that summer and autumn, I played quite well and even brilliantly in spurts. I was fourth in the John Player Classic, second in the Dunlop Masters. Ironically, the best golf I played that autumn, indeed perhaps ever, came in the Piccadilly World Match-Play against none other than Lee Trevino. We met in the semi-final of a 36-hole match, and after not playing particularly well in the morning I was four down at the lunch break. I don't remember what I had for lunch, but whatever it was I ought to have eaten it every day for the rest of my life, because I came out that afternoon and applied a scorched-earth policy to the course. On the first nine, I strung together an eagle, five birdies and three pars for a seven-under 29 (there's that number again). From being four down to Lee I'd gone to one up. Lee birdied the 10th to draw level, I birdied the 11th to go back to one up,

Lee eagled the 12th to pull even again, and then we halved the next five holes. On the 36th hole of the match, the par-five 18th, Lee hit two brilliant shots to leave himself an 8-foot eagle putt and I chipped my third to leave a 7-footer for birdie. Lee missed, but sadly so did I. He tapped in his short birdie putt, to beat me, again.

Despite an afternoon round of 63, I was again forced to bow to Lee. At least this time he hit shots off the middle of the club to earn his win. And I had forced him to hit those shots, since I'd played so well myself.

This exceptional calibre of play was not so uncommon for me in the days and months after Muirfield. I was still capable of some magical golf. Not everyone goes round Wentworth in 63 at the Match Play. (Though, as at Muirfield, despite the overall quality of my play, it was a mistake at the death that cost me. I missed the final green with my three-wood, and then missed my 7-footer.) As with Muirfield, at Wentworth I was utterly convinced I was going to beat Lee, and I even looked upon the match as a way to gain a small measure of vindication. But Lee simply had something I didn't. Call it luck, call it fate, call it whatever you like, he had it and I didn't.

So, at the end of 1972 – the Year of the Mex – I stood back and took stock. From a family perspective, life was continuing to expand joyfully with Vivien and me and the fun we were having with our two boys just about every day. This family stability was so important to me after Muirfield. I was a more emotionally fragile person, full stop. But let's be clear on what I mean by that. I've always been a very emotional person in a positive sense – this was often how I performed to the heights I did. I think I used the term 'inspirational' earlier in the book to describe my style of play, meaning that when I was feeling the juice flowing through me I was a tiger, I was on fire to hit shots and make putts and compete and win and show the world what

I was made of. But every adrenalin-charged performer – whether it be an athlete, an opera singer, a stage actor, or even a CEO at an annual meeting – has an inverse to his or her public persona, an opposite side to the energy and charge of the public face. For me, after Muirfield, there was many a day and night when I was a wreck, when I wondered if I was going to be able to recapture that dynamism. I suppose the answer was no, since I never did win another Major, but my point is that I'd have been quite seriously depressed – even clinically depressed – if I hadn't had my wife and children there to help me work through it. Not so much to forget about it – because I have never forgotten it – but to help me put it in perspective. Which I badly needed at the time. Honestly, I don't know how players who have nothing but golf in their lives cope with the pressure and stress and the failure. Professional golf is a wolf that will eat its children unless you can protect against it happening. I had Viv protecting me. I always had Viv.

I suppose, from a playing standpoint, when I looked back at 1972 it was fairly easy to see the positives. I'd won on the US Tour at Jacksonville, had earned just over $110,000 and finished 32nd on the money list, no small feat given that I really only played half the year there. On the British Tour I'd won the Viyella PGA, earned a bit over £16,000 and finished second on the money list behind Oosty. Toss in a semi-final appearance in the Match Play, and my third at the Open, and one would have to say that it was a year of no little success.

But that was the surface interpretation. Despite my two wins, one on each Tour, it was Muirfield – Lee's chip-in and my three-putt – that defined the year. It was a fulcrum point. It changed me, and not for the better. When his chip hit the bottom of the cup, and my par putt did not, nothing was ever going to be the same again.

*

Through the middle part of the Seventies a criticism began to come up frequently, a criticism I sometimes heard not just from the tabloid Press (which I would have just ignored) but from commentators and even the odd fellow player. People began to say that I was losing the plot because success had gone to my head. They said I had stopped practising. Basically, people were saying I'd stopped working, that I was no longer committed, lazy, looking for easy marks and unwilling to make the sacrifices necessary to scale the heights required for victory in Majors.

This was and is such utter rubbish. I'm still offended by it. How can anyone besides me know how much I practised and how much I needed to practise in order to make the most of what I had inside me? How can anyone but the player know what he or she needs to do to draw the most out of their well? It's such a complex mix, the making of a player, and it's such simplistic nonsense to imply X number of buckets of balls equals Y level of success.

When I was a younger pro I practised incessantly. It was an obsession; I had to get it right, to crack the code. I started with nothing – old hickories, hacked-up balls, no lessons – and it was only through pure resolve and desire that I made it happen. I *made* it happen. It didn't fall in my lap. I was fascinated as a youth by the golf swing, by the mechanics of using my body to make the ball go where I wanted it to go in the way I wanted it to get there. It's the way with every driven youngster, I'm sure. You work and work and work, and then, one day, you realize that you actually can do these things you have set out to do. As I got older, through the late 1960s, I began to ease off practising so hard, not because I felt in any way smug about my game, but because I was *comfortable* with my game. It seemed to me it was just a matter of keeping the machine well oiled; when you've got a purring Ferrari you don't take it apart and put it back together every day – you simply look after it properly, make sure it's running the way it ought to, and then you let it do what it's meant to do.

Still, this didn't stop me from feeling guilty here and there about not practising more, particularly because so many of my colleagues would come in from a round and go straight to the range and bash balls, whereas I was more likely to head back to the hotel. I do remember at one point early in my time playing in America I became so self-conscious about not practising more that I began to go to the range and practise just for something to do, just to fit in. But I started playing worse, so I gave that up.

Every player needs to find that balance, the mix of what works best for them, both as golfers and as people. Vijay Singh has spent half his life beside a bucket of balls, whereas Carlos Franco wouldn't know what a bucket of balls looked like if you gave him a hundred dollars to go and find one. Everybody's different. Johnny Miller used to take considerable criticism because he once said he understood the subtleties and mechanics of his swing so well he could fix a problem just as easily sitting in an armchair and visualizing it as he could working through it on the range. Bobby Locke, the old master, tip of the hat and giving nothing away, was a genius in many realms, one of them being the ability to go to the range and hit half a dozen easy wedge shots, then stride to the first tee and proceed to win the Open.

There are distinctions to be made with the nature of practice, anyway. If you have unsound mechanics, practising is only going to reinforce those bad habits. Secondly, there is far too much emphasis on the long-game practice. Young players can hit bucket after bucket after bucket of balls, but the plain fact is that it's the short game that turns a good player into a great player. Tiger Woods hits the ball miles and can curve a shot any which way he wants, but he (not Mickelson) is the final authority around the greens and is also one of the deadliest putters to ever play the game. Simply cast your mind back to the 2005 Masters.

His long game was good, but not great. It was his short game, particularly his chipping and wedge play, that won him that tournament, capped off with his now-famous chip-in on 16. This is a bit of a misapprehension in my opinion, this focus on practising the long game, particularly in the last few decades. Even someone like Gary Player, renowned for his work ethic, made his living with his short game. He was forever hooking the ball all over the park, but it was his wedge and putter (and incredible determination) that bailed him out time after time.

Golf is a game of opposites in so many ways. We always hear from our parents and our teachers and our mentors that hard work is where it's at, that the people who work the hardest are the ones who will do the best. I'm not here to disagree with that; I want my kids to work for what they have, the same way I worked hard as a young man to achieve what I achieved. But golf is not like every other pursuit. It is not an open-and-shut case that those who work the hardest will have the greatest success. Even when you reach the pinnacle of achievement and become one of the world's better players, it is still a very personal thing. And some people don't need to work that hard at it. Many will work too hard and do more harm than good. Golf is not always about sweat equity. I think this is because the game is so much about the mental component once you reach a high level of mechanical proficiency. Once you have a solid game, and once you *know* you have a solid game, then it becomes a matter of figuring out what conditions are best for drawing scores from that game. That's all it is: what suits you best. People could say John Daly should practise more, give up smoking, give up drinking, give up marrying, start playing conservatively. Maybe. Maybe not. He's won an Open and a PGA. How many golfers are going to do that?

The point is that there is no direct correlation between the number of balls you hit and the scores you'll make. Hogan famously said that he dug it out of the dirt. That's all well and good for Hogan, but it might not be the case for everyone. Some people have games that need a tight rein and the whip, others know how to gallop without it. But I have never been a believer in the rule that says relentless practice is everything, particularly once you know your swing. I think you practise hard as you develop your swing. Once you know your swing you hit balls for the purpose of maintaining that swing. For the life of me, I don't understand the predominance the 'gurus' have on tour now. Especially since none of them are any good as players, certainly not at the professional level, anyway. I remember Lee Trevino's great line about the upsurge in teachers, 'Show me one of those guys that can beat me and then I'll listen.' It's the truth. Today there just might be too much information out there, especially for younger players who are more easily influenced than experienced players. Where did common sense go? Where did simple fundamentals go? Somebody once said to me that of all the senses common sense is the least common. It just might be the case out on the practice range. As I said earlier, teaching has become a money-making industry, and what it promises is, to me, largely fraudulent.

The truth is I don't really derive any actual pleasure from hitting the golf ball any more. If I play now with friends, as I do once or twice a week, and hit a pure drive, straight down the pipe, knock a 2-iron on the green, and leave myself a 15-foot putt for eagle, then that's all well and good, but that's what I'm *supposed* to do. I'm a professional. I've been there. I've done that a hundred thousand times. It's when the ball *doesn't* go where it's supposed to that my emotions are engaged, so to speak. Hitting the ball off the middle of the clubface is what's meant to happen, and when it does, well, then that's just the way things ought to work. Of course, all this is certainly affected by the knowledge that even if I stripe a driver and a 2-iron to 15 feet on a long par-five I will still be left with a putter in my hands.

I never really did play golf for fun, at least not once I got serious about it and knew that I had it in me to be one of the best. I played to be as good as I could be. It was something that I saw I could use as a way to express myself, to express my competitiveness, to use as a way out of my upbringing, to show the world who I was. And then once I learned how to do it, once I knew how to make the ball go where I wanted it to go, then it became simply about beating the other guy, about winning tournaments. I was never in it to be second. It was never about the inherent value of the golf shot, other than for the result it produced. I suppose it might have benefited me had I been different. It's hard to look into that crystal ball and see what might have been. I look at various players now, and it seems to my eye that Tiger Woods, for instance, has retained a genuine curiosity about golf shots and still seems to enjoy hitting the ball. It's about winning for him, but it's also about the strike, the shape, the flight. Good on him. But I wasn't like that, and there's no use pretending I was. It was about the competition, the achievement. There was never any of that mystical joy to the game for me in the way it's sometimes portrayed – you know, the dew on the ground, the first light, the clear air . . . If I want that I'll just go take the dog for a walk.

It's funny, Peter Thomson, who, as I've said, is one of the smartest people I have ever met, and is someone I will forever respect, once said that he never worked very hard at the game, either. 'It's a game,' he said. 'And you shouldn't work hard at a game to any degree.' But he played well for so long despite not working hard at it, despite not practising that much, because he loved the simple playing of the game. Sad to say, but once my putting finally went south for good, golf became virtually the only thing in my life that made me unhappy. And why do something that makes you unhappy?

I took a ridiculous amount of criticism – lazy, didn't practise, didn't care – once my game began to decline. But I knew my game. I knew my swing. Anyway, most of the criticism about being lazy or not practising was misplaced, since my problems never were about hitting the golf ball. I could always do that. It was putting that held me back, a sad fact during a time in the game when it was beginning to become clear that putting is really what golf is all about. It's even more the case now. Mike Weir won the Masters a few years ago and had 102 putts for the week. At Augusta! You'd have to be shanking it to not win with so few putts. The person who wins each week is always going to be the person who is having a great putting week. And sadly, as time wore on, most notably in the Seventies, the person having the great putting week was rarely me.

When I stop and look back at everything – and I mean *every-thing*; the Opens, the early success, the Ryder Cups, the Senior Tour, the barren Seventies, even my weekly game with my pals – the one thing of significance that always returns, like some cursed boomerang, is my putting woes. It was always a psychological factor, even when I had great weeks with the putter, which were significant *because* they weren't the norm.

Early in the 1973 season, it was apparent to me I was not the player I'd been the year before. The area most to blame, and which was most obvious to me if not always to the public, was the state of my putting. As I said, there was never an issue from tee to green. I could still strike the ball as well as anyone. But then I'd reach the green. My heart rate picked up. My breath became shorter. I felt a nervous tightness in my forearms. My fingertips simply didn't feel connected to my eyeballs – that strange, necessary link between sight and touch all great putters have. It had become mechanical for me on the greens, utterly without feel. There was no confidence, and now fear was starting to make itself felt.

My dreams started to wake me in the middle of the night. I'd hit a ball and it would end up in a kitchen sink and would be stuck in the plughole. Then I'd be in the sink myself trying to get the club back, but unable to because of the sides of the sink. I would be desperately trying to extract this ball from the plughole, always unsuccessfully, and I'd wake up rigid with frustration. In another dream, I putted and the ball went under a huge wardrobe, so I got down on my stomach with my putter and tried groping around under the wardrobe looking for the ball, trying to fish it out. I often had a dream where I was playing golf with three other fellows and we were teeing off. There were these large sliding aluminium doors in front of the tee, and when the other three teed off the doors were wide open. When it came my turn to hit they closed the doors so that there was the tiniest little slit to hit through, perhaps a foot wide. I'd be thinking, *Shit, how am I going to hit it through that gap?* In yet another dream, I would be trying to hit a full shot out on the course, but for some reason a wall was erected directly behind me and I couldn't take a full swing or generate any clubhead speed.

They were all terrible dreams, full of frustration, and forever lacking resolution, so that I always awoke feeling conflicted, incomplete, unable to draw any comfort from my night's sleep. It got so bad at times I was afraid to go to bed.

There was no doubt the pressure I felt from the public and Press in Britain didn't help. My sensitive nature meant I was very finely attuned to my environment, to what was going on around me. I knew anybody who had anything to do with British golf expected me to keep rolling along to bigger and better things, as if two Opens were just my warm-up. Not that everyone was so daft as to expect me to walk away with every Major, but more that it was assumed I'd be dominating the events on the European Tour (where I'd decided to concentrate my efforts beginning in 1973). When that didn't happen, when I played very well but didn't totally dominate (and let's remember, I *was* the leading money winner on the European Tour in 1973), I began to hear the same thing at every Press conference, from every fan, in every tabloid, on every TV and radio show: *What's wrong?*

From as early a day as I can remember, my natural inclination when pushed or challenged has always been the same: to push back even harder, to prove the naysayers wrong. It was that way with Shanko. It was that way starting out on the British Tour. It was that way when I decided to test myself in America. Every challenge someone threw out, every question raised, I tried to answer forcefully. And so, when everyone began to ask me, *What's wrong, what's the problem, why aren't you winning?* my response was to put my head down and press even harder.

Which I did. I chanted to myself, like a mantra, that my putting slump was only a phase, and that what would carry me out of it was going to be perseverance. Translation: *I'm not going to let this bloody thing beat me!* I tried every putting style I could find. I used every type of mental strengthening I could. And I kept on playing as much as I ever had. The result was that my putting deteriorated even further. What I should have done, of course, was take time off. It was exactly the same problem as after I'd won the Open. I ought to have taken some time to replenish the batteries, but pushed it too hard instead. Now I pressed too hard and played worse. This brought more questions, which made me press even harder. I said once in an interview that it got so bad at times I was actually afraid to go to the golf course because I had quite literally forgotten *how* to putt. That's no joke. You might think I'm just using a turn of phrase, but I'm telling you straight. I was so confused, beset by so much conflicting information wrapped in cocoons of emotional and psychological complexity, that I couldn't clear my mind enough to properly read a putt and then direct it holeward.

Sure, I made the odd putt, but pick your saying: *Even a blind squirrel finds a few nuts. A stopped watch is right twice a day.* You have to understand, even when I *made* a putt there was no confidence to be gained from it, because I simply had no idea why I was missing *or* making them.

I kept on because of this bullheaded determination, but also because I felt a true obligation to the fans and tournament organizers, and even to the European Tour, which was in its delicate infancy. I was often paid appearance money, and so I had to show up. But I began to play so badly that sponsors started to include a clause in my contracts stipulating that in the event I missed the cut, I would only be paid a partial fee. How could you blame them? I ought to rephrase that: it wasn't that I was playing so badly, so much as that I was scoring badly. This poor scoring was always circling back to one thing alone – my putting.

The odd thing is that to most fans who were just casual observers of the game – meaning the average fan who watched a few tournaments here and there, but particularly the Majors – it must have appeared from a historical perspective that I was a good putter. After all, I'd putted extremely well in winning at Lytham and at Hazeltine. But to close followers of the game, and especially close followers of my game, the wasting disease that was my putting confidence would have been plain to see.

Most fans simply do not understand the nature of the pressure, that constant hunger from the public and Press to reproduce brilliance. The pressure is probably impossible to convey, but let me try: Imagine that from your earliest years you direct every ounce of your emotional and physical energy towards one thing and one thing alone (with me it was winning the Open). Imagine that as you mature you actually begin to show signs that such a dream is within reach – this has the effect of only intensifying that desire, that hunger. It becomes all you think about. Then imagine that as a young adult you have success on the first of the steps towards that goal. Now it's not just dreaming, it's reality. The pressure moves to a whole new level, because now you start to know in your gut that if you *don't* get there, it might be because of a failing inside you; that the elements for attainment are now demonstrably there, and they simply await an application of intensity and hard work and perseverance. Next, envisage that the day comes when you reach this goal, when everything you've devoted the majority of your life towards actually comes to fruition. You win the Open! You win an Oscar! You win the Booker Prize! Whatever. You've made it. You have actually arrived at precisely that place you wanted to be.

But the next day, you're a bit off. For whatever reason. It doesn't matter what the reason is. You don't dispense the magic that you did the day before. Then you realize, in a hurry, that not only is the whole country watching you, but that they have actually invested a part of themselves into you and your magic, your success. This is a great honour, but at the same time it's a burden. You never asked to carry everyone's hopes and dreams. But you do. It's a very unhealthy psychological fact, but you start to understand that a great percentage of the sporting public actually live their lives through you, through replenishing their inner emotional lives with how you perform. Nick Hornby, in his wonderful book *Fever Pitch*, talked about this in some ways, about being a hopelessly addicted Arsenal fan, in that it became about so much more than simply appreciating a sport from an aesthetic level. I don't remember exactly how Hornby phrased it, but it struck me how he wrote about those times when it was physically painful to be a fan, whether Arsenal won or lost, because if the team won you couldn't possibly have real life match the intensity of the joy and if the team lost life was an empty wasteland until the next game and the next chance for redemption. Now *that* is over-invested. And it speaks to the other side, too, to what it was like to be a sports hero in Britain in the Seventies, to the scariness of having so much emotional hope placed on your shoulders

After Muirfield, it became clear, at least to me, that every time a member of the Press or public asked, 'What's wrong?', what they were really saying was, 'How could you do this to us? I believed in you. I put my trust in you. How could you do this to *me*?'

That is pressure.

I was eating my heart out over the whole thing, day and night. It was murdering me inside, and don't ever make the mistake of thinking I didn't care. I bloody well did care. I cared with everything I had. I would read these articles being published not just in the tabloids, but in the broadsheets too, saying the most awful things about me. That I didn't need the money any more (which wasn't true), that I had no hunger any more and didn't want it (which wasn't true), that I'd had the soft life too long now and could no longer make the sacrifices necessary to win (which wasn't true), that I didn't care any more (which was the absolute opposite of what I was feeling). In fact, I made decisions in those years based almost entirely on my caring too much, but I was roasted for those decisions, too. One such decision was to try and play on the US Tour again in 1975, when I was offered my US PGA Tour card back through being exempt for having won the US Open. I accepted, thinking that perhaps a return to the competitiveness of the US Tour would help. It didn't. (It was also the right year for me to try it, since I was actually unable to even enter Britain at the time. It all had to do with setting up residence in Jersey: if I'd returned to Britain, I would have been deemed a domiciled Briton returning home. This peculiar legal limbo caused me to miss the 1975 Open, in which Tom Watson beat Jack Newton.)

I was roundly criticized by many American pros for accepting something – my Tour card – they thought I didn't deserve to have handed to me, yet I was also slagged back home for leaving the European Tour, even if briefly. It didn't help my game, either. I won about $11,000 and finished 123rd on the money list. It was an unhappy experience in just about every way. I took the whole family with me. For fifteen weeks, we drove all over hell's half-acre in a station wagon, renting houses and apartments. It was unsettling, not just for me, but for the whole family, not least because we had just had Tina, who was born on 27 March in 1975. Poor little thing, dragging her around the world like that, and poor Vivien, having to look after a newborn, as well as two highly energetic little boys. Bradley was five and a half, and Warren was two and a half. Can you imagine the chaos? But it was a necessary evil, in that I had to find out if it would help me or not. So at that level it was a positive thing, but we were all relieved, I think, when I played so poorly we figured I might as well just go back and play poorly in Europe. At least then we could live at home. I did bounce back and forth a lot even up until 1978, but I knew I would never return to America to play full-time on the regular Tour.

Perhaps a more balanced person – or at least a person with a more stable relationship to money, a person less stubborn – would have handled the situation differently than I did when my game started to sour in 1973. I couldn't release my anger and tension on the course, because in golf that would only intensify the pain. I began to get depressed about it all, which doubled the scope of the problem. What I should have done, of course, was to just say, *Sod it all. I'm taking a few months off to let the pressure bleed away, and to hell with all the appearance money and endorsements and Mickey Mouse tournaments.*

But I didn't. I tried to play my way through it. Maybe Peter Thomson would have taken a break. Lee Trevino would have made a joke about it and laughed his way through it (although he's a much more serious person when out of the limelight). But players like Trevino back in my day, and someone like Fred Funk today – players who seem able to turn the pressure elsewhere – always somehow manage to make you think, and possibly make themselves think, that it's all just a game and that none of it is really of much consequence. I was never able to turn this trick. It was of *great* consequence to me whether or not I performed well. And the worse I performed the worse I felt about myself. The worse I felt about myself the more it affected my performance. The more my performance became a drag on my career and even on my legacy, such as it was, the less interest and enjoyment I derived from the game and from competing. It was a nasty emotional spiral, and it didn't take long for it to all go down. Especially since every single time I ventured out of the front door somebody was asking me what was wrong with me. If there *hadn't* been anything wrong, I'm sure I would have started to assume there was.

A big part of the problem, as mentioned, was that I'd become the fan favourite I had always hoped I would be. This attention was the proverbial double-edged sword. When I was on form, when birdies were the expectation and pars a disappointment, when I was in full flow and attacking the course with all the excitement I could find, then being a fan favourite was a huge advantage. I was always able to feel the collective will of the gallery; for whatever reason, I always had this sixth sense for what the crowd was thinking and feeling. And when I was charging around the course and the galleries were there with me, urging me on, getting as hyped up as I was, it only motivated me further. I wanted to do it for myself, but for them, too. And often I did get the job done. But every rainbow is connected to a storm cloud, and so it was with my ability to feel and interpret the mood of the crowd. When I struggled I could sense the anxiety seeping from the gallery. I could almost physically feel the tension gathering in their bodies, a tension which transferred itself to mine. Even worse, there were times I was able to pick up on a strain of hostility the frustrated fan inevitably projects at times – *I've been behind you all the way, Jacko, and now you're playing like a berk. You're making me look like an idiot for supporting you.*

What this brought about was, to be blunt, even lousier putting. The mood of the crowd never affected my ball-striking, at least to no significant degree. But from 1973 on (though I'd also had moments of confusion and anxiety for years before) I became a lost man on the greens, as hopelessly without direction as a Sahara explorer separated from his caravan in a sandstorm. Sure, I was holding the putter, but I had no idea what I was doing with it. In fact, there were times I would walk to tap the ball into the hole – after yet another miss – and I would realize I couldn't even remember hitting the approach putt. Had it been a 30-footer? A 50-footer? A 10-footer?

It was a complete lack of flow, a fatal absence of connection between mind and hand. It's all in the hands and fingers, putting. The best orchestral conductors don't consciously move their hands in mid-performance (*Okay, now here, then here, a finger there, a sweep of the palm just now . . .*) but rather intuitively allow the music in their heads to flow out of their fingertips into the baton and from there to the orchestra – they aren't even aware of what their hands and fingers and wrists and arms are doing; it's all instinctive. Practised, yes, but unconscious during the performance. The best putters see the line and speed, and make a stroke; they are not conscious of the mechanical action they are engaging in. I became the opposite. I became so focused on trying to find a mechanical solution that it paralysed my instinct. Which only made things worse. I tried looking away from the ball as I drew the putter head back. I tried turning my gaze away from the ball as the putter head made impact. I putted with my eyes closed. I tried putting left hand only, then right hand only. I tried to putt with my hands separated on the grip. I opened my stance, closed it, widened it, used thick grips, thin grips, and then in one moment of utter desperation a putter with no grip at all, just a metal shaft.

None of these seemed to work, surprise, surprise.

It got to the point where some days I was almost literally unable to draw the putter back. It took a singular act of willpower just to draw the blade back and make contact, let alone think about holing a putt. It was craziness, and it was eating me up, but just to show by way of example how even the people who loved me had no understanding of what I was going through, my dear old dad came to watch me in a tournament one week. It was not a good week on the greens, as was becoming the norm. We were driving back from the tournament after the last round, and he said to me, 'Tony, do you have any idea how much you're letting your fans down when you go and miss little putts like those ones you were missing?'

Oh shit, I thought. 'Dad, for Christ's sake,' I said. 'Do you honestly think I missed those on purpose? Don't you know I couldn't miss those with one hand and my eyes closed if it was just out playing a game with you and your pals? I'm trying so damn hard I can't move. Don't you understand that?'

He didn't. I don't think he ever did understand, even up to the day he died. He lived a couple of years into my senior career in the mid-Nineties, and I used to call him and chat with him pretty regularly, and he would come over and spend the winters with us. He used to say to me when I was on the Senior Tour, *Tony, I don't understand why you're not beating all these guys. You hit the ball so much better than them.* My dad never did have a real sense, I don't think, of the hell that playing tournaments quickly became once I couldn't putt. By the mid-Seventies I dreaded going to the golf course more than anything else (even though I still won occasionally, such as the Scandinavian Open in 1974). All I knew was that there was a hole with a flagstick in it at the end of every hole. People used to ask me – they still do – *What's your favourite golf course?* The answer? None of them: they all have greens at the end of every hole. And the only rule I now understood as central to golf is, *If you can't putt you can't play golf.*

This axiom is even more true today than it was thirty years ago. I grew up in an environment where ball-striking ruled. It was all about the swing, about being like Hogan, where the motion and the contact was the nut of it all. If you mastered that, they said you had mastered the game. It was all we thought about, all anybody thought about, really. And there were good reasons for this, beyond the obvious one that being a great ball-striker makes it a slightly easier game to play. But ball-striking was the key then because the greens were such rubbish in the Fifties and Sixties. Everybody missed putts (well, everybody except for Bobby Locke). But as time went on the greens became better and better. It's now reached the point in 2006 that golf is a masquerade. You watch it on the television and they show most of the long shots. Well, that's such bullshit. It's like covering a dinner party, and focusing on the *hors d'oeuvres*. That's not what it's about. The game is 60 per cent putting now, if not more. They can all hit it flush nowadays. *Everybody* hits it great. The unusual player nowadays is no longer the superb ball-striker, it's the person who *isn't*. The guy who hits sixteen greens in regulation . . . so what? If he doesn't cash them in, there's no benefit. Like I said before, Mike Weir wins the Masters with 102 putts. Christ, we used to take that many for three rounds and still be in the hunt.

The heavy irony associated with putting being such a focus is that if you're struggling on the greens it's like a slap in the face to be hitting it great tee to green. You hit a perfect tee ball, the perfect second shot in there with a 4-iron, and you're 5 feet from the cup. Well, there's no rule that says two shots out of the meat of the club means you deserve to make the putt and convert the birdie. Golf doesn't work like that. You have to shrug off the missed putt. But when you play round after round, week after week, year after year, where you are knocking the stick out of the hole and missing half a dozen putts a round under 10 feet, it wears on you at a deep emotional level. You lose your ability to care. It's simple: if you can't putt you can't play golf.

We're all different, but that's just the way I've always felt about these things. Let's face it, it's a bloody impossible game anyway. All we ever do when we play well is come close to doing what we do in our imaginations. We get as close as we can to not having the game make a fool of us. But at a certain point in my life – a point I was rapidly approaching in the mid-Seventies – I began to feel I'd had enough. The stress was eating me up. I wasn't sleeping. I was locking myself in the toilet after some rounds and literally crying my eyes out because I didn't know what was happening to me and I couldn't see a way out. Simply trying harder was not going to work. Everybody knows that often the harder you press, the worse you get. You can't play Major-winning golf simply through trying hard; it has to flow. Today you look at fellows like Retief Goosen and Ernie Els, and they're practically asleep on the surface. That can only help, because they are turning the pressure somewhere else, and good on them. But that wasn't something I had in me. And I wasn't the only one, I can assure you.

The pressure is always there, for everybody, and don't let anyone ever tell you any different. I often thought of Bobby Jones, for instance. Everybody says, *Oh, he quit at twenty-eight because he had nowhere else to go, he'd done it all, what was the point?* Fine, maybe that was part of it. But he used to get himself worked up into such a state of nervousness, it would eat at him. He was always getting mobbed, too, and that didn't help calm him down. They say he quit because he was getting sick and because he'd achieved everything he wanted to achieve. That's just the half of it, if it's even part of it. He didn't quit because he was getting sick. He quit because the game was *making* him sick.

And then there was Byron Nelson, quitting the game when he was, what, thirty-five? He went on and on about making enough money to buy that ranch and leave the game, just so he could be this gentleman rancher even though he was still a fantastic player. Don't believe it. He quit because he'd set such an impossible standard with his eleven wins in a row, and he knew in his heart that was the best he was ever going to be able to do. Every time after that he stepped on the course, he'd be measured against his best and would always be found wanting. What's the fun in that? He quit because his nerves got to him, and he knew in his heart he'd never reach that level again. I want you to understand that I'm not blaming him. Quite the opposite. If anybody knows the pain of going out there and putting up with all the hassle every single day, and not getting the satisfaction out of it, it's me. In fact, I only have the greatest respect for people like Jones and Nelson; for their golf, of course, but also for their ability to know themselves well enough to be able to say, *Enough is enough. I'm looking after me now.*

I ran into Tommy Bolt's wife in the Dallas airport seven or eight years ago, and we talked about this very issue. She told me she knew Byron Nelson's first wife quite well – the lady he was married to when he was most active on Tour – and that she told her she spent every night cleaning up Byron's puke in their motel room because of the state of nerves he wound himself into.

The bottom line on all this is, why would you keep doing something that makes you sick? I won the Open and US Open, and after that I was supposed to win everything with one hand

and the other tied behind my back. And living in Britain, there was nowhere else to go. I knew it. I battled on. I never, ever, stopped trying and had two or three close calls after that, but this syndrome of trying to prove to the world, and especially to the British public, that I was still there was making me sick and unhappy. Unless your ass is in the seat, you can't know what it's like. And there were people, especially throughout the troubling period of the middle and late Seventies, who would always be telling me, *Oh, Tony, just go out and play for fun. Don't take it seriously. People don't care. They just want to see you. Just don't care so much. It doesn't matter.* Well it bloody well did matter! It mattered to *me*. I couldn't pretend not to care. That's not who I am, which is why golf still makes me unhappy when I go out and hit it pure and shoot 73 or some bloody crap score because of my putting – because I *care*.

Without question, living in Britain was also part of the problem. There just wasn't anywhere to hide – a far cry from the way I might have felt living in America, where there's room to hide if you need it, where there's space and scope to accommodate all the names. Maybe this is one reason so many of the big stars from America were able to perform to the degree they did. I do know that Jack, for instance, seemed to have the ability both to try as hard as hell (in other words, he never tried to pretend he didn't care) and yet calmly to accommodate any amount of pressure. He could be really fiercely, consciously, working at it, but he also had this uncanny ability to cut himself off from the frenzy of it all. He was both a tornado and the calm at the centre of it. I could never get over the fact that Jack could sleep in on a Sunday of a Major when he was in the lead and had a late tee time. Me? Sure, I could sleep . . . until a bird farted outside, up a tree, down the street.

I think a huge part of it all was that I was mentally and emotionally spent. Vivien, ever the wise voice, made the suggestion I ought to have listened to, but didn't. *Just take a year off, Tony,* she said. *We'll survive, and then you'll come back fresh and excited to play with your mind clear.* I didn't listen. Even if it didn't cure the problem, it wouldn't have made it any worse, and I'd have got some rest out of the deal. I didn't pay attention the way I might have to that bit of advice, but thank God Vivien kept her head, her sanity, and her balance when I felt I was losing mine. I once said to someone that it was during these few years of my life that golf became a completely different thing to me from what it had been when I was growing up. Then, it had been a source of total fascination, a kind of puzzle I worked on every day, one that gave me constant challenge and pleasure. But by the time I was thirty years old, in 1974, the game was a source of mental anguish. Obviously, one has to avoid being overly dramatic about these things, because there must be thousands of people around the world every day who suffer genuine physical and emotional life-changing torment, and that must be respected. I've got perspective on that, trust me. But within my purview, in the world I knew and experienced every day, I was in hell.

14

Having self-awareness never made it any easier for me to step out of the door and go play golf. I didn't know what to do about all my problems. The only option I could come up with was to play a bit less, not out of any belief that it would bring about a 'cure', but only because it might help, in the way it might hurt less to jab yourself in the head with a fork five times than it does fifty times. It was agony, but at least there was less of it. Even so, there were still times when the embarrassment was almost too much. One of those awful moments came one year during the Madrid Open. I had a putt of no more than a foot – it might have been less – on the last hole, an uphill par-five overlooking the city. I addressed the putt and stroked it holeward, and somehow managed to hit it twice before it got there. My nerves were jangling like a teenage lover's. It was a one-foot putt! You could line up a one-foot putt and *try* to hit it twice and have trouble doing it. It's easier to make it than to hit it twice. I was a basket case.

I suffered in silence. I think probably only Vivien knew the level of agony I was going through, but it was difficult to explain it all to her since she wasn't a top-flight golfer. A writer once asked her about what it was like for her going through the pain of watching me struggle, and her response was typical of her – straightforward and honest. 'It's depressing to see it,' she said. 'I've often walked round a golf course and wanted to scream or cry, but that's part of loving someone and having a husband. Sometimes the comments on the course were upsetting – like, he's useless, he's choking – and I would try to shut myself off from them, but I might let them affect me and come off the course feeling quite uptight. He would come home and we would discuss it and try to help each other, but there was not much I could do, except talk about why it might happen. It was difficult to understand what was happening, because it's not a technical thing. I haven't any insight into it, as I haven't gone through it myself, and when it comes down to it I'm not the one who actually does it. But you're part of a person, and it is your business. I'm pretty easygoing, though I do get wound up at times. I hide my feelings. I've learned to bottle them up, cope with them.'

I think only someone who has been through that kind of pressure and survived it, or not, could really understand. I remember Jack once said to me that I only needed to hang in there, to keep fighting, and that I would pull out of it, because that's what he did. He fought through his dry patch around 1970, and eventually broke his bad luck by winning at St Andrews. This was all fine for Jack, but for him a dry spell was a different thing than for me. It wasn't so specific for him, meaning that it wasn't just one aspect of his game that had vanished, seemingly for ever, as had my putting. And it's one thing to lose something, but it's an added layer of heartache and pain when you have no idea why. This was maybe even more what kept me up at nights for years on end (which sleeping pills only ever partially helped with): it was the not knowing why. I could stand on the practice green and make good reads and decent strokes. It took me years to come to the realization that what was wrong might not have been my putting, per se. The putting woes were, I suspect, only the manifestation, the fallout, of the real problem, which was that I was simply no longer enjoying tournament golf. I was the jockey on an exhausted thoroughbred, whipping it, cajoling it, all to no avail. I realized somewhere in there how thoroughly miserable I was on the golf course. It was probably Vivien who first pointed this out to me, though it must have been obvious to most people, particularly the players I got paired with. I can imagine I was moaning and groaning all over the place every time I missed a putt or got a bad break.

I saw what I was on the way to becoming, and that was a bitter old man. Bitterness is a kind of virus in professional golf – you can easily become infected if you're predisposed to it. And once you've got it in you, it's very difficult to cure. The only way to really inoculate yourself against it is to recognize it early and take the appropriate steps; take time away, have someone help you get your priorities straight, try to interact more with the public and enjoy it rather than resent it, alter your expectations. What happens if you don't do these things is that the inherent unfairness of the game will consume you (and it feels exponentially more unfair if you're trying to make a living from it, believe me). I've seen it happen to so many pros. I saw it happening to myself.

There were so many things I got enjoyment from in life, and, as I said earlier, in the mid- to late Seventies it hit me in a flash that the only thing in my life – the one single thing – that made me unhappy was playing golf. There were so many other things that gave me pleasure and satisfaction – golf was not even on the radar screen in this respect. I took up working with wood, for instance. What satisfaction it gave me. It still does. I love wood. I love the feel of it under my hands, at the lathe. I love the look of it, whether it's a bowl I'm making or the panelling we've got up in our house. There's something so comforting about the warmth of wood. It's like when you get into some of those clubs, in Sunningdale or the R & A, you get this warmth that just seeps into your bones, the sense of the history and of all the people who've come before you. There's something that touches me really deeply about those environments, and I've always thought it had to do with the beauty and comfort of the wood that's gone into the making of those rooms. This was but one thing, one small thing, that was so much more enjoyable and comforting to me than playing golf.

But that's just me. Everybody is different. Someone like Arnold hasn't played a decent round of competitive golf in decades, but he doesn't care. Until just recently, he still went out and hacked it around, seemingly without any embarrassment at all. The television broadcast would show him making his one 8-footer per round so that they could pan a camera highlighting the crowd cheering wildly. They never showed the triple bogeys. I suppose the rationale was that he was 'rewarding' the loyalty of his Army, by sticking it out and still being there for them. Fair enough, but surely all they wanted was to see Arnold in person, not necessarily to see him play. Why not just show up at tournaments in a jacket and tie and shake hands and sign autographs if he wanted to pay them back for their support? It's a mystery to me. Same goes for Gary Player, who is still out there grimacing away, hectoring the youngsters (the 55-year-olds) about the value of doing three hundred sit-ups a day. Well, who cares? Not me. I can't imagine what pleasure anyone derives from watching an old fart wander around a golf course.

In any case, I didn't want to become a bitter and twisted person on the golf course, particularly since I was not yet thirty when this whole affliction gripped me. It was an affliction that *did* stay with me the rest of my playing career, though I took what back then might have been considered fairly radical steps. I actually tried Scientology in 1977, and although I didn't continue long with it (certainly not to the degree they wanted me to), it wasn't without value in that they focused on the positive and helped me understand I'd become wholly negative about the game. It was that same year I tried another form of psychology. I was playing in the Uniroyal tournament at Moor Park (in which Seve Ballesteros beat Nick Faldo – a lovely precursor of European strength to come; I finished joint third behind them), and I visited with my old Potters Bar pal Johnnie Rubens. He was always such a delight, so supportive, yet also practical and forever with an eye on progressing forward in one's life. He knew what I was going through, though even he admitted it was hard for him to truly sympathize because it was a pressure he couldn't possibly feel. He had just gone through his own time of enormous stress – he never really said what it was but I'm guessing it was business-related. He had gone to see a Harley Street therapist, a man specializing in hypnotherapy. Johnnie thought it might help me. I was so desperate I probably would have gone to see a man specializing in hippo-therapy if I thought it would help.

So I went. I told the psychologist my problems had gone way past just worrying about whether I'd make a putt or not; I strode onto every single green viewing it as a fresh and new opportunity to fail and make a fool of myself. I was in a state of pre-embarrassment walking on to each green. You could toss fear into the mix, because each mini-horror would be added to the next and the next and so on, all of which eventually were going to be gathered into my spectacular fall from the game altogether.

It gave him pause. First he tried to hypnotize me, but it didn't work, whether because I was just too strong-willed and resistant, or because it was all rubbish anyway, I don't know. I saw him for half an hour every day that week, and he would have me sit in one of his comfy chairs. In a calm voice he would ask me about the things that gave me pleasure, what did I enjoy doing besides golf? One day I told him that I always found cutting the grass fairly relaxing in a let-your-mind-drift kind of way.

'Well, then,' he said. 'Let's talk about that.'

He took me through the whole process of mowing the lawn: preparing the mower so that it was working correctly, starting out at one end, making my way in an orderly fashion around the lawn, creating a pleasing and thorough pattern, emptying the grass from the box, dumping it in a bag, sealing the bag, completing the job by doing the edging around the border and the shrubs and the trees, then, once the labour had been completed on such a hot summer's day, sitting out on the patio with a frosty lager admiring the work I'd done.

'Nice, isn't it?' he said.

'Mmm, yes, I suppose so,' I replied.

'Now, doesn't that give you satisfaction?' he said. 'What do you see when you look over that lawn?'

'Holes,' I said flatly. 'With flagsticks in them. And now I have to putt on that beautiful lawn I've just cut, and I'll miss, and I'll feel awful about it.'

I didn't see him again after that week, but I thanked him for trying.

There were others I spoke to about my putting travails, as well as my overall frame of mind about the game. Bob Toski once told me that he thought I was a wonderful putter, but that I just wasn't letting it happen. So I blocked out all my conscious thoughts about making putts, as best I could, and 'let it happen'. I finished third that week at Doral, but shortly thereafter I reverted back to being unable to let it happen. Ben Crenshaw told me he'd been watching me struggle for many years, and that his tip was to forget about making putts, but to just try to get them somewhere up near the hole, to focus on a 6-inch-wide pathway to the hole and direct the ball down that. It worked for a while, but I could never quite get my head around consciously trying to *not* make a putt.

When things were at their worst one year during this spell I approached Bobby Locke for advice, and he said, 'Put drop spin on the ball, Master.' I suppose he meant a couple of things by that, the first being that he did things at a very instinctual level, and second, that he perhaps consciously tried to impart some slight overspin or topspin on the ball so that it rolled itself out towards the hole without the drag of underspin. (Or maybe he'd had a few whiskies and didn't really know what he was going on about.)

One thing apparent to me was that most of the really great putters back then were people with less than spectacular long games. No surprise there, I suppose. People who grow up gifted with the ability to strike the ball cleanly and hit it where they are aiming are more likely to focus on that, because it gives them pleasure and satisfaction. They practise it more, and so get better at it. They practise putting less because they are involved in their long game. This was the case with me. Then there are those with spotty long games, people like Bobby Locke, Billy Casper, Jerry Barber, even Ben Crenshaw and Gary Player, who could be wild with the longer clubs; they were all great putters because they had to be. Otherwise, they would not have been professional golfers. Today, a player like Brad Faxon is a prime example of someone with a weak long game, who nevertheless excels almost solely due to his putting.

There are always those highly irritating exceptions, those people who seem to have it all. Ernie Els is a marvellous striker of the ball and a gorgeous putter. In my day, the only person who truly had both was Jack, but then he had everything else, too. Tiger is an interesting case, because everyone is forever talking about his power and the beauty of his swing and so on. Well, if you look at his game under a cold, hard light, he is a very much a streaky ball-striker. His mechanics are excellent, but his timing is spotty. When it's good, he is nearly unbeatable. When his timing is off, he is merely in contention. But the reason he's always at least in contention is that he is simply the best putter on the planet. You can take all the statistics and all the other information TV analysts and golf writers will throw at you about who leads the Tour in putting average, who makes the most putts, who is best from long range, who is best from short range, and you can toss all that out the window. Tiger contends nearly every time he plays because he makes an obscene amount of putts, and he does it not just on Thursday on the 1st hole but on Sunday on the 72nd, and everywhere else in between. He also possesses that brilliant short game, and he never allows his putting to let that short game down. In other words, you could put Tiger in pretty much the worst greenside predicament you could imagine, but he would still conjure up some magical way to get it within 6 or 8 feet. And then he makes the putt. *Every time.* This, I think, is the underappreciated genius of Tiger's game – how rarely he misses that 6-foot putt for par. It just doesn't seem to happen. The logical extension of this is that Tiger does miss a lot of greens in regulation. If he ever attained the ball-striking consistency of, say, a Kenny Perry he'd be virtually unbeatable.

All I know is that if I'd had Tiger putting for me in my heyday, I'd have won twelve tournaments a year; that's how good my ball-striking was, even during the years I was petrified to step on a green.

But step on greens I did. It was very hard for me to slow down, let alone to stop playing altogether. For one thing, I was simply too full of this notion that one must work one's way through trouble, that the only honourable solution to a problem is to plough through it. Retreat was not an option. Also, I felt

considerable pressure to keep playing and keep up a busy schedule because we were financially on a high-wire. Everything was
fine as long as I kept earning, but there was simply no way I'd
have been able to quit and take some time off. I faced all kinds
of obligations. Today, these elite players have millions in the
bank and they can afford to suit themselves. It wasn't like that
for me. It was all about chasing security, as it had been from the
start – a financial security I never, ever felt I had in my life. I
couldn't quit the way Nelson or Jones did. I couldn't take a year
off. I had obligations to sponsors, to my family, an obligation to
myself to make the most of this opportunity in life (even if it was
making me miserable). I was being squeezed at both ends, inter-
nally and externally, like I was caught in some ever-tightening
vice. I was employing people in Jersey, gardeners, butlers and the
like, and we were also helping out both my parents and Vivien's
parents. Taking a year off would have meant a hardship for both
sets of parents. Contributing to their well-being was an obligation I was happy to assume, but it was still an obligation.

There was a terrible family tragedy in these early years of the
Seventies that threw us all into a spin, and which changed our
living circumstances somewhat. Viv's parents had emigrated to
Melbourne in the late Sixties, trying to escape the Troubles in
Northern Ireland. They took her younger brother, Frank, with
them, but her older brother, Billy, stayed on. Anyway, in late
1969 I went to Melbourne to play in the Australian Dunlop and
I took my dad with me. We stayed with Viv's parents when we
there. They lived in the St Kilda district and we had a lovely time
with them. But while we were there we saw that young Frank,
who I'd got to know a bit when they still lived in Northern
Ireland, had turned religious. He'd become besotted with some
preacher or other. I don't even remember what faith it was, but
I do recall it was some wacky offshoot Church. In any event, it
turned out that he was manic-depressive. It was all very sad,

though they did get him on medication soon enough, so that he stabilized for a while. One day, however, he took his parents out for a drive. His dad, Viv's dad, had bought a car even though he didn't drive. One Sunday they were out for a family drive, the three of them, Viv's parents and Frank driving, when Frank stopped the car near a railway crossing, got out and just threw himself under a train right in front of his parents. This was in 1973.

I answered the phone when Viv's older brother, Billy, phoned to tell us. I hung up and went to Viv and said, 'Prepare yourself for a shock. Frank's dead.'

She collapsed straight away in my arms, out cold, so I put her on the bed and left her there for half an hour or so. It was an unbelievable shock. What a tragedy. Viv's parents were never comfortable in Melbourne after that. By the time they knew they could no longer stay in Melbourne we were living in Jersey. We had a house with a kind of archway to drive through, and on the other side of this archway was a little two-bedroom cottage. Jersey is notoriously tight about who can live there, so we had a whole song and dance to go through to make it happen, but finally they were given permission to move to Jersey. So they packed up and came to live with us. It was perfect: they got to see a lot more of their grandchildren, and whenever we were away it was like having a caretaker for the house, that added bit of security. They were lovely people, and we loved having them with us, which is why they also joined us when we went to Spain in 1983.

Yet another obligation I felt I had during this time was my growing sense of duty to the fledgling European Tour. You look at it now, and it's hard for people to understand it's only been thirty years since it was a piddling little sprat of a Tour, just an idea in the heads of a few dreamers. It's very recent history, is all I'm saying. And frankly, people like Mark McCormack and John

Jacobs needed me playing in Europe to make it viable. They knew it and I knew it, and that was okay. I understood, and I wanted to make it happen to the degree that I was able to be central to it. There was really only one key world player in the early and mid-1970s who supported the European Tour, and that was me. You often get a picture painted that it was Nick Faldo and Seve Ballesteros who really got the European Tour started, but they didn't really come along until 1976. I was there nearly full-time trying to get it going as early as 1973.

A heavy irony is that even this European commitment was detrimental to my putting; I can remember playing on greens in Germany in the early Seventies that were worse than most American fairways. But I thought I had a responsibility to Britain, to the European Tour, and so I played there, which was crazy when you stop and think about it, because Britain never really did anything for me except take my money with high taxes. Yes, it is true that I was paid many appearance fees to stay in Europe and play on that Tour, and that was something I greatly appreciated. I also felt it was appropriate. However, in another of those odd twists of fate, these appearance fees also became millstones around my neck. I knew I was being paid by people to produce a certain kind of golf, and when I didn't produce that level of golf I was racked with guilt. It was yet another thing contributing to my plummeting self-esteem. *Jesus, Tony,* I'd be saying to myself week after week, *you're taking these people's money because you're the main draw and yet you're struggling to break par. What the hell is wrong with you?*

Overall, it was a difficult time to be a sports personality living in the UK. Financially, I often felt conflicted; being so popular everybody wanted me for this, that, and the other. Open a store. Give a talk. Do an interview. It seemed as if everyone expected something for nothing. It was all about favours, and never about earning a living. Too soon I found myself doing a million things for people and not making a penny from it. I remember Michael Caine once said to Laurence Olivier that he had no choice but to go and make movies in America, because although he earned a knighthood and all kinds of accolades, Olivier never made a living working in Britain, or at least not the kind of living he ought to have been making. We don't talk about money in Britain, or we didn't back then, and so it was hard to say these things. But it was not easy to make a living in Britain, not easy at all – well, not a living anywhere near the same as my peers in America. This was the group I measured myself against. In every way. And I was starting to lose sight of them.

15

There were other financial issues that began to surface in this turbulent time of the middle to late 1970s. Mark and his group at IMG were getting me the odd contract, but I was hardly having to choose from too many suitors. One area they got me into ended up nearly being the financial death of me years later, and that was the whole Lloyd's of London fiasco. This was around 1979. IMG came to me and said that they thought it would be a good investment. The way the whole Lloyd's thing worked was that you showed a certain amount of worth, after which you could underwrite a greater amount than that in insurance. I suppose it was all part of Mark's plan to help me diversify my income, so that I had a few business deals here, a house or two, some investments such as Lloyd's. All fine on the surface, but it won't do a whole lot of good if the investments bankrupt you. IMG believed Lloyd's was a way to earn income without having to invest great amounts of my time. I confess it seemed reasonable then, since so many of the big-name British politicians and hierarchy had been in Lloyd's for years. The downside, as I was to find out, rather shockingly, was that they could come after you if things went sour. Yes, you could make the money, but the risk was that you were putting your name and your personal worth down as collateral in the 'unlikely' event of a significant setback. Perhaps that was in the fine print.

I never cashed a single bloody cheque. I was in it six years and I even had to sign a couple of cheques to cover things during that time. Finally, after six years, I'd had enough (and by that time, it was up to me to handle it myself, since I'd left IMG in 1983). There was no point in staying in it. The money I had in it was tied up doing nothing, and I wasn't earning a cent. I investigated getting out, and was duly informed that it would take three years to extricate myself and my money from Lloyd's – three years during which I was also accountable and responsible. By now it was into the late Eighties, and I still wasn't able to get out. Nor could I give it my full attention, either, because of the other ways in which my life completely unravelled and then got stitched back together again (which I'll come to soon enough). By the time the whole great mess got sorted out in the courts under the Thatcher government, the directors were held liable for the company's meltdown. I was told I could either fight it through the courts and possibly end up on the hook for £300,000, or pay restitution, immediately, of £100,000. There was no way I could afford £300,000 or even £100,000. I was hearing stories of bailiffs entering people's houses and literally taking the paintings off the walls. People were committing suicide over the whole thing. I ended up waiting too long and was on the hook for £300,000. I was out but was furious, disgusted, and frankly worried that it might seriously damage the new life for my family that I was trying to start. Naturally all the IMG people who had counselled me to get involved had moved on by then. There was no responsibility, no accountability.

There were other issues with IMG. In 1974, for instance, I went down to South America on an IMG exhibition tour. It seemed exotic and interesting, though of course one still wanted to be properly compensated. The arrangement was to go and play matches in Chile, Colombia, Venezuela, Argentina, and so on. The compensation was to be $4,000 a match and all expenses for the family were paid for. My first reaction was, Is that it? And they said, Yes, that's what it was for the five tournaments. A total of $20,000 plus expenses. I said fine, and off we went.

There were some other top-name golfers on this tour, most notably Tom Weiskopf, who, as mentioned earlier, was a good friend of mine at the time. That was certainly part of the attraction in making the trip, since Vivien and I enjoyed the company of Tom and Jeannie. Lee Trevino was there, as well, and that was okay despite my certainty that, like a toreador to a flagging bull, Lee would find yet another way to stick a sword into me as I passed him. We were sitting at dinner one night with the Weiskopfs, somewhere in Argentina it might have been, and since we were friends we did occasionally talk money. I asked Tom how much these folks were paying him. It was the first of the five legs of the tour.

'Thirty-five thousand,' he said, matter-of-factly.

Really? I thought. Thirty-five to my twenty. But then came the real kicker.

'Yeah,' he continued. 'But I'm just playing this one and the last one, and I'll get thirty-five thousand for that one, too.'

Lee was with us for dinner that night, and he informed us that he was getting the same compensation – thirty-five thousand per event. Now I'm thinking, I've won two Majors and Weiskopf's won one. Okay, I was never going to win the Nobel Prize in mathematics, but to me those numbers weren't computing. When I said something to IMG about it, their reply was simply that it was what they could get for me, because there was a 'European budget' and a 'US budget' to pay players with. Please. Did they expect me to simply accept that? I won the fourth tournament in Caracas, and following that gave them a less than cordial goodbye, skipping the fifth tournament altogether. I took the family to Barbados for a holiday instead. IMG were less than impressed, but so what? In the end, what could I do but add it to the list of things telling me I was not respected or valued by IMG the way I wished I had been? I was practically sweating blood trying to work myself out of a horrific slump; I don't think IMG was working quite that hard to ease my worries about my family's security.

Throughout this decade of despair, there was at least one constant in my golfing life, a constant that was not without pain but which at least had a few moments of camaraderie and intrigue and even insight, perhaps because it was a team event. I'm talking about the Ryder Cup teams that I was part of on every second year of the entire decade. In a way, probably because the British team was always expected to lose and always did, there was less pressure on me than in individual events. I didn't suffer quite the same anxieties I did in normal tournament play. Consequently, I didn't play too badly in the Ryder Cup throughout the seventies. This is not to say that I enjoyed them all; that would be incorrect. Nineteen seventy-seven was a very difficult tournament, even though we hosted the Americans at the course where I'd had so much success – Royal Lytham. The outcome in the end was not great – a 12½ to 7½ defeat – but it was the personal issues that upset me.

Our captain that year was Brian Huggett, a European Tour player who had never really done much outside of Europe, or in Europe for that matter. Still, he was a decent enough player, and in fact he was having an acceptable year in 1977. Yet he put himself forward as wanting to be Ryder Cup captain, and you could tell he was almost desperate to get it. I didn't understand it myself. Why wouldn't he want to play? He was still good enough, in my estimation, to be playing and God knows we needed the help. So, when it came time to pick the captain, based on the voting of the PGA Committee, of which I was a member, I voted against him and voted instead for John Jacobs, primarily because I thought Huggett should be playing. However, he'd obviously done the correct amount of lobbying beforehand, because he was elected as captain, and that was that.

When it came down to it, I thought he did a very poor job. These were things I must have subconsciously taken note of, because six years later I did things very differently as captain. To begin with, not once did Brian talk to the players about any of the pairings. How daft is that? Why on earth would you not talk to the players themselves and find out who they like, who they gel with, whose game they feel suits their own? As far as I could tell, he just sat in his hotel room and came up with the pairings on his own. Perhaps he put all the names into a hat, and just paired people as he pulled them out. I have no idea. There seemed little rhyme or reason to it to me. I was learning lessons all along on the kinds of things it takes to be a good Ryder Cup captain, though as often as not these were lessons of the negative variety: learning what *not* to do!

Huggett paired me with Eamonn Darcy the first day, which was okay, but the fact is that Eamonn and I are very dissimilar people. There was no problem between us, but no particular rapport or relationship either. Even players who had an obvious rapport, and who had proven effective in the past as a pairing – partnerships like Brian Barnes and Bernard Gallacher – Huggett chose to separate. What was the logic there?

My befuddlement with Brian's captaincy techniques turned to irritation the next day, a heavy, cold day. He paired Eamonn and me together again. This resulted in us losing badly to Dave Stockton and Dave Hill (and to be fair, I didn't play very well). But afterwards we made our way to the clubhouse for some lunch. After a bite, we tossed on our rain gear and wandered back out to watch Mark James and Ken Brown come in. We caught up with their match at the 17th hole, and stood where their drives had ended up, though we were off to the side, near the gallery. Some of the other members of our team were with us. Huggett came over to us in his buggy and said, pretty much straight to me, 'Where have you been, practising?' I told him that Eamonn and I had not been practising, but had finished our match, then gone in for a bite, since it was already late in the afternoon and neither of us had had anything to eat since breakfast. There might have been a hundred people standing within hearing distance of us as Brian shouted out, 'You should have been out supporting these lads!'

'What the hell do you think we're doing right now?' I shot back. 'We've just walked all the way out here from the clubhouse, and we certainly can't play for these guys.' He was way out of line, and I wanted to tell him so, but I knew it was the wrong place for it – something that apparently hadn't occurred to him. I hauled him off to the other side of the fairway and told him straight off that I didn't give a damn what his opinion was, and that there was no way he ought to have spoken to me like that in front of the public. It was unprofessional and rude, and it certainly didn't bolster team morale.

After the matches ended for the day I went back to my room to relax and have a hot shower. About thirty minutes later the phone rang. It was Huggett informing me I'd been dropped from the team for the singles matches the following day. He said he was 'sorry' to have to inform me of this decision.

'No need to be sorry,' I said, and hung up the phone.

It was personal and spiteful, and I was never able to forget it (though we did bury the hatchet to some degree years later). Peter Oosterhuis said publicly he thought Huggett was making a major mistake. Eric Brown talked to me about it. But no one else really said much, and the whole week left me with a very sour impression of what it meant to be a Briton at the Ryder Cup. Huggett played people like Ken Brown and Mark James ahead of me that final day. Brown had never won an event in his life, and James had the honour of holding a single title – the Lusaka Open from Zambia. A couple of months later a writer ran into Oosterhuis in the US and asked him again about Huggett's mean-spirited decision. 'Ludicrous,' said Oosty. 'Tony won the Open on that course. Whatever happened, however he was playing, it was the captain's duty to have Tony play.'

If 1977 was difficult to swallow, it was small beer compared to the antics of Mark James and Ken Brown in the 1979 Cup. The matches that year were held at the Greenbrier in White Sulphur Springs, West Virginia. We lost 17–11, and this was no huge surprise, I suppose, given the recent history we'd experienced. It was disappointing and even somewhat surprising to me, however, since 1979 was the first year we added Continental Europeans to the team. This was an electrifying move in my opinion, adding a buzz of excitement and anticipation to the event. It was a move I'd championed and had been behind from the start. The addition of Seve Ballesteros alone was reason enough to get excited. What a man he was! What a player! There have been few players in the history of the game with charisma and talent in equally massive doses. Seve was one of them. Not that he played perfectly that week. I think he was a bit nervous, and it showed at times. He was barely out of his teens, after all; I think he'd turned twenty that spring. He had a losing record, but it was just a tune-up for him, a prologue to his Ryder Cup heroics in the decade and a half that followed. Neither was it a satisfying a week personally. I ended the week with a 1 and 3 record.

But the real significance of that week for me was again of a personal variety, and again of a negative brand. Mark James and Ken Brown behaved so abominably, in my view, in West Virginia that I've never since been able to talk about it without shaking my head and feeling my blood pressure rise. They didn't show up for team meetings. They wore the wrong uniforms. They didn't stand for the national anthems. They refused to help their partners look for balls in the alternate shot format if they happened to hit it in the trees. A cameraman would come round with film rolling to take the kind of footage we'd all had taken hundreds of times in our lives, and both of them would hold magazines or napkins in front of their faces so that the cameraman couldn't do his job. James signed the menu at one team dinner, and then was told the menu was for a local priest. He asked for the menu back and added 'son of a bitch' after his name. Ha ha.

It was a pretty disgraceful performance, I thought, and since they are both intelligent fellows it could only be that they acted this way based on a conscious decision to do so. It was not simply accidental or inattentive or a failure to recognize certain protocols.

John Jacobs was team captain that year, and my feeling was that he was too soft on them. If I'd been captain that year I would have packed them on to the next plane, and said, *Get the hell out of here, and I never want to see either of you again!* You can't operate a team with members acting like that. We had ten other guys trying their hearts out, men who cared, and who managed to act like grown-ups. Then there were these two buffoons undermining every one of us. It got so bad at one point that Vivien and Bernard Gallacher's wife actually confronted Mark James outside the dining room one night and said to him, *Just what the hell do you two think you're up to?* That's how bad it got. It didn't go unnoticed, to be sure, and in the end the European PGA levied the largest fine to date against them afterwards. They deserved it.

*

There were so many things about the 1970s that I look back on now and see how representative they were of my general state of mind, which was a kind of brooding frustration, a confusion, a wandering around searching for answers.

There were my issues with Dunlop, for example. I was under contract to use their clubs and advise them on a Tony Jacklin model. I went to the factory and inspected the model destined to have my name on them. They were hideous red, white and blue things, and I instantly told them they needed to be changed. Even the shape of the head was all wrong. They took note of everything I said, took pictures of me with all the staff, said all the right things, and then some months later the clubs came out exactly the opposite of what I'd advised them to do. I was furious, particularly because all the suggestions I'd given them about what I wanted on the clubs with my name on them had been used to create a separate line of clubs *without* my name on them! I immediately instructed Mark McCormack to call Dunlop and have every single club with my name on it withdrawn from the market. No little turmoil resulted. Soon after I got a letter from Dunlop asking me to not interfere in their work in the future. This whole imbroglio started a pattern of many years where I went back and forth between Ping clubs and Dunlop clubs.

There was also so much running around all over the world, doing corporate days, playing in tournaments where I received appearance fees, doing exhibitions in places like Japan, where I happened to be quite popular. I was also constantly buying and selling cars, never seeming happy with one or the other (though some of them were fantastic cars).

And why did I do all these things, why was I constantly chasing my own tail? Maybe I was running away from my putter. Perhaps it was that search for security I had always been on, a quest for the peace and contentment I thought being wealthy would give me. I have no definitive answer to that question.

Perhaps it was a combination of all of them. It's funny, I remember telling a writer quite some time ago (I think it was in 1979) that I was going to start being more careful with my money, try to protect what I had. I said in this interview that if I thought that after everything I'd done up to that point in my life – with all the worry, the anxiety, the endless practice, the relentless travel, and all the other sacrifices of the previous ten or fifteen years – there was to be nothing to show for it at the end, except for memories, then I would die. Perhaps a bit melodramatic, but I was being honest. It was the most awful feeling to consider it as a real possibility; it would be just like starting all over again. But then it hit me. 'Oh my God!' I said, 'maybe that's what I need.'

Perhaps that *was* what I needed, to go back to the beginning and start over, at least metaphorically. After the despair of 1979, I would have given anything to recapture that feeling, that surging sense of excitement and possibility, that I'd had ten years before. I was at one of the lowest points in my life as the decade closed. I was always good at putting on a brave face, at making people think things were fine. Yet the reality inside was radically different from the public façade I tried to maintain. My putting was abysmal, which meant golf was abysmal. We were not financially settled. Inside, in my soul of souls, I was struggling to know who I was and what the hell I was supposed to do with the rest of my life, even though I was only thirty-five.

My life has always been about living fully day to day, trying to make sure that no matter what I do I do it with passion and conviction. It was always about the passion I brought to life. It had been an amazing and improbable journey to that point for Viv and me, but there was no doubt I had stalled out. I knew it. She knew it. Because playing the game of golf was making me so unhappy, I was simply unable to pour my enthusiasm and being into it. I was a man of passion with no professional outlet for that passion, a professional golfer who hated playing golf. The fatigue of treading water was overwhelming me, so much so that I was starting to sink. As the new decade began, I could hardly have said the Eighties were looking bright and shiny in their possibility. I needed something in my life to inspire me, to motivate me, to give me new lifeblood. I knew I needed something, but I had no idea what it was or where it was going to come from.

The answer wasn't far away.

16

The thing I hope people understand, perhaps more than any-thing else, is that deep down I'm a very sensitive person. I don't just mean expressive or perceptive, able to reach my emotional side if I need to – those things you can take as a given. What I mean is that I filter life and experience primarily through my feelings. It's always first and foremost about how I *feel* about something, that initial emotion, even intuition. That's really just our subconscious, though, isn't it? It's gut instinct, the sub-conscious, intuition, trusting your inner voice, your emotional core. I have absolutely no doubt that our subconscious, or whatever you want to call that central place deep inside of us, tells us everything we need to know about people and situa-tions within moments of our first encounter: the first ten seconds after we meet someone, the first ten seconds after we're in a spot that is going to need a decision down the road. Deep, deep down we just *know* what we're supposed to do. Our subconscious has done the sums. It's that simple. After that, it's a matter of our conscious selves paying proper atten-tion, listening, acting upon what we already know inside. I'm sure we've all come to a point with someone or something, and said, 'You know, there was something not quite right about that guy from the start.' Or, 'I'm not surprised she went on and made a huge success of herself, I could see it the first time we met.'

I have always felt things deeply and with intensity, and have always been open about it. It's who I am. Nor would I wish to be different – not for a moment. I don't mind admitting I'm the type of person that cries at movies I love, or who feels a lump in my throat when I hear a song lyric that moves me. You get what you're dealt. I think it came from various parts of my family. My granddad was tough as old boots, that boy, but he wasn't without emotion. We used to go on visits and he was always watery-eyed when we left. I always noticed it. I think singing had something to do with my development as a romantic sort, too. My mum, as I mentioned earlier, was a great singer, but even when we went on car trips the lot of us – Mum, Dad, my sister Lynn and me – would be singing away in the car. *When you are in love it's the loveliest night of the year.* We loved the lyrics, and I always paid close attention to the lyrics, especially the ones that were more sensitive or had some romance in them. I couldn't help it. I just loved them, and still do. In fact, in 1971 I cut an album – *Tony Jacklin Swings.* The highlight was my rendition of 'Come Fly With Me'. I thought it was pretty damn good, if you're asking for my thoroughly unbiased critical opinion. But it was always about the lyrics for me. That's where the meaning, the feeling, is. *On the big night, on the last night, we had the big thing.*

I could go on and on. I must have the lyrics to two hundred songs etched into my brain. Practically every Elvis song. Sinatra's stuff. Half the songs the great Jerome Kern wrote. I loved them all, and always seemed to get into the emotional angle of the song through the lyrics and through thinking about them and what they meant, how they made me feel. It spirits you away, and was the sort of thing dreams are made of, or my dreams, anyway. It was in so many song lyrics that I found a belief within me that I could be raised up and out of my circumstances. It was all emotion, is what it was. I am easily moved, especially by romance and inspirational stories (which, sadly, is why I have always been so genuinely upset when people turned out bad or not what they seemed – because I was so ready to believe in the best of what they offered and never wanted to believe the worst). To be brutally honest, this aspect of my nature probably hindered me in my golfing life, as a player, at least in terms of having a career with some longevity to it. There's no rule that says that emotion will help you in golf. When things are going well, it's all passion and glory and everything right with the world; when they're not and you wear your heart on your sleeve, well, it can be a very painful game in a very public way.

In the early 1980s, I was beginning to flounder. No sense denying it. I'm not trying to make excuses for anything. I've never done that with any aspect of my life and never will. But I was at a very frustrating and even depressing stage of my life. I was only thirty-eight when I quit playing tournament golf in 1983. I just couldn't do it any more. But I *am* a golfer. Golf has defined my life in so many ways (though as I said earlier I've always viewed my life as less about golf than the incredible experiences and the emotional voyage I've been allowed to have on this earth). But in the early Eighties I was lost, in a very real way. What the hell was I supposed to do with my life? Thirty-eight is not that old. Especially when the one thing you are expected to earn most of your living from is precisely the one thing, the only bloody thing, that makes you unhappy. It was an impossible situation, and I can tell you there were many gloomy days and sleepless nights.

But my nature saved me. It was soon to be the very thing that transformed the Eighties from what looked to be a long trudge through an empty desert into some of the most fulfilling experiences of my life.

Okay, you know that I'm talking about the Ryder Cup. But what I need to do before really getting into the Ryder Cup captaincy years is to fully dissect what went on with the European Tour, with its formation and leadership. These things are central, I think, to understanding what went on with the Ryder Cup and even with the European Tour in the Eighties and since. In fact, it's central to everything I feel about European golf, where it's been, where it's going, and the part I played in that. It's not an entirely happy story, I'm afraid.

The European Tour is a calamity, or at least it was for decades. Now that it's under new management, as of 2005, perhaps there's hope for a renaissance. I'm not passing judgement on people in particular, at least not those currently running the show. It's important to me that you understand this. In fact, George O'Grady, who took over from Ken Schofield as Executive Director, is a first-rate guy. I respect George. He's smart, he's committed and he damn well should have been the one running the Tour a decade ago. He is the hope for the renaissance I was talking about. Anyway, what I feel I need to say about the Tour and its formation, and the way it went about its business roughly from its inception in 1971 to when George took over on the 1st of January 2005, is something I'd want viewed in an historical sense only. I wish the Tour well from here on in, and would love to see it grow and be successful . . . but if it happens it's going to be without any involvement from me. I'm done with it.

It's not for me to make personal judgements about whether someone is a good man or bad man. But I can have an opinion on whether they are good at their job, and in my opinion, as someone supposed to be the very face of the European Tour around the world, Ken Schofield wasn't good at his job. It's an opinion. Sure, as the saying goes, opinions are like arseholes; everybody's got one. But my opinion is an informed one, and I do not think that the European Tour benefited over the course of thirty years from having Ken Schofield as its Executive Director.

He started out as an office boy, essentially. John Jacobs had been appointed the Tournament Director-General of the PGA on 10 January 1971, and it was that date that marked the official birth of the European Tour. I think John Bywaters was the Secretary, George Simms did the Press & PR, Arthur Crawley-Bovey was Tournament Director. Anyway, Ken was in there somewhere doing something with George Simms in the Press Office, and by 1975 he got himself appointed as Executive Director. He retired at the end of 2004. Thirty years he had that job. Incredible.

I suppose the root of my issue with Ken is that I don't think he represented the Tour as professionally as I thought he should have. It may be hard to understand some of these comments, if you are someone who has kept up with the golf world and events off the course. For instance, it was Ken who gave a speech on my behalf at the World Golf Hall of Fame induction in 2002 (the year I was also made an Honorary Member of the R & A). *What?* you might say. *Why on earth are you slagging off the guy that spoke for you at such a huge event?* Well, the fact is that I never did ask him to do it. The Hall of Fame people asked me if I had anyone in mind to speak, and I said, Well, no, not really. My dad was dead. I don't like to ask other people for that kind of favour (for instance, I just never would have imposed on someone like Sean Connery to do it, even though we've long been friends). And so when the Hall of Fame staff said, *Well, Ken Schofield is going to be around anyway, and he certainly is familiar with your career, he could do it,* I said, Okay, why not?

The whole Hall of Fame thing leaves me with a slightly bad taste in my mouth, to be honest. I don't mean being associated with it or going to visit it – I'm delighted with the fact that I'm in there, and I really think it's a place that's going to come into its own. But it still feels slightly tainted for me, from a European perspective, because it was difficult for me to understand on what criteria other players were inducted before me; players who'd never won a Major, for example, or who didn't even seem especially interested in being inducted.

Another reason I'm unhappy with the way Ken ran the Tour is that it isn't nearly the financial power it ought to be. Sure, the prize money has grown in the past thirty years, but that's just going to happen over time, isn't it? How could it not? You only have to compare the way the PGA Tour has grown and prospered, compared with the European Tour, to know that the European Tour wasn't run anywhere close to the same level in terms of business acumen. It doesn't take a rocket scientist to figure it out. I'm not an economist, but it seemed to me the Tour was run as a kind of private playground for decades, all while the players who *were* the European Tour didn't make nearly the living, or the retirement pension, that players on the PGA Tour made. It's like Tim Finchem said when he took over from Deane Beman (who was a genius in the way he ran the PGA Tour): 'I was handed the keys to a Mercedes, and all I've had to do is keep my foot on the gas.' Schofield handed O'Grady a bloody Lada as far as I'm concerned.

It would be the polite thing to say, *Oh, yes, this was unfortunate, but I'm not bitter or angry or hurt about it.* But that would be a lie. I *am* bitter and hurt by what happened with the European Tour, and I'll talk more later about how things finally came to a breaking point in 2000, the point where I decided I just couldn't have anything more to do with them.

I've said in this book that passion is what I'm all about, that living with a combination of vitality and integrity is what has always fuelled me. I think it's safe to say that my passion and sense of integrity were activated by the way the European Tour went about its business. Perhaps it's more accurate to say these characteristics of mine weren't activated, so much as they were antagonized.

The circumstances around the 1981 Ryder Cup instilled in my mind deep suspicions about the way the Tour was managed. The 1979 Cup had been such a fiasco, in my book, with Mark James and Ken Brown and their antics. When the time came for the team to be chosen for the 1981 team, John Jacobs was captain again. After the qualifying period had ended Mark James stood twelfth in the points standings and I was thirteenth. Neither one of us was an automatic pick. I'd played in seven straight Cups, but Jacobs picked James ahead of me. I was stunned. No – worse than stunned. I was disgusted. Granted, my game wasn't on top of the world any more, but I was hardly casting about struggling to win the Jersey Net Amateur. (By the way, whatever I think of Mark James I have to make it perfectly clear that I have always had the utmost respect for his game. The man is a tenacious competitor and he can play golf, flat out.)

So, I didn't get chosen. They asked me if I would still attend the matches – you know, wear a blazer, shake hands, represent everything good about European golf. You can imagine the answer I gave them. But that wasn't the only crime committed that year, in my book. Don't forget, it was to be the second instalment of the Ryder Cup featuring European players, not just players from the UK. A three-man committee – comprised of John Jacobs, Neil Coles and Bernhard Langer – got together behind closed doors prior to announcing the team selection and decided to ban Seve Ballesteros from competing.

What were these men thinking? I have no clue. I remember

being almost literally lost for words when I heard their decision. Upon recovering, the first words I was able to speak wouldn't be suitable for family listening, I can tell you. I think the reason they gave had something to do with Seve accepting appearance money for playing in certain events, and there seemed to be some discrepancy as to whether this disqualified him or not. It was nonsense of the first degree.

I suppose it's only right to mention that I was, early on, one of the first on the European Tour to accept appearance money. IMG negotiated these fees. I mentioned them earlier, how they actually became a millstone around my neck. But it was just something the European Tour had to ante up for. I was playing golf in America, Australia, all over the world, and if they wanted me to play in the Swedish Open or the German, an appearance fee was simply the reality. Particularly since for much of the early and mid-Seventies I was the only world player to play regularly on the European Tour. But let's be clear: I was playing in Europe because I *wanted* to play in Europe. It was where I wanted to be. I wanted to support the start of the European Tour. I was very explicit about that.

The world has changed now, however. The money is so big everywhere that I think it's a huge mistake for the European Tour to have kept on paying out appearance fees, which they must feel they had to over the years for players like Seve, Faldo, Langer, Olazabal, and on to Woosnam, Monty, Clarke and Westwood. It's a mistake. I think nowadays the European Tour would still command a lion's share of the European players, just because the players like playing near home. It's that simple. It's easier, it's where the kids are in school, it's where their wives are happier. You don't need the appearance money to that degree any more, because the tournament prizes are big everywhere. I mean, look at the PGA Tour. You sure as hell don't have appearance fees there.

But as for their decision to ban Seve, I thought, *God help us*. We had at our disposal in Seve not just the top player in Europe, but possibly the best player in the world. He was pure magic. Not only did brilliance flow out of every single move he made, but it rubbed off on everyone else, too. What an unforgivable decision, and to this day I still don't quite know how it was arrived at. I think Jacobs wanted him, but Coles didn't. I certainly don't attach much blame to Bernhard for it, and Seve never did, either. But I was livid and mystified. Seve, of course, was deeply insulted, even hurt.

The boys on that team got their heads handed to them on a platter. It was a low point in European Ryder Cup history.

In April 1983 I was on the practice range at the Moortown Golf Club, hitting a few balls even though I was attending the tournament as a commentator for the BBC. Ken Schofield and Colin Snape, who was then the Secretary of the British PGA, approached me. They said hello. We chatted about this and that for a few minutes, before they got down to why they'd come over.

'Tony,' said Ken. 'The boys on the committee have asked us to come and ask you if you'd like to be the Ryder Cup captain this year.'

'Excuse me?' I said. 'What?'

'The Ryder Cup,' he said. 'Do you want to be captain?'

You could have knocked me over with a feather. I was done with the Ryder Cup, done with 'the boys' on the committee. I wanted nothing to do with any of them. My first reaction, my gut reaction, was to tell them to go to hell. Worse language may have even come to mind. But I bit my tongue.

'You're going to have to let me think about that,' I said.

They wandered off, and I went and did what I had to do that day with my commentary work, then I left the course to think about it. I was staying with good friends of mine, Marshall and Carol Bellow in Leeds. They lived just around the corner from Moortown. I talked about it with them, and I thought long and hard, first, as to what could be gained from it, and second, why in the hell would they ask me to do it?

I came to the conclusion that night that there was a lot to be gained. The Ryder Cup, representing my country and continent, was something I always had a passion for, even when I was pissed off at the people running the show. And so part of me knew instantly, almost instinctively, that this was a chance to maybe get things right. In my opinion, we'd been second class to the Americans far too long, and I don't just mean because we were always losing. The entire manner in which our side operated and in which our players were treated was, to use the American phrase, bush league. And I thought I had some pretty solid ideas on how to go about changing that.

The second part of the equation – why me? – was mystifying at first, but the more I thought about it, the more I came to the conclusion that they probably just didn't have many other options. All the other players were too young; I was the only one around who was the right age with the right credentials. Seve was still in the early stages of his career, as was Faldo. Players like Christy O'Connor were still playing okay, and anyway they didn't have the track record I did. There really weren't any other obvious candidates, and perhaps, with the savaging Europe took in 1981 (losing 18–9 at Walton Heath), who knows, maybe they had, in fact, asked someone else who'd said no. I don't know. I can't pretend to understand the minds of those guys.

Anyway, after an evening's deliberation, I went back to Ken and Colin the next day to give them my answer. I had decided to say yes, but I somehow knew that it was within my powers to negotiate things the way I wanted them to be. I don't know how I knew, but I did. But the fact of the matter is, negotiations or not, I bloody well wasn't going to do it unless they let me do it the way I wanted to. There was nothing in it for me otherwise. So in a way, it really wasn't even a negotiation in the proper sense. It was me presenting my working conditions, and if they weren't agreed to – all of them – I wasn't going to do it.

'My answer is yes,' I told Ken and Colin. 'But . . . I have conditions. I want Concorde.'

'Pardon?'

I went on.

I wanted to fly on Concorde, because the American team had flown first-class, but we always flew in the back of the bloody British Airways economy with a block of seats. If somebody spilled a Coke on you, you paid for your own dry cleaning! That had to change. We didn't have caddies, because we weren't allowed to bring our caddies over. That had to change. There was never anywhere for us to gather as a team, to eat, to plan, to chat. I said I wanted a dedicated room at the team hotel for players and wives only, where there would always be different kinds of food, beer, wine, a place for us to be a *team*. All that had to change. And the clothes! God help me. The clothes foisted on our team in years past were unforgivable crap. One year they gave us plastic shoes. Plastic. We were playing at Laurel Valley the year Dai Rees was captain, and in the middle of one round the sole of my shoe came loose and was flapping all over the place. 'Dai,' I said. 'Do you think I could get some new shoes, or am I supposed to play like this?' We had these hideous plastic golf bags standing beside those gorgeous big full-leather American bags, toted around by their own caddies. Honestly, I'm not making this up. You had to see our outfits to believe them. There were the Americans, decked out in stylish, comfortable clothing, looking the part, and then we showed up looking like some amateurs' outfit, wearing these awful clothes with braiding everywhere.

That had to change.

I finished reeling everything off to Ken and Colin. Concorde. Caddies. Cashmere. The best clothing. Proper bags. Team room. Then I added that I wanted three player choices instead of two, because if we were going to get serious about beating the Americans I needed that discretionary choice. In sum, I told them I wanted to do it all my way, exactly my way, and I wanted total control, full stop.

I stopped talking.

I remember Schofield looking over at Colin (who was a good man, by the way; he did his job very well). I'm not sure what prior agreement they had as to what conditions they were going to agree to, but in the end I got it all, every single thing I asked for. We got the Concorde. We got the caddies. We got Austin Reed, a very reputable name, to do the clothing for us. Lord Derby of the PGA consented to the three picks instead of two.

But there was one final item I had to have in order to sign on. I saved this for a later meeting, once it was clear I was in the driver's seat. Seve.

'I want him,' I said. 'He's my general.'

'If you're accepting,' said Lord Derby, 'then he's your problem.'

'I take that to mean if I accept I have *carte blanche* to move forward with Seve, and *carte blanche* with everything else I want and need?'

The answer was yes. If I could convince Seve to play, he would be approved by the PGA. Talk about a king-size IF. I was disgusted and depressed by the way the European Tour had handled the 1981 Ryder Cup, but I was positively a booster compared with the bile Seve felt towards the whole thing. I couldn't say I blamed him, obviously. But now I needed him. We weren't going to have a hope without the man I considered the world's best player at the time. I had to talk to him.

This, to me, is one of the key moments in Ryder Cup history.

I found out what Seve's schedule was over the next couple of weeks. He'd just won his second Green Jacket at Augusta, in electrifying fashion, with the eyes of Watson, Kite, Crenshaw and Floyd – all earmarked for that 1983 Ryder Cup team – watching him close up. It was an impossibility that he wouldn't be on our team. It couldn't happen. I was not going to let him *not* be on that team. I finally tracked him down at the Prince of Wales Hotel in Southport. He was playing a tournament there, and I was commentating. We sat down for breakfast, and I knew I had to be persuasive yet also very careful. Seve was a virtuoso, a genius, not just a golfer, and he had that air to him of the passionate tortured artist. Pride is among the most prominent of Seve's many fortes, and I knew I was going to have to both appeal to it and be wary of it, too. I told him what I wanted, straight away – I desperately needed his play, I needed his inspiration, I needed his leadership. I needed *him*.

After finishing my opening statement, I got to concentrate on my breakfast for the next half an hour, because that's how long it took him to tell me everything I already knew about what a bunch of bastards those guys were that banned him from the last Cup. *These people, no respect, this and that.* I nodded my head so often, I needed massage when it was all over. I had to let him get it out. I had to let him vent, as the saying goes.

When he finally stopped for breath, I thought I'd try to further my case.

'Seve,' I said. 'Your public image in Britain right now isn't great. You get too much negative press. You and I know you're bloody unbelievable. We know what you've achieved, but your publicity doesn't reflect that. There's a wedge between you and the British public and that's not right. I'm going to tell you something. If you come on board here and we can get this thing right, that'll change. And you've got to believe me that I'm going to do everything possible on my side to get it right. You can help me. I can't do the playing, but you can help me, you know that. The British will embrace you like their own.'

I meant it all. It has always been important to me that the great players get the recognition and accolades they deserve. That wasn't happening for Seve at that moment.

The breakfast lasted maybe an hour.

'I see about this,' said Seve. 'You know, maybe. I see, Mr Hacklin.'

Bloody Seve never could pronounce an English 'J' even years later. He always called me Mr Hacklin.

'Okay,' I said. 'Thanks for listening to me. Let me know.'

The next day, he approached me.

'Mr Hacklin,' he said. 'So okay. I come. I help you.'

Twenty-five years down the road, I don't think it's an exaggeration to say that Seve was instrumental in saving the Ryder Cup. You've got to understand, the tournament was dead on the vine. We got smoked in 1981. The European thing hadn't made any difference. Particularly since the best player in Europe, and on the planet, had been banned from playing in the Cup by his own association. People look at the Ryder Cup now, and see 60-million-dollar profits, huge TV ratings, excitement, anticipation and all the rest. Well, it wasn't always like that. It became that way for a reason, and that reason was what happened in the 1980s. Don't kid yourself. The Ryder Cup is fantastic now, but it was on life-support twenty-five years ago. In Palm Beach Gardens, for that 1983 Cup, there wasn't even national TV coverage. Can you imagine? How many countries is it broadcast to around the globe now? A hundred? I think there might have been some local ABC television coverage, but there wasn't anything close to national media attention. And it might have been one of the most exciting Ryder Cups ever. We started the last day tied 8–8 in points. Seve hit one of the greatest shots I've ever seen in his final-day singles match against Fuzzy Zoeller. He'd got himself into trouble on the last hole, and then hit a 240-yard bunker shot with a three-wood just up by the green, from where he got down with a chip and a putt for a par, all to score the most outrageous half with Fuzzy. That was the Cup where I thought we might actually pull it out. It was agony all day, back and forth, with us nosing ahead, the Americans nosing ahead. Then, with it all in the balance, Lanny Wadkins hit a sand wedge to a foot on the last hole, and the Americans won 14½–13½. Jack Nicklaus, who was the American captain, went out to the fairway after Lanny's shot and kissed the divot.

There was one other moment involving Seve and our youngest team member, Paul Way, that I'll never forget as long as I live. I can call it up in my memory like it was happening right in front of me. Paul was just twenty-one at the time, and had earned his place on the team through some fantastic play, but he was as green as could be. I decided to pair him with Seve, thinking Seve's presence and leadership abilities would be the best thing for Paul. It worked. They played fantastically as a team the first day, beating Floyd and Strange in the afternoon. Naturally I paired them together again the next day. Why wouldn't I? It was just common sense. Anyway, after the morning round – in which they played well again, halving with Morgan and Haas – I got wind that Seve wasn't happy, that he was grumpy about something. This was not in the plan. Seve was central, a happy and motivated Seve, that is. So I tracked him down in the locker room between the morning and afternoon rounds, and we found a private place to talk. He'd just come in off the course, and he was changing. It was damn hot down there in Palm Beach, and I remember him literally peeling his shirt off, sweat everywhere.

'Seve,' I said. 'You're upset about something. What is it? Just tell me.'

'This Paul,' he said. 'I have to hold his hand everywhere. I tell him to chip with this club. Hit with that club. I feel like his father. It too much.'

Paul was just a kid, it was true. And even though Seve wasn't that much older than Paul, Seve had experience and presence in droves. But the great thing about Paul was that, even though he did need a father figure, he nevertheless wasn't intimidated by Seve. This was key. You had to find someone to play with Seve who wouldn't be intimidated by him. Paul wasn't scared of Seve, but he was still just a kid.

'Seve,' I said. 'That's the point. You need to understand. This week, you *are* his father. Here. Today. That's who you are. That's why you're playing with him. Is that a problem? Because if it is tell me.'

Seve looked at me for a few seconds, and then you could see the penny drop.

'No, Mr Hacklin,' he said, nodding. 'For me, this is no problem.'

And that was it. Then they went out and kicked Watson and Gilder's arses that afternoon. It was a magnificent performance by both men, but an object lesson in Ryder Cup captaining. Do the simple thing. Do the obvious thing. Don't make it more complicated than it has to be.

It was on the plane back that Seve demonstrated exactly why I knew we needed him on that team. When he had everybody listening, he said, 'This is not a defeat, this is a victory.' He believed it and so did we. We hadn't won, but we'd turned a corner. We all felt it as a team, as a group, that *Hey, we can DO this*. This was not beyond our capability.

That was the autumn of 1983, and the next thing I knew it was the autumn of 1985, Ryder Cup time again. At least that was how it felt. It was just a blip, like no time at all. The Ryder Cup was back on the radar. People cared. The golf world was interested. You could feel the passion and vibrancy flooding back into the thing.

And you could say the same for me.

17

By 1983, I'd decided I'd had enough of IMG and enough of Jersey. IMG weren't doing anything for me, and it was made clear over and over, through their actions or lack thereof, that I simply wasn't a valuable client for them. It was a waste of time for all of us. So I severed ties with them.

That was about the time we decided to leave Jersey, and it didn't come a moment too soon. I could go into more long-winded explanations, but what it boils down to is that we'd finally had enough of living on a big pile of rock in the middle of the sea. It wasn't where we wanted to be, tax advantage or no. We had always loved Spain, and particularly the Cádiz area of Spain, in Sotogrande, where Valderrama is, and so we decided to relocate there. We'd had an apartment there since 1977, and had always enjoyed it.

Valderrama was, and still is, a great golf course, too. Naturally, being the only really fine course in the area at the time, that was where I played most of my golf. José Patiño, the billionaire who would go on to secure the 1997 Ryder Cup for the course, bought it right around the time we moved there, and he spent millions upgrading Trent Jones's original design, though he didn't really improve it all that much, if you want the truth.

Anyway, Patiño turned out to be a bit of a tyrant around Valderrama. It became less and less of a golf club, and more his personal playpen. He was a character, but what a dictatorial streak the man had. I think it was around 1985 or so that our gardener accidentally let our two dogs, a couple of Dobermanns, out of the yard. We had this big fence around the gardens but one of us must have left the gate open. Anyway, these dogs went scampering about the place and ran across the lawn of one of Patiño's friends. Next thing I knew, we got this letter from a Mrs Bemberg, I think her name was, saying, *Oh, your dogs have done this, that and the other. My maid's pregnant and she nearly had heart failure when those dogs came rampaging through our property. She could have lost the baby*. And so on. I wrote her back a sharp little note saying, *Madam, if your privacy is so important to you, allow me to suggest you erect a fence around your property. As normal people do.*

Bloody Patiño banned me from the course! It was all over the British press, of course. I wasn't the only one Patiño had banned. Sam Torrance had been banned as well, apparently because he'd taken an orange off a tree he shouldn't have, or some ridiculous thing like that. Really, Patiño was unbelievable. He saw a cow on the course once, out near one of the greens. He took a revolver out of his desk drawer, walked outside and shot the animal right in the head. Just dropped it right on the spot. I'm not making this up. He walked back inside and had the course workers haul the carcass away.

Not long after this, Ken Schofield and George O'Grady were in Sotogrande, along with a fellow who was the head of Volvo in Europe. They came round for dinner with Viv and me, where they proudly announced the formation of a new tournament for the European Tour, a big tournament with Volvo as the sponsor. It was going to be amazing, they said, it was going to be this, it was going to be that. The European Tour's flagship tournament.

'And,' added Schofield with evident pleasure. 'We're going to have it right here, at Valderrama.'

'No, you're bloody well not,' I said.

There was silence at the table.

'I'm banned from the course, for starters,' I said. 'So is Sam Torrance. You remember him, don't you, Ryder Cup hero? And if Patiño treats the rest of my professional friends the way he's treated Sam and me . . . well, I'll tell you what, I think I'll write to every single one of them and recommend they skip this event.'

The next morning, I got a phone call from Patiño's secretary, requesting that I meet him at four o'clock that afternoon. When I arrived I let him have it with both barrels. I said, *I understand you want the Volvo Masters here. Well, why should you have it? You just walk all over people.*

He tried to explain himself away. It was the closest thing to an apology I was ever going to get from him. In the end, he lifted the ban on Sam and me. That was enough to make me say, *Okay, I'm off your case. Get on with your tournament.*

But Patiño or no Patiño, it was a lovely spot, and a place that, once we got there, I'd hoped to spend the rest of my days, especially when I became involved in the development of what came to be known as the San Roque Club (I had also started a nice business renting out golf carts, and it was doing quite well for us). San Roque was to be my signature, in a way, a place where we lived for ever and where a golf course with my name on it existed for ever. It didn't happen. Our history in Spain and of my business dealings in Spain is a sad one for me. It was all about trusting the wrong people. Or getting introduced to the wrong people at the wrong time.

The whole San Roque project started before the 1985 Ryder Cup when I met a fellow named Martin Stuart, who'd come to Valderrama to play golf. We met, hit it off, and naturally talked about many things – our dreams, our goals, dozens of things to do with golf. One thing he said was, *I've always wanted to start a country club, my own place.* I told him that I'd always dreamed of the same thing, too. We agreed that if I could find the right land, we'd do it, and it would be called The Tony Jacklin Club.

'You find the land, I'll find the money,' he said.

Well, I found him the land and it didn't take me long, either. The location was more or less beside Valderrama. It was stunning. On what would eventually become the first tee, one view was to the golf course, the other straight out onto the Mediterranean. It was two hundred acres or so owned by the Domecq family, famous for their sherry. I called Martin and said, *I've got the land, you got the money?*

The answer he gave me (which probably should have been my first clue he wasn't all he said he was) was that he wanted someone else's opinion as a backup, another eye to make sure that the site was suitable for a great golf course. He brought in Dave Thomas, my old Ryder Cup partner. Dave had got into designing, and was getting a bit of a name for himself. Of course, Dave said it was perfect for a golf course. It was a bloody no-brainer. I mean, it was right next door to Valderrama. Anyway, Martin went ahead and acquired the land from the Domecqs, and we started the project. I began running around like a maniac trying to get this thing going. I confess I found the whole thing very exciting, but then that's me, isn't it? When I think something is worth doing, I'm going to do it. There's no room for half-measures. If you're going to do something, put your heart and soul into it, otherwise, why bother? This was worth the effort. The Tony Jacklin Club. In one of the most gorgeous parts of the world. With housing to come. It was a dream.

But within six months Martin got cold feet. I'm still not entirely sure why, though I'm guessing it was just the size of it all, the sheer scope of the project. I don't know. Maybe his backing ran out. Whatever it was, he sold it to British & European Ferries, who at that time also owned the La Manga Club. During the year or so the project was owned by the Ferry Group, it was managed by a fellow named Nigel Smith, but the Ferry Group decided to keep me on, as well. I mean, why wouldn't they? It was my concept. It was my name they could hang over the door. I was still Ryder Cup captain. We agreed I'd get paid a thousand pounds a week as a retainer to represent the club and work on promoting it, but for a year I didn't get a penny.

The result was that I had to sue them to get what they owed me. We had a contract, and I have no idea why they didn't pay me. But they didn't and so they forced me into trying to recover what they owed me. You have to remember, I was doing okay during this time, but I wasn't exactly raking in the millions. In any event, it was the principle of the thing. I had to do what I thought was right.

While this was going on, the Ferry Group sold the property and concept to the Asahi Kanko Group from Japan. The arm of the company overseeing the San Roque project was run by a Mr Shun Tezuka. I still can practically feel my teeth begin to grind at the memory of him and of the way he acted in the whole affair. It was Dave Thomas who introduced Shun to me when Shun first came over to Spain.

The project had got under way with Dave doing the design in consultation with me. It really was turning into a magical spot. I was Director of Golf. Right around the time the course really got up and running, they started the housing end of things, and Viv and I decided this was it, this was the place. We committed to building a superb house there. Time passed. I was busy with various Ryder Cup duties. I'd hired a site manager, if you will, someone to handle a lot of the golf operations, but also a person to liaise with Shun for whatever needed doing. It was shaping up beautifully.

I'm cutting ahead a bit, but a couple of years later Shun decided he needed his own project manager. Who does he hire but Nigel Smith, the very fellow I was suing! He more or less put Nigel in charge of the whole bloody project, above everybody on the organizational chart. I was flabbergasted. I went to him and said, *Shun, what are you doing? I'm suing this guy. I can't work with him.*

Shun's answer was that I had to work with him whether I liked it or not. Life became very unpleasant in San Roque after that. There were so many problems. I had an accountant I cherished, a fellow named Lionel Becker, who was my neighbour in Sotogrande. You could have trusted Lionel with your life. He was a gentle, sweet man, and I remember the two of us once going to a meeting with Nigel to talk about this lawsuit. Nigel was simply abusive. He was yelling and screaming at us. And this was a guy I was supposed to be working with at San Roque? It was impossible, but Shun either didn't understand or didn't care.

It got so bad towards the later Eighties that I knew I could no longer live there. Even though I'd sunk nearly a million pounds into constructing a brilliant house right on the course, it was becoming impossible to stay.

Yet this was only one of the headaches and financial losses associated with San Roque. We'd hired my brother-in-law, my sister's husband, to be the contractor for the house. I basically helped him come to Spain and get set up as a builder under my name – the company was called Guts SA – to help him get a better life for himself and my sister. He was in charge, and for a long time it was coming along wonderfully. Lionel, my accountant, was in charge of everything, of handing over cheques and overseeing the house project. But Lionel dropped dead of a heart attack while everything was in midstream, and, I was later to learn, he was keeping many of the details in his head.

The record-keeping was perhaps not as wonderful as his personality, because there was a lot of documentation we couldn't find. To be brief, it turned out that my sister's husband had only put £600,000 of the £840,000 we'd given him for the house into the house. He'd used the rest to pay off business debts. And it was gone. He blamed his business partner. By the time I learned the full truth of what he'd done, it was the early Nineties and we'd already left Spain.

The real blow on San Roque came when we learned that Shun was claiming possession of the property and house we were three-quarters of the way through finishing. Of course, my plan by then, by the time we'd left Spain, had been to finish the house and sell it at what would have been a reasonably tidy profit. It was going to be a stunning house in a stunning location. I had that in my side pocket, that million pounds or so. But now San Roque were invoking the Spanish law that said if a residence is 'abandoned' the ownership reverts to the previous owner. I even tried to get the European Tour to advocate on my behalf, since I'd personally helped them acquire a property and a house on the San Roque site that they use to this day as their continental European base. But Schofield wasn't able to help out, to whatever extent he tried.

It all meant years in the courts, hiring lawyers, arguing case after case. It was relentless and bloody utterly exhausting. Vivien and I had built a house at San Roque to demonstrate we were deeply committed to the place and the project. That wasn't abandonment, that was commitment. As I've said before, if you do something, do it with full enthusiasm, with passion. You don't just do these things on a whim, on a hope. You must commit. We did. And we paid dearly for it. It was devastating, and even today if you say San Roque, or even Spain, to me, all I think of is sadness, missed opportunity, loss.

There are other reasons for that sadness which I link with

Spain. Reasons that are much more human and deeply emotional and crushing. I shall come to those.

In between 1983 and 1985, the excitement surrounding the Ryder Cup seemed to have taken on a life of its own. That whole two years was a blur. I can hardly remember it as a passage of time, even. It was simply 1983, nearly beating the Americans, the return of Seve, a rejuvenation of the Ryder Cup spirit, a move to Spain for our family (with Viv's parents, incidentally, who came along with us from Jersey), the whole excitement of planning and beginning the Tony Jacklin /San Roque Club. Then, bang, it was 1985 and time for the next Ryder Cup. On British soil, at The Belfry. The American captain was Lee Trevino, and I was just glad he and I weren't going to have to play one another. There was no telling what he might have done to me. Seriously, there was no problem with Lee. He was professional and personable, of course, as he always was. In fact, in a way his native enthusiasm and gregariousness matched my own, now that I wasn't playing.

There were certainly hard decisions to make before play began, the hardest by far being my decision to pick Jose Rivero instead of Christy O'Connor Jr. Christy was so hurt it was years before he spoke to me again. They were so close on the money list, but Rivero had won a tournament at The Belfry that year. I can put my hand on my heart and tell you there was not an ounce of personal bias in the decision either way, but Christy took it hard and took it personally. I picked who I thought would be best for the team, plain and simple. The opposite happened later on, in 1989, when I picked Christy ahead of Philip Walton. Christy and Philip had won about the same amount of money, but Christy had played fewer tournaments. Also, he was using the short putter, whereas Philip was using the long putter, which made me trust Christy's putting more. Well, after I announced the picks, Christy came at me like a long-lost brother the next time I saw him, shaking my hand, thanking me. 'Excuse me, Christy,' I said. 'I picked you because you're the best choice for the team. End of story.'

The behind-the-scenes preparation at The Belfry in 1985 was key, too. I worked closely with Brian Cash, the general manager of the place. He was a right character, a good bloke, and he did everything absolutely spot-on for us, from the team rooms to the food, everything. And I worked with him on the schedules for the players throughout the week. I was trying to minimize their ceremonial duties. I said flat out that they would do one cere-monial cocktail party, one, and that that could only be after the official flag-raising when they all had their jackets and ties on anyway. My mission was to win the bloody Ryder Cup, not to be nice to be everyone.

One very vivid memory I have about the 1985 Cup was that Nick Faldo was going through a divorce. It was a struggle for him. Nick may play the good-natured joker nowadays on TV, and he's a great commentator, to be sure, but he's an emotional fellow, too, and his marital troubles were really weighing on him the week of the Cup. He just wasn't up to it emotionally. I played him the first morning with Langer. They lost badly to Cal Peete and Tom Kite. I took him aside and asked him if he thought he could play.

'You've got to tell me, Nick. Are you fine? You just don't look like you're firing on all cylinders. Can you go out again? Or do you want me to put Ken Brown out with Bernhard this after-noon? You've got to be honest with me. I'm talking about the team here.'

He looked at me and said, 'Put Ken out.'

I put a hand on his shoulder, shook his hand. 'Thanks for that, Nick.'

It took a big man, a real man, to say something like that, and

Nick is a man. That's what you call commitment and humility. I took him out and didn't play him again until I had to, in the singles, where he lost to Hubert Green.

The key moment of the whole Cup that year might have come on the second day, when Craig Stadler missed a little tiddler on the last green to give him and Curtis Strange a half with Bernhard Langer and Sandy Lyle, which meant our lead was 9–7 instead of 8½ to 7½ going into the singles the next day. The putt was too short to miss. Really. I remember saying to whoever was standing beside me at the time, 'Jesus Christ.' My immediate reaction was to actually feel sorry as a human being for the guy. Stadler was gutted and we were all stunned, frankly. You don't want to see something like that happen. I mean, it was the kind of putt he should have made with his eyes closed. Stadler and Sutton went out later that afternoon and got run over by Seve and Manuel Pinero, losing 5&4, but to Stadler's credit he came back the next day in singles and took out Woosy 2&1. Still, that missed putt was a gigantic boost for us as a team.

Also instrumental, I'm convinced, was one of those gut-instinct captain's moves I made during the last practice round. I'd partnered Jose Rivero with Seve. In the practice rounds I was watching them closely, the way they played as a team, and I could see – I don't exactly know how, probably because he was just playing bad – that Rivero was totally intimidated by Seve. So, that last afternoon of practice, they were walking down the 14th or 15th fairway, and I pulled Manuel Pinero out of his partnership with Jose Maria Canizares and put him in with Seve. Rivero was just too awed by Seve. But that wasn't going to happen with Manuel. He was an older man, a wonderful, lovely man, and though he had high respect for Seve (who by this time, remember, had won the Open, again, at St Andrews, in such thrilling and memorable fashion), Manuel was not overawed by him.

I have such fond memories of Manuel from that Cup. I remember when we did the singles draw and I put Manuel out first, and he found out he was going to play Lanny Wadkins. He must have jumped six feet off the ground, that's how excited he was to be playing such a pivotal role for the team against one of their talismans. Wadkins wasn't the easiest guy to like, sorry to say. Bit of a cocky fellow. And when Manuel kicked Lanny's ass the next day, and we saw it up there on all the scoreboards around the course, what a boost that was! But, you see, Manuel was a perfect example of why I knew I needed to have three captain's picks instead of two. He would not have made the team if I'd had just the two picks. And even though I knew he wasn't the most physically gifted player, he was as tough as they come. So mentally strong and an absolute rock in match play. He was a tenacious little bugger, always wielding some kind of magic with that wedge of his, and when he got his teeth into Lanny's pant leg, there was no getting away for Lanny. He was done. That was a huge, huge point for us on that final day, particularly because we'd started with that 9–7 lead, and Manuel's point meant we had a three-point lead with eleven matches out on the course. In the end, we went on to win by a fairly convincing margin, 16½–11½.

I think it's worth mentioning here, too, that I perhaps began to think differently in 1983, and certainly in 1985, about the role of the captain in picking the order of the singles. It used to be the case, as a matter of course, that the marquee players were always saved for the last. The captains just did it that way. That's why Jack and I ended up playing one another in 1969. The captains didn't think about it. They just pencilled in names and always put their strongest players in the anchor positions.

But when I began to think about where to put Seve and my other strong players I remember thinking, *Well, what bloody good is Seve to me in the anchor spot if we've already lost?*

What's the point of that? And so I decided to put the real strength of the team straight up the gut, as it were, right in the middle of the lineup. Now, I'm not saying I'm a genius or anything, but, well, it worked. And it really was something I made a *decision* on. It wasn't a slip of the pencil. I didn't go around consulting all the players about where they'd like to go and so on (though I did speak to Seve maybe two or three times about tactical things in the four Cups I captained). My view on that was always, directors direct and actors act. Captains captain and players play. It wasn't being arrogant or uninterested in consultation. It was just that I knew what I was doing. I don't know how I could phrase that more simply. I'd been around that block a few times. And I trusted my gut. I did. I truly trusted what my insides were telling me. I think that self-belief rubbed off.

The image often associated with the 1985 Ryder Cup is that of Sam Torrance draining his final putt for victory, for team victory, and raising his arms skyward in utter joy and celebration and disbelief. He had a tear or two in his eye. He wasn't the only one. I was bawling like a little baby. What an astonishing turn-around. A few years earlier the Cup had been on death watch for lack of competition. Now it was on its way to becoming the massive event it is today. It was also taking a different direction. The Americans had been beaten, for the first time in twenty-eight years. I wish I could even say that it was extra-special, as a captain, to beat Lee Trevino, the man who'd caused me so much grief, but that wasn't really part of it. It was about more than me as an individual, or any of us as individuals. It was about representing where we were from. It was about Europe, and we were the champions. It was euphoria. It was beautiful. It was freshly made history and it will never be forgotten.

We were in America in 1987, at Jack's Muirfield Village in Ohio. Jack was captain of the American team, the first American team in a generation trying to earn the Cup *back*. By this time, I was well seasoned in the captain's role, and I fully understood it was my job to give the players everything I could to make them as comfortable as possible, to do whatever I could to take the pressure off them in every way, shape and form. I wanted them to be thinking about one thing and one thing only: performing to the outer limit of their abilities. It was about me doing my best so that they could do their best.

Of course, this began to get more difficult and complicated as time went on, often for the most ordinary of reasons. One of the players wanted to bring his two-year-old child along in 1987. Well, to me, that wasn't what the Ryder Cup was about. I never took my kids to the Ryder Cup. I was there to do a job. But this fellow wanted to bring his little kid. So you need a room for the nanny, and then that room has to be right beside their room, and it was a room I'd originally designated for players only . . . you get the idea.

But I had to be accommodating, because I didn't want to piss anyone off. My job was to not piss anyone off, because if they were pissed off, they weren't going to perform to that outer limit. So my job was to accommodate them and motivate them, and I knew – again, it's just plain common sense – that the easiest way to piss off these guys was to not accommodate them. Some of the players were more difficult than others, and at times it became very tedious to meet everyone's requests, but I did it without showing that it felt tedious. I did it because it was the best way to make sure we accomplished our mission.

The overall impression I can still so easily recall from the 1987 Cup was that it was just done *right*. Everything was perfect. The course was great. The accommodations were great. Our hosts, Barbara and Jack Nicklaus, were unfailingly gracious and generous while also being competitive in exactly the best way.

I remember we landed in America as the champions, brimming with excitement and confidence. I told our players that if our one-point loss in 1983 had been the stepping stone to our victory in 1985, then our victory on British soil in 1985 was our stepping stone to victory on American soil in 1987. To me, it was a progression. We were quietly confident. It was a marvellous year to be captain, because we had great returning strength and experience from the previous Cup, but we had new blood, too. What a roster I had! Seve, Faldo, Langer, Woosnam, Sandy Lyle, the new face of Jose Maria Olazabal. All of them true greats who would end up with multiple Majors on their résumés. I remember when we landed at the airport someone from the Press stuck a microphone in my face and asked me what I thought was going to happen that week.

'Oh, we'll win,' I said, simple as that. I meant it. It wasn't a boast. It wasn't a challenge. I wasn't trying to anger the Americans or motivate my own team. It was just what I thought, what I *felt*. Question. Answer. Next?

I had a simple strategy for the 1987 Cup – I was blessed with an incredible roster of upper echelon talent, in my opinion. Nothing against fellows like Howard Clark or Eamonn Darcy; they were great players, fighters, and they worked like hell for that team. Eamonn, in particular, was magnificent in beating Crenshaw in the singles. But I just felt that year that we were going to live or die by the performance of our big guns, and so I decided to ride them hard. The way I saw it, I couldn't afford to put a man who was a class act on the sidelines. So it was the big boys who worked around-the-clock shifts that week. Seve, Faldo, Langer, Woosy and Olazabal all played in every single match, and they were all bloody fabulous, although I remember in particular that Langer was exhausted that week, for some reason. He approached me at one point early on, and told me that he was tired and wasn't sure he could be at his best if he played every match.

'Bernhard,' I said to him. 'You are a great player. You're a champion. And I, as the captain, can't afford to have you on the sidelines. It's people like you that dig deepest at moments like this.'

I could almost physically see the tiredness on his shoulders, but I thought I had to push him through it.

'I'm going to have to play you. I'm sorry. You're a champion, and great players find a way to get it done. You'll find a way.'

Which he did, winning three out of four with his partners, and then adding a half in the singles. It was majestic.

But that was just me doing my job, you see. Everybody has their limitations, but it was up to me to find the right buttons and then push them the right way. To get the best out of everybody, and to combine the various talents. As I said earlier, I am intensely fascinated by the way people work, and this was the most intense laboratory you could imagine in which to observe human behaviour. I loved the challenge, and loved feeling successful at finding ways to motivate people. It felt, in a way, like what I was born to do.

And so, in the end, victory was ours again. It was also the dawn of what would become one of the greatest, if not *the* greatest, partnerships in Ryder Cup history, that being Seve and Olazabal. They won three of four matches. We had a five-point lead going into the singles, and when Eamonn, Bernhard and Seve – playing near the bottom of the order – secured two and a half points out of three, we had won. It was hard to fathom, really. Two in a row. Victory on American soil!

It was pandemonium in our camp. There were tears everywhere and a massive party broke out amongst our team, but I didn't stay that long. I went back to my hotel room, poured myself a Glenmorangie, sat with Viv and reflected. It's hard to describe the combination of exhilaration and exhaustion I was feeling, the comedown from such an absolute adrenalin high. All

I knew was that it was time to sit quietly for a moment and try to absorb the immense satisfaction, the achievement. The only way to do it was to sit and let it sink in, and it was one of the most peaceful and gratifying moments of my entire life. Viv and I clinked glasses. It felt wonderful to be there, with her, just the two of us.

18

The 28th of April 1988.

Who among us can know why we're here? Why we have what we have. Why any of it gets taken away. Is it the lucky ones who get punished? Or the unlucky ones?

I was playing golf at Valderrama with Sean Connery and John Fitzpatrick, the racing driver. It was a perfect Cadiz spring day – lovely sunshine, light breezes coming off the Mediterranean. On the 11th tee, we heard a golf cart coming our way. It stopped in front of us. Dave Thomas's young son Philip was in the cart. He got out and walked over to us, and the second I saw him I knew, deep down inside, that something was wrong, though there was no way to know what it was. I had no premonitions, no fore-shadowing, I only knew something was desperately wrong. His face was twisted up in a mask of sadness.

'Philip?' I said.

'There's been an accident.'

I walked toward him.

'Vivien,' he said.

I dropped my club, got in the cart with him, and he ran me back. The whole ride back he wouldn't tell me what had happened, only that there had been an accident. It was his father who'd found Viv. In the estate we lived in the kids were allowed to zip around on these little mini-scooter things, as long as they didn't go on any main roads or the highway. Viv had just popped out to go down to the local petrol station to get some petrol for these scooters. She'd had a headache that morning on the golf course while playing golf with her girlfriends, so she took a couple of aspirin when she finished and that, she thought, was that.

Dave found her. He was driving down the road and he saw our Mercedes. It had ploughed into the metal fence right beside the gas station. He stopped and went to check it out. Philip was with him. He opened the passenger door because the car was against the fence on the driver's side. Vivien wasn't conscious but was still alive. Dave heard her make a choking, guttural noise.

A last gasp, literally. She died then. My Viv.

It was a cerebral haemorrhage, an aneurysm. She'd been driving, just out doing her errand, minding her own bloody business, not causing a moment's grief to a single soul in the entire world. And then she was gone. Forty-four years old. Dave pulled her body from our car and brought it back to the house. That was where I saw her. I never got to say goodbye. I didn't get to kiss her one last time. She was dead in my arms when I held her and wept on her clothes.

Things were already starting to happen. The police had come to the house, just as part of normal procedure. The doctors came and pronounced her dead, which triggered the whole mad Spanish rush of having to bury people within twenty-four hours of their passing. It was insanity, and thank God I had people around me who were close. Viv's parents, who were living with us, were devastated, though I will never ever forget Viv's mum's first words to me when I went in to tell them what had happened. There was nothing to do except be blunt, and so I told them Viv was dead. 'Oh my God,' said her mother. She looked at me. 'What will you do?' It had to be crushing for them, since they'd already lost their son, Viv's brother Frank, to the suicide they'd witnessed years earlier.

You can't know. It was over. My world was gone. It had ended in an *instant*. Everything that I was was over and done with. It all came to an instant stop. Golf. Houses. Designs. Ryder Cup. Everything. Gone.

I was crushed, devastated, but more than anything that day I was just stunned, lost in disbelief. Dead? Viv? It couldn't be.

It wasn't like cancer, where people waste away and you see it happen and you can say goodbye. Viv was fit as could be, and in the twenty-two years we were married she never once spent a day sick in bed. Then she was gone. She was there at breakfast and gone by dinner.

Sean Connery was unbelievable for me and my family. He took charge at the church, doing a reading. Everybody came for the funeral, which, as I say, was the day after she died. The boys came from boarding school in England. Nick Faldo came. Ken Schofield came. A few of the Spanish Ryder Cup boys came. My parents were there. The funeral ended. Everybody offered their final condolences. Then, naturally, people went back to their lives. Three days later I was in the house, going to bed by my self, alone.

Can you imagine? No, of course you can't. Or at least I hope you can't, because the only way you can know the pain and complete dislocation I'm talking about is if you've gone through it, and I hope you haven't had to because it's a bloody living nightmare, hell on earth. I'd been cut in half. I was lost, angry, confused by the world's irrational unfairness. I did a lot of talking to myself in the days and weeks that followed, and also had many a long discussion with Johnnie Walker. Some of those long nights I thought of suicide. Who wouldn't? It just couldn't be true. Some days I couldn't see any way at all to carry on. Other days I thought I could. I knew, finally, that offing myself was just something I did not have inside me. I was a person who carried on. I had children. I had responsibilities.

Small bits of time passed.

Larger blocks of time passed.

For weeks I don't think I had any idea where I was or what I was doing. But gradually, you do start to come to some sort of terms with it. We didn't do anything wrong. It wasn't anyone's fault. It wasn't about deserving or not deserving it. It wasn't fate. Or destiny. It just *was*.

It was awkward in the public eye, or even with friends. Some people avoided me altogether because they didn't know what to say or do. Perhaps they stayed away because they themselves were so shattered they wouldn't have been able to stand being close to me. There were other friends who did come around, but then they seemed to try their best not to talk about it, as if they thought that's what would be best for me, to chitchat about anything except Vivien, when, of course, what I most desperately wanted to do above everything else was talk and talk and talk. If you can't talk about it you can't get it out.

It took me years to put Vivien's death in any sort of perspective. Today, right now, 2006, I will tell you about it, and it still makes me weep. It's one of those things you just don't ever, ever, get over. No matter how happy you can make your life again – and believe me, my life today is a source of absolute daily joy. But I will still cry if I sit down and talk about Viv with you. I can't help it. You don't get rid of a traumatic shock like that, and I'm not sure you want to forget about it, either, because it's who you are, it's what you're made of, and you can't pick and choose. You are the sum total of your experiences.

Even so, it was hard all the time. Years later I would run into people I hadn't seen in ages, and they'd say, *Hey, Tony, how the hell is Vivien, anyway?*

Oh, well, she's dead, I'm afraid. That was always out there. You're telling the story for years on end.

The whole thing took on elements of the surreal, because of Viv's death but also because of things that happened to those around us. After Viv died Lorna Townsend called up and told me how sad she was and how she so desperately wished she could be there in Spain to comfort me and be with me. Lorna was the wife of my old pal and 1969 Ryder Cup partner Peter Townsend. Two years later, she died of the same thing. Brain aneurysm. She was forty-five.

Peter Green was a very good friend from the early days when we'd travelled to South Africa together. One year after Lorna Townsend died, Peter's wife, Jenny, died. Of a brain aneurysm. She was fifty.

It was simply beyond the pale, the kind of thing you can't let enter into your imagination as possible. But it happened. I remember telling Arnold Palmer about it one day a few years after the fact, and he was incredulous. He wondered what the common link could have been, if it might have even had something to do with a medication or even the birth-control pill.

Lorna and Jenny's deaths happened in the years that followed Viv's death, but 1988 on its own was a desperately sad and horrific year, and not only because of Viv. In some ways, it was almost macabre. Earlier that year, in February, we'd had a dinner party. My friend Manuel Corillo and his wife were there. Manuel was an *aprecador*, which is a sort of partner to an architect in Spain, someone who helps find the real estate and does the planning and permit acquisition. He was friends with Juan Luis Bandrez, the wealthy owner of the ferry company that operated between Spain and Morocco, and Bandrez and his wife were also at our dinner party. Bandrez was a fantastic guy. He bred bulls for the bullfights and had a huge estate where he and I did some shooting. The last couple at our party were the Chinese couple who owned the restaurant near us that we ordered out from and ate at regularly. He ended up cooking the meal, just because we thought it would be something unique.

There were four couples at that dinner party in February. In March, Manuel died suddenly of cancer. In April, Viv died. In July, the restaurant owner had a stroke and was paralysed for the rest of his life. And in December, Bandrez was confronted behind his desk by a steward he'd fired from one of his ships. The steward demanded his job back, but Bandrez said no, what was done was done. The ex-steward pulled out a gun and shot Bandrez in the head, murdering him where he sat.

Nineteen eighty-eight.

It was like something out of an Agatha Christie novel. Only this wasn't make-believe – it was real. The final, sad twist was that after all these awful deaths, Philip Thomas, Dave's son, the young lad who'd come out onto the golf course to tell me there had been an accident, had an accident of his own. He crashed his motorcycle on the roads around Sotogrande and died. I'd fallen out with Dave Thomas by then, over my unhappiness with the way he did business, going behind my back, dropping me on projects without informing me when it suited his purposes. (Dave and I get along okay now; we've let bygones be bygones.) But business wasn't relevant to any of this. I went around after Philip died and offered my condolences.

I knew what he was feeling. I truly did. There was no sense to any of it. It's one thing to say that loss happens to all of us at some point. It's another thing entirely when your life becomes unrecognizable – *in a heartbeat*. Vivien and I were a team. And I'm not just saying that because it's a way of saying we had a good marriage – I mean it literally. We were a unit. Every single thing I'd done and achieved in my life had been accomplished with and through her. And then one day . . . it was all gone.

19

Days, weeks passed. I suppose I played some golf here or there with my pals. Maybe I went around to some friends' houses. I know I cried myself to sleep many a night. I just had to survive, that was all. Once you decide you're not going to kill yourself, then you just have to get on with it. There's not much choice, is there? You can't sit in a room all day, not eating, not brushing your teeth, staring at the walls. Sooner or later, you step out. You move around. Gradually the world seems less cast against you, and you try to press forward. I was also doing my damnedest to be there for the people who needed me. I talked regularly with Warren and Bradley and Tina. They all seemed to handle it in different ways, ways that shall remain private to them and their memories of their mother.

About six weeks or so after Viv died, I decided to accept an invitation to play in a tournament called the Four Stars, which was run to essentially replace the Bob Hope Classic up at Moor Park, a sort of British version of the Palm Springs tournament. (There was a huge celebrity component, all of it devoted to raising money for charity. This was a tournament, incidentally, that the British Press ultimately ruined by accusing Hope and other stars of arriving on a 'sea of champagne' and other such nonsense, like the fact that they were paid to appear; well, of course, they got paid! That's the way the world works – celebrities get paid to loan their name to something, usually for much less than their normal fee, and it's charity that benefits. But the Press decided that wasn't a good enough cause, and they browbeat Hope and the others so badly they decided not to come back, which meant the end of the tournament.)

Anyway, I thought it might be good for me to get out of the house, literally. I'd been slowly coming to grips with the fact that my life had to continue. You see, even though I was thoroughly devastated, I also have something of a pragmatic, survivor's streak in me. A streak now emerging, which was saying, 'Okay, Jacko, you're grieving, and that's okay, and you can take your time to let it happen, but that doesn't mean you can't also try to get back into the land of the living.'

So I went to Moor Park. At one of the dinners they had for the event, I was at the head table. Terry Wogan, the BBC disc jockey was there. Joan Collins was down the table, and she was sitting close to Bill Wiggins, a bit of a man about town and something of a partier. Princess Margaret was near me, as was good old Jimmy Tarbuck, a pal of mine for ever who is one of the funniest men in Britain. At one point, Princess Margaret, who was a good sort, noticed Joan Collins and Wiggins getting on rather well. She leaned over to Jimmy.

'Mr Tarbuck,' she said. 'Who's the gentleman with Mrs Collins?'

Jimmy said, 'It's Bill Wiggins, Ma'am.'

Princess Margaret nodded. 'I see. And what does he do?'

Jimmy, who knew Margaret well enough to say this, leaned in close. 'Well . . . I think he gives her one, Ma'am.'

'Really.' Princess Margaret sat back, let the slightest smile cross her lips. 'He must be very good at it.'

We roared with laughter. God, it felt good to laugh like that;

it was almost as if something had broken free inside me, a part of the glacier chipped away.

In any case, I was at that tournament with my friend Malcolm Brooks, who was caddying for me, and one day we went into the lunch tent to have a bite. There was a girl there serving lunch, and what I noticed right away, no sense denying it, was that she was a lovely young lady. We hit it off, had a good chat, a laugh or two, and then I went back out onto the course. As I did, I thought, *Bloody hell, I've got to move on sometime*, but on the other hand I knew my mind wasn't really working properly. I was still a bit of an emotional basket case. That's no excuse for anything. It's just a fact. Viv had only been dead six weeks, and I was still absolutely in a state of shock, even if I was only now trying to emerge from it. But I started thinking, *Okay, I know I don't want to spend the rest of my life alone. I know that.* I also thought, *Jesus, there's no way I could stand to start up a relationship with someone as old as me, someone with the same kind of baggage I've got.* I felt I needed to meet someone younger, someone I could begin fresh with.

I saw the girl again. Her name was Donna Methven. We chitchatted back and forth nicely enough, I asked her out, and to cut to the chase, we had an affair. Little did I know at the time she was sixteen years old. Or so she said. She said a lot of things that later on turned out to be distant cousins of the truth. Anyway, we met often, whether for lunch or dinner or some sort of liaison. We went down to Bournemouth. Quite frankly, it was wonderful to have simple human contact, that warmth of being next to somebody. She seemed a pleasant girl, and I'm not going to lie to you, I was very physically attracted to her. This went on for a month or so and I decided to take her down to Spain with me. It was all on the up and up. I wasn't trying to hide anything. Viv's parents knew she was there. Tina knew she was there. It was just me trying to make my way back into the world, and if the first step I had to take was to have an affair with a woman younger than me, well, there are much worse crimes.

But then my life changed. Again. In a flash. It was another of those times I've talked about, when my life turned on its axis and became in one moment something completely different than it had been just that one moment earlier.

In August, Malcolm was over for a visit and he told me that I ought to pop over some time to my neighbours, the Greenlees, who lived more or less around the corner. My house was located near the 18th tee and the Greenlees were behind the 17th green.

'Why's that?' I asked him.

'You just should. There's someone there you should probably see.'

He was being a bit inscrutable, though I suppose I knew what he meant – there was an attractive woman over there, was what he was saying. I can't recall exactly what my reaction was to his suggestion. After all, I already had a bit of a thing going at my own house, though it was becoming increasingly clear with Donna that, although we were having a good enough time, she wasn't going to be any sort of long-term answer to my loneliness and desire to once again create a sense of family.

So I kind of ambled over to the neighbour's, just to say hi, to shoot the breeze a bit. I ran into the neighbour, Astrid's sister, as it turned out, who took me outside. And there she was. Astrid Waagen. She was sitting by the swimming pool. Her two children, A.J. and Anna-May, who were eight and six at the time, were with her. They were visiting from Miami. The first thing I noticed above all else was that I saw why Malcolm had recommended I pay a visit to the neighbours. Astrid was, and still is, a beautiful woman. And she was a woman. Not a child. I introduced myself, we got to talking, and it was plain to me that she was the woman I was now meant to be with. It was magical and yet somehow also obvious. *Right*, I thought. *Of course!* It had only happened one other time in my life, and when it had happened with Viv it stuck, it lasted, and it was real. That's why I trusted the feeling. I just knew. I trust my instinct, and when I looked at Astrid my instinct told me, *This is one fabulous, perfect woman, and she will be your partner for the rest of your life.*

You could see that she had already had a life, that she had had her own set of experiences. To me, she looked, I don't know, a bit forlorn. I found out soon enough what the source of her inner sadness was. We saw one another at group things a couple of times before we finally went out for dinner, just the two of us. We hardly touched our food. We sat in the same seats for five or six hours, just telling each other our life stories. It was a deeply touching, wonderful night, and I felt so free, finally, to talk about whatever I wanted to talk about. She felt the same way. She had not had an easy go of it, despite the fact that she'd already had a rather glamorous life for many years. She'd been married to Alan Kendall, the lead guitarist for the Bee Gees, and had managed their books and affairs. But they'd had their difficulties, and when I met her they'd been divorced for five years. (The happy postscript is that he and Astrid remain on very good terms. In fact, when Anna-May was married a few years ago, one of Astrid's cherished memories of the wedding was Alan and I walking Anna-May up the aisle and Alan and I walking Astrid down it!)

When I say that Astrid looked forlorn when I first laid eyes on her, I suppose I also mean that she looked lost to me. That was something I knew about, because I sure as hell was lost. I can see her now, sitting by the pool at her sister's house, quiet but a bit sad as she watched the kids jump in and out of the pool. Don't get me wrong, I didn't feel sorry for her. Not in the least. I'd hate to be misunderstood, because that wasn't it at all. But in those first ten seconds I looked at her my mind and body were doing the sums. It was about empathy. I was tuned in. I was attracted to her, and simply saw who she was. That's all. It's what I've felt all along. I saw where she was and I knew I was there with her and she'd be there with me. It was plain as day that she was a tough, resilient, deeply honest and supportive person. I was in love with her the day I met her, and that hasn't changed an ounce, nearly eighteen years later.

The funny thing is, her memory of how we made our connection is rather different. She was at the house while her sister was out, and her sister had told her to expect the architect to come by. So she hung around with the kids for a while, expecting some architect to show up. A couple of hours later I was walking through the door with her sister, who introduced us. 'Astrid,' she said. 'This is Tony Jacklin.'

'Big deal,' Astrid will say now, laughing, as she tells the story. 'Tony Jacklin, Tony Shmacklin. I thought he was the architect.'

Astrid's sister explained that I was Tony Jacklin, 'the golfer'. That didn't make much of an impression, either. She told me later she wondered why her sister thought she might care that I lived on the golf course and played there. What was so special about that? In fact, as I mentioned, the first couple of times we had the chance to talk and be around one another was in mixed company, in larger groups, backyard cocktail parties and the like. At one of those drink parties, in front of other people, she asked what I did for a living, and I said, 'I play golf.'

'Yes,' she said. 'But what's your business, your occupation?'

'I'm a professional golfer,' I said. 'Golf *is* what I do for living.'

She seemed genuinely surprised, and if she was having me on, she was damn good at hiding it. 'Really?' she said. 'You can make money doing that?'

Suffice to say she was not gold-digging.

Astrid will happily elaborate on her version of our first meeting, and it's sweet, even if, or perhaps because, she had no bloody clue who I was. (And why should she have? She'd toured the

globe with a rock band a bloody sight more famous than me.)
She said when she first saw me she felt an instant electricity, that
she was tongue-tied, and that she briefly had to go back inside
and stand in her room and compose herself before she could
come back out! I'm inclined to want to believe every word of
that . . . but I wouldn't be surprised if there's a just a bit of embel-
lishment in there. She's as much a romantic as I am, if not more.

I took her out the morning after our dinner date to show her
the San Roque course, which was well under construction by
then, this being the end of August. It was coming along beautifully, and I was proud and excited to show it to her. It was my
baby, my legacy (well, at least *then* it was). All she remembers is
me showing her a big pile of dirt and not knowing what she was
looking at. She teased me later about me being so proud of my
'lump of dirt'.

We left the site, and as we were driving back, Astrid thanked
me for showing it to her. 'You'll have to bring me out again
when it's done,' she said. 'I have to go back to Miami, but I'll
come back in a couple of years and I'd love to see it then.'

I glanced over at her. 'You're not leaving.'

'Pardon me.'

'When I met my first wife,' I told Astrid, 'I saw her across the
room. I knew I was going to marry her. It's the same with you. I
know it, in my heart. Don't go back to Miami. At our age, we
don't need to play games. We know it. We know we're in tune.'

If you got to know Astrid, you would soon learn that you do
not, under any circumstances, dictate terms to her. Many have
suffered the consequences. But I didn't know that then, so I was
allowed to get away with it, I suppose. She forgave me. And she
never did go back to Miami.

Of course, I still had a sixteen-year-old girl lounging beside my
pool under the impression that she and I were an item. I've

always been an honest person, and hand on heart, I never told Donna one thing that wasn't true. And so when I knew I was in love with Astrid and that we were going to try to make a go of this thing, it was obvious Donna had to get on a plane and go home. That was all there was to it. There'd been no promises, no whispered pledges. We were just having fun in each other's company, and now it was over.

I told her so in plain language. This brought on a terrible wailing and shrieking and bawling, none of which stopped until the door of the plane closed behind her on her way back to London. She'd been a shoulder to cry on and she never said a mean word to me, and vice versa, but I was glad to see her go. I now had the rest of my life to look forward to.

How was I to know, of course, that sweet Donna Methven would step off the plane at Heathrow and barely take the time to pick up her luggage before marching straight into the offices of the *Sun* to sell her story for a reported £75,000! Unbelievable. The next morning the shit hit the fan, and it was suddenly a media frenzy right outside our bloody house. The phone was ringing off the hook. The doorbell was ringing. What the hell was going on? A friend rang up and told me the *Sun*'s headline.

'*JACKLIN SEDUCES VIRGIN, 16.*'

It was a certified madhouse.

We took the phone off the hook and stopped answering the door after the first journalist showed up and barked at me, 'Is it true you were having a wild sex holiday with a sixteen-year-old virgin?' Within a day and a half we had the Press literally camped out on our front lawn, and my sexual prowess was being itemized on the front page of every tabloid.

I bundled Astrid into the car and we got out of town as fast as we could, hightailing it into the hills, up to the stunning Hotel La Bobadilla behind Malaga, where the King of Spain used to stay. Dave Thomas was the only person who knew where we were, and every day we'd phone back.

'Dave, are they still there?'

'Oh, for fuck's sake,' he'd mutter. 'Don't come back. Stay where you are.'

There were headlines every day.

'JACKLIN HAS RUINED MY DARLING DAUGHTER.'

'MADE ME A WOMAN.'

And on.

Meanwhile, Astrid and I were enjoying a rather blissful get-to-know-one-another time in the Bobadilla, which is a fantastic spot. It was quiet and romantic and lovely. I think we were gone nine or ten days, and when we came back we were slung low in our seats with our hats over our heads. The storm had begun to blow over a little by then, mostly because of dear old George Best. Bestie was a true friend, a great man, and he did me a huge favour that still makes me laugh every time I think of it. Right around the time Astrid and I were coming back from Bobadilla, the Press in London somehow, for some reason, asked Bestie what he thought of the whole Jacko Seduces Virgin controversy.

'Virgin?' said Bestie, grinning away. 'Her? I don't think so. I fucked 'er when she was fourteen.'

Well, you can imagine the bedlam. The Press went bananas. It was madness, and I can tell you the tables rather turned on poor Donna. One of her pals came out in the Press saying she was upset by the way Donna had treated 'Mr Jacklin', who had in her opinion treated Donna quite well. Then the Press got hold of a photo of Donna topless in Thailand from at least a couple of years earlier, where she was frolicking with a group of similarly unclad teenagers.

I was off the hook, and after that every single story in the Press leading up to Astrid and me getting married that December was of *Jacko and his new Norwegian love*, or some other shorthand gossip-sheet stuff. It was all so ridiculous, but I was never more thankful for Bestie's nature than I was that autumn. He had one of the best lines of all time in my book, when he said, 'I spent a lot of my money on booze, birds and fast cars. The rest I just squandered.' I was deeply saddened when he passed away last December. We won't see his like again.

There was, unhappily, another task I felt I had to perform that autumn. Once Astrid and I set a date to get married, I knew I could no longer look after Vivien's parents. They were lovely people, and I never failed to get on with them, and Astrid liked them, too. But by this point I'd been putting a roof over their heads for a decade. What a terrible time of it they'd had. My God, I mean, I may have had it rough, but so did they; seeing one child throw himself beneath a train and then having another die right under their noses. It's not right to lose a child before you go, let alone two. I'm sure they were shell-shocked.

But – and this may sound hard, even if I didn't mean it to be – I had to get on with my life, a new life, a life that wasn't ever going to have their daughter in it again. That was over. So I phoned Billy, Vivien's brother, who was still living in Melbourne, and I said to him, 'Look, Billy, I've got a problem. I've taken care of your parents for ten years. We all know what's happened, and I just need to get on with my life, such as it is.'

I had no concrete idea of what that life was going to be yet, but I knew I needed my freedom, and that I simply couldn't be responsible for them any more. Fair or not, it was how I felt. I'd looked after them financially, put a roof over their heads, ensured they had a good lifestyle. But I couldn't do it any more. I told Billy I thought they should move back to Melbourne to spend their last years with the only immediate family they had left.

Billy hummed and hawed, but finally he knew I was right, and even if I wasn't 'right', his parents were still ultimately going to be his responsibility. I put them on a plane in Malaga, and they went back to Melbourne. We were sad to see them go, but they needed to get on with whatever time they had left, about eight years as it turned out. And I had to get on with my life. It might have seemed harsh, but it was the right thing to do.

On the 29th of December 1988, Astrid and I were married in the Gibraltar Registry Office (because we didn't want hordes of press there; incidentally, this was also where John Lennon and Yoko Ono were married). It was four months after we'd met, eight months after Viv's death. It was a quick courtship, yes, but it was only as it was supposed to be. The proof of the validity of our decision is still in evidence every day; we are still together, still ridiculously in love, we still make each other laugh all the time, whether it's just sitting around the dinner table or crossing oceans. It's an amazing, nourishing, love-filled relationship, but more than anything we just have a hell of a lot of fun together.

After our wedding, I suppose it would be fair to say I got busy on two fronts. First, we began trying to have a child together. I had my three with Viv, and she had her two with Alan, but we very much wanted a child of our own making. It was a process of agony, heartache, considerable pain for Astrid and, ultimately, joy. Astrid had three miscarriages, one of them very late in the second trimester. It's the kind of pain that feels universal in some ways, because most of us try to have children at some time in our lives, and we all know how wild the swings of emotion can be. But it's also a pain that finally has to remain rather private, since it's nearly impossible to describe how one's heart breaks unreservedly for that little being who fails to make it into the world. Our desire to have a child together was finally made real when we managed to bring our dear son Sean into the world in

1991 (I say 'dear' because he is very dear to us, even though he's now into being everything a teenage boy will be . . . enough said!).

The other thing I got busy on as 1989 dawned was the Ryder Cup coming later that autumn. You'll understand that I'd let my attention wander from my captaincy, given that my life had sunk in a shot to the bottom of the sea, but it was now resurfacing. After our thrilling victory on American soil in 1987, the Cup was being held back on home turf, at The Belfry. It wouldn't be accurate to say I had the captaining thing down to a science, because what I knew about the job, above all else, was that it was an *art* and not a science. I never wavered in my self-belief about my ability to motivate people, to pick good partnerships and to put out good singles orders. I just felt good about it. And that Cup was something I was really looking forward to. We owned the Cup and we were defending on home soil.

I hadn't fully decided before the Cup began, but I was having inklings inside that it would be my last. I suppose my reasoning, even if it was only partly conscious at the time, was, 'What's left to do?' If we won, which I fully expected us to, it would be three in a row, and if we lost, then that was likely to be a signal some new blood was needed anyway. Probably with that partly in mind, I was determined we were going to make it one to remember.

Yet again I was gifted with a splendid lineup, a roster of stars who were truly on form, winning Majors everywhere, and yet still hungry for victory. I was always amazed and glad at how the Ryder Cup captain's job never palled for me. Never, ever. There was always a passion for it, always that sense of energy and enthusiasm when it was time to get busy. It was a perfect kind of situation for me, one which was all about golf, but in which I was also able to bring into play my fascination with, and insight into, people and their individual motivations. I loved that! What would motivate this player, that player, what would push them right to the outer limit of their own expectations and abilities? I knew a little something about this, after all. Perhaps this was one of the things that was so gratifying about it all – because I had done it, because I'd been to the top, when I talked the players listened. Simple as that. But it was truly a situation of mutual respect; I also knew first-hand the pressures they were experiencing. It was all golf, and I never had to touch a putter – what more could I ask for?

If it was a perfect situation, the opening was made even more perfect, if that's possible, when the American captain Ray Floyd presented me with an early gift. I wasn't expecting it, though I did think it was awfully considerate of him. I hope he wasn't offended when I failed to respond with an equally massive gift. I think I'm a generous person, but there are limits.

At the opening ceremonies, in front of the whole world, but most importantly in front of me and my twelve players – and I mean literally in front of us – Raymond announced how proud he was to be the captain of a team made up of 'the twelve great-est players in the world'.

I think my mouth opened slightly. My jaw may have dropped a bit. Had he really said that? Surely, he'd said twelve *of* the greatest. But no, my ears weren't playing tricks. He'd said 'the twelve greatest'. He really had. The twelve greatest players? Was he trying to make a joke?

I looked down the line of chairs beside me on the stage, down to Seve, Olazabal, Bernhard, Woosy, Faldo, down the roster of Europeans who held Green Jackets and Claret Jugs sitting there listening to Raymond blatantly insulting them.

The twelve *greatest*?

Really, I said to myself. *Oh, really!*

You might have thought I'd be offended on behalf of my play-ers, but I was far too delighted by Raymond's going-away gift to me. Talk about having it handed to you on a platter. I didn't need anything else to motivate my guys. It was unbelievable!

Our big guns never let Raymond forget, either, at least in their actions. Seve and Jose Maria went undefeated as a partnership that week, and Jose Maria added a singles victory to give him 4½ points out of 5. What a performance. And who of the world's 'twelve greatest players' did Seve and Jose Maria manage to get lucky against? Tom Watson, Tom Kite, Curtis Strange, Mark Calcavecchia, Payne Stewart, Mark O'Meara. Obviously, Seve and Jose Maria were damn fortunate to beat those titans. I can't remember if I ever actually did thank Raymond for his gift. Perhaps I ought to have.

I am partly teasing Raymond here, because he's a good man, and he was, after all, only trying to motivate his team. His wife Maria was wonderful that week. It was Astrid's one and only time to attend the Ryder Cup in a formal role, and she enjoyed it immensely. Maria really contributed to that, helping Astrid out in so many ways, which Astrid always appreciated and never forgot. It was not all smooth sailing for Astrid and me as a couple at that event. There were still people I hadn't seen since Viv's death, and inevitably I had to discuss it, often with Astrid there. She was patient and understanding and generous through-out, though the same can't be said for some other people. Even before the Ryder Cup took place, Dave Thomas, my old Ryder Cup partner whom I had fallen out with by 1989 over the San Roque debacle, said to me, 'Why are you taking Astrid there?'

I asked him what he meant. Why wouldn't I bring her? She was my wife, for heaven's sake.

'Well, because,' he said. 'Because the Ryder Cup was always yours and Viv's thing. It was about you and Viv.'

I just shook my head. How do you respond to something like that?

The definitive moment of the whole competition, in the end, was Christy O'Connor Jr beating Fred Couples. Freddie's a good fellow, but I'm telling you I saw it all coming. Or at least I saw something coming. On the 17th green I thought I saw the slightest hiccup of tension affect Freddie's stroke. He always has this kind of shrugging loose air to him, but there was no relaxation in that stroke. I told Christy this as we walked to the next green. *Stay focused*, I told him. *I don't think he's quite right.*

The 18th at The Belfry is a long brute of a par-four, with water curving in and out all down the left side. Only the longest hitters can carry it far enough to cut off a big chunk of the hole, and Christy wasn't that long. So he hit his drive, a decent enough shot, but he was left with a long approach. Freddie got up on the tee and pulled the shit out of it, but he's such a long hitter that he actually carried his ball out onto this little peninsula no one in their right mind would ever aim at, especially under that kind of pressure. But he was dry and now he only had an 8-iron to the green. I was beside myself, because this was a key moment in the Cup; my guy's got a 2-iron in his hands and the other guy's got an 8-iron. But I was walking the fairway with Christy, and something inside me still wasn't convinced Freddie was steady.

'Listen to me, Christy,' I said. 'Just knock this sucker on the green. Something good is going to happen. Come on. Just one more good swing for Ireland.'

He struck that 2-iron so damn pure I wonder if he even felt the contact. It must have been absolutely buttery. It flew to the green and stopped 6 feet from the hole. Freddie was rattled something awful, because he hit the worst-looking 8-iron that bailed way right of the hole. The rest was history. It was a massively important point, given that, surprisingly, some of our big artillery didn't play their best that day. Christy and Freddie shook hands and that was that. We'd won it again. Through a tie, yes, but the Cup was still ours.

Three in a row. Who'd have predicted that? Nobody, that's who. They'd have put you in a straitjacket if you'd walked into a bookie's in 1981 and put a hundred pounds on Europe winning three Ryder Cups before the decade was out. It was absolutely stunning, and surely it has to rank with some of the all-time-great team achievements.

If I had to look back over the four Cups it's clear to me that Seve was the key component. I'm happy to take credit where credit is due, and false modesty is something I can't stomach. I was damn good at being captain, and was proud of the skills and talents I brought to the job. In some ways, it was the purest expression of who I am in the golf world. But Seve made the Ryder Cup what it is today. Every person who has anything to do with the Ryder Cup, or who enjoys the Ryder Cup, should write Seve a note and thank him. It wouldn't be what it is now if Seve hadn't come on board, though I also need to emphasize that he always showed the utmost respect for my leadership and decisions. He never challenged me and always put very high stock in my captaincy. Still, the loyalty he showed to 'Mr Hacklin' rubbed off on the team, and had the effect of making us more of a team. Having him out there playing the Ryder Cup was like putting the best singer in the world on stage at Carnegie Hall. I was the conductor, he was the soloist, and everyone else was the orchestra. It was where he was meant to be. He was full of passion, and that stage was his destiny. He was such an inspiration to the other players, and I just let that happen wherever it took root. Why wouldn't I? He was so enthusiastic, so driven, so full of self-belief. This is why for the life of me I will never understand the stupid bloody decision by that committee banning him from the 1981 Cup.

Funnily enough, all these years on, I don't really feel that Seve and I have any particular bond. Sure, we'll still talk whenever the chance comes up, and he will always have my respect and admiration, as I know I have his. But he's his own man, Seve. Even then he knew as well as I did that we weren't in this thing to be pals, to have a laugh and a couple of pints. We were dead serious about it from the start. We were in it to get a result, to make history. We were on a mission, and we joined forces to accomplish that mission.

And that was how I viewed it when I finally had to announce that I was done with being captain. There was nowhere else to go with it. I was told I could carry on as long as I liked. But why would I? It was mission accomplished.

It took a long time to get over Vivien. I'm not going to say it didn't. But Astrid was always patient, always there for me. She knew about loss. I was totally committed to her, of course, but that didn't mean part of my hardwiring wasn't still set to Viv. It was only natural that every now and then I'd blurt out something like, 'Pass the TV remote, will you, Viv, love.'

Astrid would look over. 'Did you just call me Viv?'

'Did I? Oh, Jesus, sorry, darling.'

And the like.

But it was just something in my brain, and it took a long time to work through it. Astrid and I talked about it, we cried about it. To her, it wasn't just about my healing, or our relationship, but also about our future ability to create a family together. She has the most incredible maternal protective instinct. It's one of the most powerful things I know. She would defend her family to the death. She's a beautiful, sensitive person, but if you crossed her over something to do with anyone in her family, she'd knock your bloody block off, make no mistake. She's the real deal, and trust me when I tell you that she is the one person above anyone else on the planet who holds my respect.

Now that Astrid and I were married and trying to start a new family together, and now that the whole Ryder Cup captain thing was over and done with, my financial affairs took on an added importance. I wasn't a player any more. I wasn't a captain any more. I was a 45-year-old guy looking for work. There were plenty of irons in the fire, and we were also coming along, or so we thought, on the construction of our house at San Roque. Like I said before, little did we know at the time that my sister's husband was in trouble with his business and would use hundreds of thousands of pounds of my money to try and get out of it. There were also the growing problems surrounding the whole San Roque Club project. I'd given up on it being what I'd first hoped it would be. It was never going to become The Tony Jacklin Club, and Shun was not the man I thought he was. Basically, the whole San Roque dream was off the rails as far as I was concerned, but as the Nineties opened, Astrid and I still thought it was somewhere we wanted to live. After all, we were building a wonderful house and it was still a sublimely beautiful part of the world. That never changed. Astrid liked it, and almost more than anything else in my life at that point, what I wanted to achieve was to make Astrid happy, this incredible woman I'd been so lucky to have come into my life.

Sadly, it became an intolerable situation. I almost couldn't stand to look at Shun, after the way he'd treated me by hiring that Nigel Smith fellow. It also became painful to be around the golf course itself. It was supposed to be part of my legacy, part of what I was going to leave behind, and because that hadn't happened, it always tore at my heart a little bit to walk on it. I'd put so much of my very person into that project, so much of my life-force, and to see it come to nothing, or at least 'nothing' as far as I was concerned, was very painful, very hurtful.

Lastly, the whole place reminded me of Vivien. It's a hard thing to say, but I felt as if part of me wanted to stay and part of me wanted to go. The part that wanted to go, to get on with my new life, was, in the end, the bigger part. When we left Sotogrande for good, it was complicated and painful, but necessary. It was time to move on.

20

We thought we'd died and gone straight to heaven. The house was called Quoth Quan, and it was in the hills of Lanarkshire, near Biggar, pretty much equidistant, heading south, from both Edinburgh and Glasgow, though Edinburgh was the easier place to get to. What a gorgeous house and property. My God, you'd have to see it to believe it, the way it was set high up near the Tinto Hills, on a 167-acre property. When we bought it it was fifteen bedrooms and we turned it into eleven bedrooms with extra bathrooms and an office. The back of the house looked over the garden and then over the heather and down to a farm at the back, which a man used to rent from us to graze his sheep and cows. The land kind of rolled along, and if you looked straight out, you'd see the Tinto Hills, five miles away as the crows flew. What a place it was. Astrid always called it her dream house.

Life in the Scottish countryside was bucolic and wonderful. We had Sean in 1991, and Astrid and I were continuing to love each other fully while also helping each other heal in our own ways. I was doing a fair bit of shooting in the hills, which I loved. I wasn't golfing much, but I didn't miss it, I can tell you. In the autumn of 1991 I played an honorary role in the Ryder

Cup at Kiawah Island, the infamous and unfortunately named War on the Shore (a lowpoint, in my opinion, in Ryder Cup sportsmanship history), at which Bernard Gallacher first acted as captain, and which the Europeans ended up losing in such dramatic fashion when Bernhard Langer missed that last putt under such stifling pressure. (Ironically, this was the Cup where I had to perform one of the most heartbreaking tasks I've ever had. Steve Pate had been involved in a car accident, and on the final day's singles matches he couldn't play, so we had to sit someone down as per the rules. The name in the envelope was David Gilford. Bernard came over to me and said, *Tony, I've got to run off and meet with the Press, can you just go and tell David his name was in the envelope and he's not playing?* I pulled David aside and said, 'David, Pate can't play, and the envelope has come into play. Your name was in it. You're sitting out today.' The poor man was gutted. It was the worst thing I ever had to do in the Ryder Cup and I wasn't even the captain.)

In any case, life was grand, even though there were rumblings of a financial nature. I didn't feel quite busy enough, and we were living in a house with staff, a house we'd paid a lot for and which we then renovated to an extensive degree. To cut to the point, by 1993 Quoth Quan was costing us £300,000 a year to run and pay off, but my annual income might have been £200,000. We were dropping £10,000 a month on the place. On top of that, we had the whole Lloyd's of London fiasco coming home to roost, and it was looking like that was going to cost me £300,000. Finally, I was in the middle of taking a million-pound burn from Shun down in Sotogrande.

In short, we were sinking, fast. It's hard to believe, but it was true. There was no major income stream, except for the stream flowing out. It was a drastic situation, and it all seemed to come about so suddenly. One day, walking around our land, I looked out over the heather and I said to myself, *There's only one thing*

I can do, and I know how to do, and that's play golf. I've got to get my ass to America and play the Senior Tour.

I was forty-nine then. And at that age, I made what I truly consider one of the most courageous decisions of my life. I decided to play professional golf again. But I have to remind you; I wasn't playing golf then. And let's be clear, I'm not just talking professional golf or tournament golf. I was barely playing *any* golf. I was too busy off in the woods shooting, living my life, being with Astrid and Sean and the other kids. Sure, I did the occasional clinic here or there, and kept my swing intact enough to not look like a fool when I did play, but the fact is that I hadn't played a real round of golf in a dozen years. Not one that counted for anything, anyway. And don't forget I'd quit because I'd become a gibbering idiot with the putter.

But what other options did I have?

The Senior Tour was in full swing by then, and I thought, Bloody hell, there's a lot of money out there, money being made by guys I used to beat. It seemed the only option to me. We had to go to America. That was where our only chance at financial rescue lay. Perfectly ironic, isn't it? Twenty-five years earlier, as a young pro, I knew the place I had to go if I wanted to be the best was America. That was where the best were, and I had to be there. And now, in 1993, America was where the money was, plain and simple. And I felt we had to go. In July of 1994, I'd be eligible for the Senior Tour, and I set my mind to it.

So we put Quoth Quan up for sale. It was yet another troubling process in my real-estate history in that it became obvious we were never going to recoup what we put into it. In fact, in the end there was only one seriously interested possible buyer as winter began to threaten. And if that buyer went away, it meant we were going to be on the hook for ten grand a month through the winter, because there certainly wasn't going to be anyone buying that place in January. Waiting until spring to sell would have meant stalling my plans for the Senior circuit. I was anxious to get things going, because I wanted to get over to America and start practising and working out and acclimatizing. Once I'd decided that the Senior Tour was the way to go, I got dead serious about it. This wasn't joking around. We were going under financially, and I was all business about playing well. I've never gone into anything without trying my best and giving it my full attention, my passion and energy, and this wasn't going to be any different. At least, that was my initial mindset.

Anyway, the fellow who was humming and hawing about Quoth Quan finally decided to buy the place, but only after we'd agreed to throw in some extras for nothing, such as a beautiful snooker table I'd paid £5,000 for. So he signed on the dotted line, and we were free to start making plans to go to America – me, Astrid (who then and always loved Quoth Quan dearly, and was sorry to leave), our two-year-old son, and our other children. The move was on. It was back to America. We arrived on 30 October 1993.

It's imperative at this point to highlight how much Astrid's support and friendship and her own kind of steel meant to me during these times (and every day since). I had been a fortunate fellow in my early life to have met and married a woman like Vivien, but I believe it to be true that I was *even* more fortunate to have met and married Astrid in the second phase of my life and of our lives together. I've said before that I'm not some lone wolf, some solitary individual who thinks he can do everything on his own. I thrive in a close relationship and I need it in my life. And thank God Astrid came along.

You see, in the same way that a building must have a solid foundation, no matter what you furnish it with, Astrid provides a foundation for us. She's as solid as Everest, and her basic dignity, her common sense, her fun nature – my God, all these things have sustained us through some very rough times. It was all fun and games early on in life, and perhaps that made it easy to romanticize the overall state of things, but character comes through when people are under pressure, and Astrid's character is as great as they come. In fact, she has often seemed to me to be at her best, her most resilient, when the times are toughest. Of course, it doesn't hurt that she also happens to be a gorgeous woman with a fantastic sense of humour! She is the second great love of my life, full stop.

It's clear to me now that I needed, and have benefited, more from having Astrid in my life than any other person. One can't compare apples and oranges, of course, and love is a mystery, yet I suspect I'd have managed in life at some basic level without Vivien. But I'd be lost without Astrid, and I don't mind saying it. She is the biggest part of me, and has been almost since the day I met her.

Jack and Barbara Nicklaus went so far beyond the call of duty and friendship that it's impossible to properly quantify it. Any attempts I make here will fall short. They were there when we needed them, simple as that, and they always have been. The truth is that we were skint. Jack and Barbara put us up in a guest house on their property in Palm Beach for a couple of months while we got sorted out. I don't think Jack ever sensed that we were broke, but he was instrumental anyway in getting me set up to represent the PGA National club. As part of the deal we got to live in a house on the course. It was a godsend. Jack and Barbara have long been among the most decent, *good* people I have ever known. It's what life's all about, isn't it? Finding the good ones, and cherishing what they bring to your life. I've been so blessed in my life to have met so many quality people. Those are the people you don't forget. Astrid will always hold a special place in her heart for Barbara, and if Astrid decides someone has that place, it is very significant indeed.

Even with the PGA National deal, this was still a very, *very* tough time. I was eight or nine months away from making my debut on the Senior Tour, and there was no guarantee, none, that I was going to make a single red cent. I had no idea how I'd perform, though I was always confident. But during this time before getting out on to the Tour, I wasn't bringing in any real money from anywhere. We had a load of furniture on its way over from Scotland, but we had nowhere to put it. We had a house full of kids. It was toughest of all on Astrid, of that you can be sure, though my self-esteem wasn't exactly at an all-time high. I had always seen myself as the provider for my family, but it just wasn't happening as well as I wanted it to.

The PGA National thing helped a lot, and things took another solid turn for the better early in 1994 when I talked to Tom Crow, who was then the head of Cobra. He and I agreed that I would use Cobra clubs for five years and receive an annual fee of $150,000. This in and of itself was great. But what Tom did – and I can never thank him enough – is that he made the contract active from 1 January of that year, a good six and a half months before I'd even be *eligible* to start playing the Tour. He must have sensed that we were in a bit of financial trouble. I can't tell you what a relief that was. Finally, there was a bit of money flowing into the coffers.

And so I got to work, remaking myself into a professional golfer. In a sense I was learning to play golf again. That's no joke. I mean it. It had been so long since I'd picked up a club with scoring in mind that I'd literally forgotten how to do it in my conscious mind. Part of me was excited by the challenge. I knew I was doing it because I had to, but I also knew there was part of me that was still fiercely competitive. Part of me still wanted to prove that I could play. I wasn't in this to finish thirtieth. I was doing this to win.

The way I chose to prepare was to enter mini-Tour events.

There were all kinds of them back then, all around the Palm Beach area. You paid $500 to get in an event, and if you finished in the top third you got your money back. If you won, you got $4,000. I was practising all the time, as well as getting up every day at six in the morning and walking 4 miles before I did anything else. I won one of these mini-Tour events. Then I won another one. Then I almost won another, barely losing to Jerry Kelly, who went on to some success on the PGA Tour. I could feel my game returning, and by the time July rolled around and I celebrated my half-century on the big ball, I was ready to take on the other old boys. It wouldn't quite be accurate to say I was 'pumped' about being out there, but I felt ready, I felt properly prepared, and I thought I would do well.

As it happened, I won on my fourth time out, at the First of America Classic. It was a massive relief and actually somewhat emotional, but in hindsight it was emotional for what you might call the wrong reasons. It was partly about the thrill of victory, of performing your best, of showing your best self, but it was also such a relief and a vindication. I'd done the right thing. I had rewarded the faith of people like Tom Crow at Cobra. I was making some money. I could start to pay back people who'd helped me out, like my friend Joe, who still lives with his wife Cynthia near us in Bradenton; he was there for me when we badly needed it in earlier days. In fact, I called Joe right away after winning. It was an emotional victory for me because it meant perhaps we could start crawling out of the hole we had somehow found ourselves in.

In any case, winning right out of the gates like that took a lot of pressure off me and I was able to play the season out and make some decent money. I won again the next year, at the Franklin Quest Championship, which produced a lot of the same feelings of relief and gratitude, primarily for the money it brought in. Looking at it from the outside, you'd have said it was a highly successful first two years on the Senior Tour.

But the joy was gone.

I was spinning my wheels and I knew it. The putting started to get bad again (and it's worth pointing out that in both my Senior Tour wins I three-putted the final green). Astrid was out there at first, pushing Sean around the courses in this great big bloody stroller with these huge wheels. It was fun at first, but then she started staying home with Sean, which meant I was out there thirty-five weeks a year on my own. I was a basket case. I was cooked, again. Golf had become just a means to an end, and I was only doing it to help our financial situation, which was much worse than I knew at the time; Astrid hadn't told me the full horror story of our troubles because she thought the worry and strain of it would negatively affect my performance on the course (which she was right about). Also, by this time we'd moved from Ibis in Florida, where we were building a house, up to the Greenbrier in West Virginia simply as an austerity move. It was just a cheaper place to live, that's all.

It's important to remember, though, that I expected our situation to improve literally any moment. I had every confidence the whole San Roque thing would be resolved in our favour. That was a million pounds sitting over in Spain that was mine. How could it not be resolved in our favour? We were in the right, and that was all there was to it. Isn't that the way it's supposed to work?

But during my time on the Senior Tour there was a fatal absence of one thing – passion. I just didn't care about playing the game. It had become a job. But I couldn't do it that way. Golf was never a job to me. *Never*. It was always what I was good at, and what I was driven and focused and passionate about. If that emotion wasn't there, the game didn't hold much for me. There are an endless number of zombies out on the Seniors Tour, these guys robotically turning up and cashing cheques, but I just couldn't be one of them. I didn't have the robot in me. I could see it for myself. Astrid could see it. Anybody who really knew me and knew me well could see that I didn't have an ounce of passion left for competitive golf.

Yet the Senior Tour changed our lives around. Why? Because it was what finally got us to America to live. It was where I should have been living thirty-five years earlier, if not for the advice of Mark McCormack. The Senior Tour was not where I belonged, but it brought me to the place I did belong, and so I was glad I tried, even if it only confirmed what I probably already knew about me and competitive golf. It's funny (in light of my experience on the Senior Tour), I remember saying to Mark in 1969, when he had me storming off to America for four weeks the day after I won the Open Championship, 'I can't do it, Mark. There's no more beans left in the tin. My try's all gone.'

It was the same on the Senior Tour. Simple, self-explanatory – my try was all gone.

You can't win before you play. The wonderful Roberto de Vicenzo said this to me at the Masters one year; it might have been 1971 or 1972. We were paired together and I'd gone charging out of the gate, trying my guts out on the first day to win it all in a rush and make it all happen. I was pressing, I suppose. He saw this, and after the round pulled me aside to try and tell me to relax, to let it happen.

'You can't win before you play, Tony,' he said, smiling gently.

He was right, but it's also true that you can't win if you *don't* play. You've got to tee it up to have a chance. In other words, you've got to take the risk to earn the reward. And the higher your goal, the more painful it can be to fall, and the harder it can be to get back up. I knew that on the golf course, only too well. I also knew about it in life. And I knew it when it came to earning a living off the golf course.

By the time I left the Senior Tour and we'd moved up to the Greenbrier in West Virginia, it was painfully clear that I was never going to earn a living from the actual playing of golf. That wasn't on the cards any more. I'd done my best, had won a couple of times, had proven that I still had enough game to do it. But it wasn't making me happy; in fact, it was making me miserable again. That meant the income had to come from somewhere else. But where? One of the real problems I began to face was that when you haven't got financial security the tendency is to chase things more than you otherwise would. You aren't as sound in making decisions. Sure, it's as easy as pie to be objective and selective when you've got a few quid in the bank, when you're secure. You suit yourself then. But if you're putting on a front, and you've got the name without the financial security, you take chances you otherwise might not. You perhaps don't listen as closely as you ought to to the subconscious voice that knows what's going on. America is the land of opportunity. There is no doubt in my mind about that. It's full of people who want to better themselves. The sky's the limit. But with this exuberance and high-aiming mentality, you naturally find a lot of, well, bullshitters, to be honest. It comes with the territory here, but if you can sort through and get to the right people (people like Kevin Daves, the developer behind The Concession) then America is a great place to live in pursuit of your dreams. The greatest place.

But I wasn't always getting through to the right people.

It was in 1997 that we moved up to West Virginia, and that was the worst of the times, by far. Poor Astrid, trying to balance everything down in that little office she had in the basement of our house. She always liked looking after our household books, and she was, and is, good at it, but it was an awful time for her, doing her Mrs Doubtfire impersonation five hundred times over, trying to decide which fire to try and put out first. I know there were nights she'd go down to that office at three o'clock in the morning and look at her desk and all the paperwork and bills, and think, Which one do I pay? And how much? God love her for keeping the house from falling apart. It was a very, *very*, stressful time.

Not that I wasn't busy. I was running here and there doing the best I could to make a go of this, a go of that. But because I am by nature an enthusiastic person, and because I was, frankly, rather desperate at this point in our lives, I simply got involved with the wrong people a few times during these dark financial days. It's very difficult at times to know what to do, because the bigger your name the bigger the crook you attract. And this is a bloody sight more serious when you're clutching at straws in your financial life. Your whole focus becomes simply putting food on the table, and keeping a roof over your head. You become obsessed with that end of things. (Although it's important to understand that though they were dark days at the bank, they were nothing like that in our family life. We always had a great time together, Sean was growing up into the intelligent, funny boy that he is today, grandchildren were starting to arrive – it was a wonderful family time. It was also really enjoyable to spend some time getting to know Sam Snead better, because Sam lived at the Greenbrier; it was enjoyable and yet also so ironic, given his objection to Jack conceding my putt in the 1969 Ryder Cup.)

I suppose what I'm getting at overall is that sometimes in life you pay a price for your enthusiasm, for being a person who gets emotionally engaged with people and their ideas. Because, to me, it was all still about having a passion for life. That's never left me and never will. And if someone came to me with what sounded a fine business idea, well, I got on board. I got excited. I lent my passion to the project. Sadly, few of them bore fruit. You get in with chancers, and too often the wrong thing happens.

There was a marquetry project I got into with some fellow, and we were going to do a Ryder Cup collection of furniture. This was a project I was very excited about because it's such a keen hobby of mine. Anyway, I introduced Marshall to everybody, from the CEO of the PGA of America to the British PGA to the marketing guy on the PGA Tour. He did nothing with it, and I made nothing from it.

There was another fellow who approached me while we were living in West Virginia wanting me to get involved with him in developing a golf centre in the marina in Bradenton, Florida. A golf range with floating balls you could hit out into the water, a golf academy, houses, shops, the whole works. I was intrigued, and essentially he offered me a half share in the project. He squired me around, taking me to Disneyworld in Orlando a couple of times, showing me a variety of attractions we could include in the project. He wasn't a complete fraud, because when we got the papers signed to go ahead, we did in fact get the range and academy built. But he was the most incredible control freak. The guy, who shall remain nameless, made José Patiño look like Gandhi. The whole thing ended up being a bit of a disaster, and in the end I took a cheque for fifty grand for my share in the academy, which allowed me to wash my hands of him.

But it got me to Bradenton.

That was what made it all worthwhile. I loved the quiet, relaxed air of the place right away, and I was always telling Astrid when I'd get back to West Virginia, 'You know, this place is all right. You should check it out.'

The truth is she didn't much like it at first, mostly because it's so flat. By now it was around 1999, 2000. West Virginia was okay, but damn it was cold in the winters. I'm just getting too old to be that cold for half the year. Who needs it? And I had a feel for Bradenton almost from the start. It felt warm, cozy, quiet, and yet there was also a distinct air to the whole

Tampa/Bradenton/Sarasota coastal area that felt exciting and new, as if it was poised to burst into something fresh. I can tell you now that that sensation was a significant understatement. In a way, the place actually matches my personality – it's friendly and easygoing on the surface, but there's also a part of it that's really surging and enthusiastic and getting on to bigger and better things. I love that about the area. It's like you can have it both ways here. You can be relaxed and comfortable, casual, but at the same time nobody's going to look down their nose at you for wanting to do business.

In any case, I think it would be fair to say that Astrid took some winning over. In 2000 we decided to rent a house in Bradenton for a year, and once we were here we came to appreciate it even more. We found an excellent school for Sean. The Bradenton Country Club is a friendly place with a wonderful old Donald Ross course to play on, and they offered me an Honorary Membership. And then we found a house for sale that actually backed right on to the course. That sealed the deal. We bought the house and have been there ever since. It was the right thing to do, and the opportunities that have unfolded for me here are beyond anything I'd imagined. If you asked me, *Was it worth it to go through all the pain and trouble of San Roque and Quoth Quan and being skint in West Virginia to end up in Bradenton doing the things you're doing now?* the answer would be, *It absolutely bloody well was worth it.*

But there have been other events in the last few years that I feel I have to talk about. The year 2000 was a painful one for me in my golfing life. What happened quite simply broke my heart. It just got too bloody much and I had to stand up and say, *Enough of you lot. I'm done.*

At the Open Championship of 2000, held at St Andrews,

while having a drink before the Champion's Dinner, I got into a conversation with Seve and Nick Faldo about the overall state of the European Tour. They were disgruntled, to say the least. There were many, many concerns, but the biggest of them all was that they felt there was no accountability in the hierarchy. Okay, the Tour wasn't completely falling apart, but on the other hand nobody had any way of knowing what kind of shape it really was in, and where all the money was flowing from and to. In short, there wasn't a scrap of accountability or transparency to the whole operation. Michael Bonallack, the former long-time Secretary of the R & A, was there with us as well, and finally he said, 'Well if you all feel that strongly about it, do something about it.'

The penny dropped. He was right. It wasn't about whining, it was about trying to make some changes, and the best way to make changes is to act. So we acted. Jose Maria Olazabal and Bernhard Langer got in on it as well. The press labelled them the Big Four when they called for an Extraordinary General Meeting of the players of the European Tour. The purpose was simple. They wanted the players – who are the whole point of the Tour, aren't they? – to gather and vote on a course of action to bring more accountability to the way Schofield and his cronies ran the operation. The recommendation was a full audit of the Tour's book. I was back in Bradenton by this time, but I was being kept up to date by the boys, all while I was on the phone day and night talking to as many Tour players as I could to get them informed.

You have to remember something here, too. There was nothing in it for those fellows, the so-called Big Four. Or for me, either. All four of them were already wealthy, so there certainly wasn't a financial motive. None of them had any designs on power of any sort, because they were all players, not administrators. None of them was doing it for the ego, or for the attention, because they were already more famous and well-known than they needed to be. The point is, all of us were doing it for absolutely the right reasons. We had poured our lives into the European Tour, into helping form it, trying to make it something special. And it was galling that it seemed to have become the private playground of a few administrators. You look at the way the PGA Tour went about its business compared with the European Tour and you'll see what I mean. Granted, it's a different economic market, but even taking that into account, the difference in professionalism and financial clout is embarrassing. And the divergence of approaches between the two is also striking when it comes to the way they use and market their stars. Look at the way the PGA Tour has always marketed its stars. They become huge, these people. I'm not just talking about Palmer and Nicklaus. Look at Watson, Kite, Couples, Norman, Price. All fantastic players. But none of them (well, except for Watson) could hold a candle to Seve. But was Seve made the face of the European Tour? The dashing, swashbuckling Spaniard slashing his way around the globe! The man could have been on a par with the movie stars if the Tour had properly exploited his awesome gifts. But did they? Seve never heard from Ken Schofield, except for the odd speech at a Tour dinner. Was Seve bitter? Well, I don't presume to speak for Seve, but I feel pretty confident saying that he feels he did more for Ken Schofield's career than Ken Schofield did for his.

In the end, our efforts in pushing this into the public eye were about making the Tour better, putting it on track to be what it could be – a strong, properly run, world-class sporting operation – instead of what it was. And the best way to start making those changes was to examine the money. Wasn't that what the Deep Throat mole fellow said to Bob Woodward in the whole Watergate thing? *Follow the money.*

And so the Big Four recommended at the Extraordinary

General Meeting that it all start with a full audit, a thorough examination of the books. Schofield and his gang made all the proper noises in public about being fine with that, about letting anyone anywhere look at whatever they wanted, and so on. They agreed to put the matter to a vote, and if the membership of the Tour requested an audit, then an audit it would be.

Well, next thing we knew the ballot question came out, and on it there was not one question – *Do you want an audit of the Tour's books? Yes or No?* – but two questions: Do you want a full audit? Or a partial audit?

Can someone explain to me what a partial audit is?

Of course the result came back with a 'majority' of the votes calling for a 'partial' audit of the Tour's books. It turned out the whole thing was handled by Arthur Andersen, of Enron fame. And when Arthur Andersen tabulated all the results, did they then turn them over to an outside third party for a proper and thorough scan? Why no. They privately delivered the results to the very people who were being challenged by the vote.

I don't even know how to express my disbelief at the whole thing. I'm still shocked to this day that the whole country didn't burst out laughing. I do not know how you arrive at a vote for a partial audit, and I still don't even know what a partial audit is. Common sense dictates that it smacks of bullshit. How can they expect any rational, reasonably intelligent human being to believe that a partial audit is valid and in the best interests of the players on the Tour?

That was it. I was finished with the lot of them after that. It was much worse for the Big Four. They did it with nothing but the purest of intent, and in the end the press hammered them. Faldo is now doing a lot of commentating for ABC. Seve nowadays is embroiled in his own inner fight to find out who he is. Langer is still playing well, but looks to be getting ready for the Senior Tour to me. And Jose Maria has been playing more and more in America the last few years – surprise, surprise. They lost the PR war, of that there is no doubt, but to me it was nothing but a black eye on the Tour, a mark of utter dishonour that you would treat your greatest players, your very lifeblood, with such an appalling lack of respect.

21

I woke in the middle of the night. We were living in Bradenton in our house backing onto the golf course. It was 2002. I had golfed a few times in the recent past with a man named Kevin Daves, a developer in the Sarasota area. He was the force behind the construction of the new Ritz-Carlton in Sarasota, and he'd been trying to get Jack Nicklaus to build a golf course attached to the Ritz. I also knew that Kevin was fond of the Arnold Palmer/Bay Hill idea, in which the name attached to the project also lived on site, or at least had a house there.

I bolted awake this one night, quite literally. Just sat upright in bed. The idea was in my head, almost fully formed. *The Concession*. Just like that. Jack and I. The link. The concession of the putt from the Ryder Cup at Lytham in 1969. A golf course, a superb golf course, that would exist long after we gone and dust. I had a vision of the whole thing, a project in honour of a moment.

The next day I called Kevin and we met. I blurted out my idea and, well, he loved it. Kevin is a quiet man, but he showed his enthusiasm right away. He and I went to see Jack and the manager of his design company. Jack said he'd be involved, that the idea appealed to him. We found the land inland from Sarasota, and Kevin got to work securing the funding. It took some time to make it happen, and there were a few moments when it looked in doubt, but it's now a reality. This is what happens when you find yourself lucky enough to be involved with people who do what they say and say what they mean, instead of chancers and bullshitters. Incredible things happen, things you can put your faith in. And from a financial standpoint, it's turning around my whole outlook. I stand to do well by it, but honestly the money is just one component of what I've earned from it. It's been immensely gratifying to do, and so educational to observe the process.

It's hard to believe looking back three years to see how far The Concession has come. The course opened last January, and the housing is going gangbusters. I mean, you have to see this bloody place to believe it. It's magnificent. The course is Jack's best. I believe that, I really do. I consulted with him on the design and I'm proud of the impact I had on it, but it's his baby. It has a slope of 155, the highest in the state of Florida. It's so good we're going to apply for a future Ryder Cup. I'm not just saying that. It's a masterpiece of a golf course, routed through some of the prettiest wetlands and oak groves in the entire state.

The housing is stunningly gorgeous, and one phase of this development is known as Birkdale, in honour of that moment Jack and I shared, and the other phase is called Lindrick, after the course where I first witnessed a Ryder Cup in 1957. There are hundreds of houses and not one under a couple of million. I'm telling you, my jaw still drops when I drive through the development. I came to Kevin with the concept, but he turned it into the kind of thing that only a man with dreams *and* guts could envision. You'd have to see it to believe it, honestly. Overall, it's a billion-dollar project. It's staggering to me that this all came about because I bolted up in bed one night with an idea, and because I put this idea in front of a man with patience and vision and determination. But I've been watching it unfold before my eyes every day for the last three years, and it's been an amazing education.

The Concession. It's part of my legacy now and I'm damn proud of it. Maybe we should memorialize it even further and institute a rule that all putts two feet and under are automatically conceded. You can be sure this would be fine by me! The club *is* called The Concession, after all.

But that's not the only thing that has gone well for me in the last couple of years. I'm heavily involved in the advertising campaigns of JJB Sports in the UK (a deal that Ian Woosnam really initiated for me). The ads have been good fun to do, and have let me express that side of my personality, the performer, the sense of humour, the professional. I've loved it, and it's been a nice boost financially (as has my involvement in the UK Golf Channel, which I hope continues to grow). But even more important than the financial and professional benefits of being associated with JJB, has been the way it has allowed me to return to my north of England roots. I mentioned in my Introduction that I've become pals with the JJB owner Dave Whelan, a good Wigan man.

What a rediscovery it's been for me! This is the England I miss so badly, I now realize. I don't miss the England of the tabloids, the weather, the island mentality. Who would? Every single one of us, all of us from the UK, would say that there are parts of who we are and where we're from that aren't perfect. It's like growing up in a family. You don't choose your family, do you? You're born, you grow up, your parents are your parents and your siblings are your siblings. You didn't pick them out of the store. They're never perfect, and neither are you. But no matter what, no matter what the faults or complaints, you love your family anyway. You love them because you are part of it, of that unit. And that's how I feel about England. I will love England until the day I die. I can't not love it. But that doesn't mean there aren't things about it that frustrate me. That's only normal and we all have that right to say what we think and feel about the things we love. God help me, Astrid would be happy to tell you that I've got my share of faults, but she loves me anyway and she always will (and vice versa).

There are always going to be things that stick with you over the years. I will never forget the sick, empty feeling in the pit of my stomach when Viv and I found that note in the car window right after I'd won the Open. It was just so sad. That stayed with me for ever, the sad feeling that there could be people like that out there.

But you can't let the bad guys get to you. This has always been my attitude towards the British tabloid Press. I'm not going to lie to you; there were some very emotional times with the British Press over the years, particularly through the Seventies. People who didn't know me from Adam were writing the most awful things about me, judging me without ever having talked to me. We all have an inherent desire to be loved, don't we? We want to do well, to get something right, to benefit not just ourselves but others. It's about progress, about what makes the world go around. But then there are people who just want to pull you down. It's always going to happen, and I find it very difficult to deal with and very difficult to understand. I'm an optimistic person by nature, but I've often been disappointed and even depressed by the downside of being in the public eye. I've always tried to do the right thing, but that doesn't mean you're not going to have people shooting at your head. What can you do but weed your own garden, and try to block out the negativity?

I have to say, regarding the nature of the Press and being in the public eye, that America doesn't treat its personalities the way such people are treated in the UK. When Tom Watson went through his divorce, did we hear anything about it in America? There was almost nothing in the papers about it. Same with Freddie Couples. Even with someone like John Daly, there isn't nearly the same kind of media frenzy over someone's private life that there is in the UK. Just look at the press reaction to Monty's marital troubles, and that will rest my case. This is the major difference between America and the UK. If I talk to someone here in the media, they write what I say and what I mean. They don't hunt for double meanings, they don't take a statement and make something of it that wasn't intended.

But I still love England. I always will, particularly the north, which truly brings out my feelings for my home. That's been the rediscovered joy for me of doing the JJB stuff. I've got to know Dave Whelan and his gang up in Wigan, and the work has taken me that way quite often in the last couple of years. We sit in the pub, have a few pints of Ruddles, shoot the breeze, and it's all as natural and easy as falling out of bed. I'm with my own. What a treat. The sense of humour. The plain-spoken directness of the people. The turn of phrase. My God, the turn of phrase, the way people there have with words and peculiar little sayings! Every time I'm back in the north, doing some work, hanging out with Dave, I am reduced to tears nearly every day by something somebody says. This is the England I love, which I will always love. A place of history, of tears in my eyes with laughter, of great friendship. That won't ever change.

For the past three years Astrid has been working on the design of our beautiful new home which is being built on our original site backing on to the Bradenton Country Club. It's got bags of character and I hope we will spend many happy years there. It's near everything we have come to love about living in America and is just a quick drive out to the spectacular beach on the Gulf

Coast, where I often go for long walks. These walks give me an opportunity to reflect, to look back, as well as look ahead.

It's been an incredible journey. So many highlights, such fantastic events, so many tough times. But throughout this unbelievable voyage it has always been about two or three fundamental things for me, things that have less to do with what happens in the end than with who you are as a person whilst chasing your dreams. It was always about passion, about pure unbridled enthusiasm for what I wanted to achieve. It was intensity, determination. To me, it was always about being as good as I could be, in everything. It's not complicated. If you want to be the best, you go flat out, you absorb as much as you can, you take everything in, ask questions, become observant. It's very simple. If you've got passion and talent, the knowledge to make the most of that passion and talent is out there. I wanted to play practice rounds with the greats, for instance, when I was coming up. I politely asked Ben Hogan if I could play a practice round with him. I certainly wasn't saying to myself, 'Ooooh, it's Ben Hogan, I'd better stay out of his way.' No. I wasn't being precocious. The point wasn't to be seen with people like that, it was to learn from them.

What Astrid and I want in our dotage, our retirement, is just to ensure that we're happy and we have the means to do what we want to do. We want to be healthy, to be well, to pursue the things we enjoy for a good long period yet. I hope I've got a ways to go. It's funny, I once said to Jim Mahoney, Sinatra's agent, that eighty would be a good number, a fine age to get to if you retained your fitness and so on. 'Yes,' Jim replied slowly, smiling. 'Eighty would be a beautiful number . . . until you were seventy-nine.

I'm sixty-one as I write this, and I suppose it's a sign of who I've always been that I wake up today and feel it's all just as exciting and fresh as it ever was. There's so much on the go, so many things still to do, to discover. So many opportunities. Most days it truly does feel as if all those roads were leading me here, to where I feel free in this place, with the great projects I'm associated with, like JJB and The Concession. I know there will be so much more to come, and I can't wait to experience it.

Of course, suiting yourself is worth far more than having a lot of money, isn't it? I look back and I know the search for security has always loomed large in my life. But I've certainly reached the point where I only need enough. I want to live a comfortable life and stay healthy, enjoy what time I've got left, and maintain an involvement in the business of golf at the level I choose. It's all a bit like the golf swing: you can make it complicated but you don't have to. The least complicated thing of all in my life is the one that's most important, and that's what Astrid and I have together. I consider myself a lucky man indeed to have her in my life, and I get excited thinking about all the things we still have in front of us.

The bottom line is we're all evolving constantly, doing what we do to the best of our abilities, and then we pass the baton. I feel incredibly fortunate to be involved with golf because the game itself was such a disciplinarian. I think back to the early days, me as a young teen standing out on the range at the Scunthorpe Country Club beating balls from dawn to dusk, and I realize that one of the greatest gifts golf has given me is resolve. That complete determination to identify what I want and to proceed towards it. No interruptions. No wavering. No excuses. You can't fake it in golf. There are no flukes. You either reach your goal or you don't. Golf taught me that resolve.

And it's never left me. I still have the same desire inside to be the best I can be at whatever it is I'm doing. Once that's in you, you don't just wash it out. It's there and it *never* goes away. I am as motivated as ever to do well the things that I do. It's who I am. But ultimately there is one thing that has always carried me along in my life, the thing I knew I could count on to be there every single morning when my eyes opened and my day began. It was always in me, and it always will be. It was my companion when I was standing on that range as a thirteen-year-old, and it's still roaring inside me as I write these last words.

The passion. The passion remains.

Index

Index

Index

Index

Index

Index